Immersive Communication: The Communication Paradigm of the Third Media Age

Communication, like the atmosphere itself, is ubiquitous and essential for humans, and, with the development of new technologies, such as ubiquitous network, big data, 3D printing, virtual reality, and artificial intelligence, it has become almost impossible to live without it. In addition, means of communication have changed immeasurably.

This book proposes a new research paradigm that incorporates new features and factors of communication and a new theoretical framework named "immersive communication." Pointing out that communication today has moved beyond the bidirectional mass communication of "the second media age" to ubiquitous, immersive communication in "the third media age," the author discusses the definition, characteristics, information structure, and models of immersive communication, using various examples including Fitbit, Apple, 5G, the Second Life, smart planet, and biological communication technologies, while envisioning future applications of the immersive communication mode.

Scholars and students of communication studies, especially those interested in the manifestations of the new media age, will all benefit from this book. It will also appeal to readers interested in new media and communication theories.

Qin Li is the director of the National Communication Strategy Research Center, an associate professor at Renmin University of China's School of Journalism and Communication, and a research fellow at the China Journalism and Social Development Research Center. Her famous publications include *Immersive Communication: The Communication Paradigm of the Third Media Age* (2013) and *Bing Media: The Theory and Practice of Immersive Communication* (2019) liqincn@ruc.edu.cn.

China Perspectives

The *China Perspectives* series focuses on translating and publishing works by leading Chinese scholars writing about both global topics and China-related themes. It covers Humanities and Social Sciences, Education, Media, and Psychology, as well as many interdisciplinary themes.

This is the first time any of these books have been published in English for international readers. The series aims to put forward a Chinese perspective, give insights into cutting-edge academic thinking in China, and inspire researchers globally.

Titles in media communication currently include:

The Patterns of Symbolic Communication
Sui Yan

China in Symbolic Communication
Sui Yan

Media Effects and Social Change
Ran Wei, Shuhua Zhou, Wenhui Luo

Communication and Community
Bin Wang

Epistemology of News Frame
Wei Xiao

Immersive Communication: The Communication Paradigm of the Third Media Age
Qin Li

Immersive Communication
The Communication Paradigm of the
Third Media Age

Qin Li

This book is published with financial support from the Chinese Fund for the Humanities and Social Sciences.

社会科学文献出版社
SOCIAL SCIENCES ACADEMIC PRESS (CHINA)

First published in English 2020
by Routledge
2 Park Square, Milton Park, Abingdon, Oxon OX14 4RN

and by Routledge
52 Vanderbilt Avenue, New York, NY 10017

Routledge is an imprint of the Taylor & Francis Group, an informa business

© 2020 Qin Li

The right of Qin Li to be identified as author of this work has been asserted by her in accordance with sections 77 and 78 of the Copyright, Designs and Patents Act 1988.

All rights reserved. No part of this book may be reprinted or reproduced or utilised in any form or by any electronic, mechanical, or other means, now known or hereafter invented, including photocopying and recording, or in any information storage or retrieval system, without permission in writing from the publishers.

Trademark notice: Product or corporate names may be trademarks or registered trademarks, and are used only for identification and explanation without intent to infringe.

English Version by permission of Social Sciences Academic Press (China).

British Library Cataloguing-in-Publication Data
A catalogue record for this book is available from the British Library

Library of Congress Cataloging-in-Publication Data
A catalog record has been requested for this book

ISBN: 978-0-367-37671-0 (hbk)
ISBN: 978-0-429-35553-0 (ebk)

Typeset in Times New Roman
by Deanta Global Publishing Services, Chennai, India

Contents

List of Illustrations	ix
Preface to Chinese edition	xi
Preface to English edition	xxi

1   Introduction   1

1.1   *Literature review: Theories on media evolution—from interpersonal communication to immersive communication 1*

1.1.1 *The first media age and the second media age 2*

1.1.2 *Evolutionary trends of media morphosis: "Coevolution and Coexistence" and "Anthropotropicness" 6*

1.1.3 *Media space, environment, and ecological theory define the relationship between media, humans, and the environment 9*

1.1.4 *How ways and modes of communication evolve to "vanishing boundaries," and how communication tools and communication relations are reconstructed 14*

1.2   *The origin and theoretical evolution of the concept of "immersion" 16*

1.2.1 *The origin of "immersion" concept 16*

1.2.2 *Immersion's application in virtual reality 18*

1.2.3 *Remote presence and immersive communication 21*

1.3   *Media technology and social development: Conditions and environment for the evolution of immersive communication 24*

1.3.1 *From "informational" survival to "post-information" survival 26*

1.3.2 *From "localized" survival to "ubiquitous" survival 30*

1.3.3 *Human beings live not only in a physical world but also in a virtual world 34*

1.4   *Limitations of existing theories and research significance 37*

1.4.1 *Media morphosis breaks through traditional spatial categories 38*

1.4.2 *The concept of "presence" has undergone a qualitative change 40*

1.5   *Summary 41*

vi *Contents*

2 The definition of immersive communication   43

    2.1 Logic of the new definition 43

        2.1.1 "Technological determinism" "decides" immersive communication as a new mode of communication 43

        2.1.2 The "anthropotropic" trend leads people to choose the most suitable things in order to survive 46

    2.2 Definition of immersive communication 48

    2.3 The breakthroughs of the new definition compared with existing definitions of communication 49

        2.3.1 Immersive communication reconstructs the three "spaces" 50

        2.3.2 Immersive communication reconstructs the relationship between media and the human being. It's the hottest and the coolest medium 53

    2.4 Summary 55

3 Morphological characteristics of immersive communication   56

    3.1 Immersive communication is human centered: Everything is media, and humans are also a media form 56

    3.2 Immersive communication is instant and anytime: The present, past, and future are integrated, and the virtual world and physical world coexist as integrated, instantaneous, and long-lasting 58

    3.3 Immersive communication is pervasive anywhere and everywhere: In "remote" presence and "ubiquitous" presence, fixed, mobile, and virtual coexistence converge 60

    3.4 Immersive communication is all-powerful: Boundaries between entertainment, work, and life vanish; cloud computing integrates everything 62

    3.5 Summary 63

4 The information content and movement mode of immersive communication   66

    4.1 Language form 67

        4.1.1 Previous media languages 67

        4.1.2 The pan-media language of the whole environment: The monitoring camera and environmental advertisements in the intelligent city 68

        4.1.3 Humans as the source of media language and information content 69

        4.1.4 The language of the virtual world 70

    4.2 The linguistic hegemony of immersive media 71

        4.2.1 Presenting ideas in immersive communication: Moistens everything softly and silently 71

Contents vii

4.2.2 *Media advertisement and the social discourse power of immersive communication 72*

4.3 *Information presentation 73*

4.4 *The paths and characteristics of information movement in immersive communication 74*

4.5 *Summary 76*

5 The model of immersive communication and its graphic forms 78

5.1 *The main communication models in communication studies 78*

5.2 *The model of immersive communication 83*

5.2.1 *The communication process: Comprehensive connectivity based on modern information technology 84*

5.2.2 *Communication relations: Human-centered communication structure 86*

5.2.3 *Communication goals and effects: The Communication Immersive Index 86*

5.3 *The model of immersive communication function: IC matrix 88*

5.3.1 *The IC matrix: Basic features 88*

5.3.2 *The meaning of the 25 intersections in the IC matrix 89*

5.3.3 *The theoretical breakthrough and research contribution of the IC matrix 89*

5.4 *The model of immersive communication process: The IC stereo helix 91*

5.4.1 *The explanation of the IC stereo helix 91*

5.4.2 *The significance of the IC stereo helix 91*

5.5 *The model of immersive communication relationship: The IC schematic 92*

5.5.1 *The explanation of the IC schematic 92*

5.5.2 *The meaning of the IC schematic 92*

5.6 *Summary 92*

6 Application and verification of the immersive communication models 97

6.1 *Application of the immersive communication models 97*

6.1.1 *General application of the immersive communication models 97*

6.1.2 *Dividing the three media ages with the immersive communication model 104*

6.2 *Case verification of the immersive communication model 105*

6.2.1 *The first media age: Lobby leaflets and unidirectional transmission 106*

6.2.2 *The second media age: Elevator television and focus awareness 107*

viii *Contents*

  6.2.3 The third media age: Panoramic monitoring and
    personalized service 110
 6.3 Summary 116

**7 How immersive communication guides the formation of
"the third media age"**   **121**
 7.1 The inevitable cause of the formation of "the third
  media age" 122
  7.1.1 The revolution of media ontology and changes in
    social productivity 123
  7.1.2 Changes in the media space and the transformation of
    human living space 125
  7.1.3 Changes in the social functions of media bring changes
    to social relations 128
 7.2 The concept and characteristics of "the third media age" 130
  7.2.1 The concept of "the third media age" 130
  7.2.2 The characteristics of "the third media age" 133
 7.3 Summary 138

**8 "Immersive communicators" and their production and
lifestyle characteristics**   **141**
 8.1 Information acquisition by immersive communicators 142
  8.1.1 Enhanced identity as audiences/recipients 142
  8.1.2 Enhanced identity as "we media" 143
 8.2 The lifestyle of immersive communicators 144
 8.3 The production mode of immersive communicators 147
 8.4 The entertainment of immersive communicators 151
 8.5 The future of immersive communicators: The commencement
  of biological media 154
 8.6 Summary 155

**9 Conclusion: Immersive communication opens a new chapter in
human communication**   **157**
 9.1 Revolutions in human–media relations 158
 9.2 Revolution of communication content 159
 9.3 Revolution of communication methods 161
 9.4 Revolution of media function 162

Afterword to Chinese edition   165
References   167
Index   174

Illustrations

Figures

5.1	The Lasswell formula (Lasswell, 1948)	79
5.2	Shannon–Weaver model (Shannon & Weaver, 1949)	80
5.3	DeFleur model (DeFleur, 1970)	80
5.4	Osgood and Schramm circular model (Schramm, 1954)	81
5.5	Dance's helical model (Dance, 1967)	81
5.6	Maletzke's model (Maletzke, 1963)	82
5.7	The display/attention model (McQuail, 1987)	83
5.8	The relationships between ubiquitous network, Internet of Things, and Internet of sensors	84
5.9	The function model matrix of immersive communication (media diagram)	93
5.10	The function model matrix of immersive communication (media diagram)	93
5.11	The stereo helix model of the immersive communication process	94
5.12	The schematic of the immersive communication relationship model	95
6.1	The function model matrix of immersive communication (three media ages)	105
6.2	Composition principle and functions of IOT	111
6.3	The elevator monitor recorded the fall of a 9-year-old boy	113
8.1	The old man is doing morning exercises in the park	145
8.2	A live sensor in the park reminds the old man: "Your heart rate is higher than normal."	146
8.3	The old man receives a remote diagnosis by a doctor	146
8.4	The doctor pulls up the man's electronic medical records and determines that excessive exercise leads to high blood pressure	147
8.5	Ubiquitous terminals tip (alert): the man's granddaughter Shizuka wants to talk with him	147
8.6	Shizuka wants to learn how to make a paper airplane	148
8.7	The old man teaches Shizuka how to make a paper airplane through video	148
8.8	Shizuka waves goodbye to the old man	149

Table

5.1	Representative intersections in the function model matrix of immersive communication	90

Preface to Chinese edition
Intelligent survival and immersive communication

We live in a time of rapid change: a great invention can be wiped out after a week, and a brilliant business can wilt in a day. In a world that is growing at a breakneck pace, there is a force that is taking over our lives with increasing power and intensity. The great changes it is bringing this very day and night are deeply subversive, yet without shadow or trace.

This kind of power imperceptibly surrounds human beings with a completely new information communication mode, interpersonal communication mode, production mode, and lifestyle. It is omnipresent and omnipotent. It leaves you nowhere to hide! This is because it carries the essential characteristics of the present and future world, based on ubiquitous networks: a new mode of information penetration with infinite energy. It is ushering in a new era that challenges your imagination and transcends any known age. This force, this core force driving the transformation of the world, is the force of modern communication.

What is communication? Throughout history, it has been a key driving force for human progress. The definition of communication itself also exhibits constant revision and expansion, a microcosm of our understanding of the world and ourselves. In the past decade, with the rapid development of modern information technology and the development of the mobile Internet, the Internet of Things, ubiquitous networks, and even biological communication technology, humans' conceptions of intelligent cities, intelligent planets, and intelligent survival are becoming a reality, step by step. At the same time, this is also bringing a set of unprecedented new phenomena, new problems, and new challenges to the field of human life and communication. This new reality strongly impacts our traditional cognitive structure of production, life, and self, forcing us to re-examine the relationships between human beings and the environment, human beings and media, and human beings and human beings.

Believe it or not, it's all around you, or even inside you. Accept it or not, its entry does not require your consent: unless you return to the wilderness, you have no escape. But I do not know whether the isolated peach garden still exists.

It is a ghost, a ghost of modern communication, wandering around the world. It's exciting, it's ecstatic; it's also worrying, even frightening. What is it, exactly? How is this power of communication constructed? What's the pattern? What changes will it bring to the world? What about the future?

xii *Preface to Chinese edition*

What drove me to write this book is a strong desire to find out what kind of new thing modern communication is, and whether there is any correlation or regulation between the law of media evolution and the law of social development. If there is a law, where will it lead human society? What is the communication mode of this new information society we are facing? How is it fundamentally different from the previous ones? How will this new mode affect the course of human society?

The process of pursuing this new communication mode and information trend that are penetrating life and changing the world is, to some extent, just like a person's process of searching for meaning in life: full of temptation and challenge, excitement and disappointment, pain and ecstasy, worry and curiosity, denial and conviction.

This process is also accompanied by grasping and melding our predecessors' theories, straddling the shoulders of communication theory giants. Media evolution rules like "coevolution and coexistence" (Fidler, 1997, 29) and "Anthropotropic trend" (Levinson, 1999, 179) led me to think of pan-mediated communication, to dialogue repeatedly with Marshall McLuhan and Paul Levinson, and ultimately to ponder one question: What will happen if we combine media theory and social development? This undoubtedly requires breaking through the limitations of traditional communication studies and adapting a multidisciplinary perspective. Starting from some fuzzy perception points, I try to explore the law of social development through multiple paths, from technological progress to fashion transition, from the landscape society to the image age, from media integration to social diversity, and from the information society to the media age. Wise men such as Jean Baudrillard showed me the framework of a consumer society, but also prompted a further question: perhaps we are already in a new social age? So is it a new consumer society or a post-information age? Or a new mode and era of communication to be defined? I felt a little too bold, but I had been haunted by a ghost and could not stop. Here is a summary of my research process and its results.

I. Exploring the law between communication and social development

At the beginning of my research, I felt only vaguely that a new thing had come into existence and was strongly affecting us, changing and determining every aspect of our life, work, and entertainment. The feeling grew stronger as the research progressed. A feeling, however, is not a theory. What exactly is this new thing? Is it possible to abstract it into a unique pattern?

This new thing seems to be as ubiquitous as air, invisible and intangible, but you strongly feel its presence and the commonalities it conveys. This commonness, if included in the sequence of communication research, may produce an extended or even transformative breakthrough in the existing research on the characteristics and objects of communication.

With this assumption and derivation, I will study the following two questions.

Preface to Chinese edition xiii

First, from the perspective of communication characteristics, human society has experienced primitive communication → one-way communication → interactive communication. What is the next form of communication?

Second, from the perspective of communication objects, human society has experienced human-to-human communication → mass communication and finally, focused mass communication. Again, what is the next form of communication?

Specifically, what mode comes after interactive communication? What object comes after focused mass communication? To answer these two questions, we need to find the common point of historical progress, which means tracing the influence of communication modes on human social changes. This needs to extend and break through the existing communication theories. However, there are few materials available for this kind of predictive and forward-looking research, and few relevant works are published at home or abroad.

At the beginning, I could not see where the research would lead, but I had a firm belief that this new thing or new law really existed and was really surrounding us. Following the glimmer of this belief, I tried my best to walk forward, discussing and consulting with professors and experts in relevant fields in the United States and China. I especially benefited from discussions with doctoral supervisor Professor Xiong Chengyu and Professor Jin Jianbin of Tsinghua University, until at last my pursuit came to the word *immersion*. From the moment I landed on that word, all my former confusion suddenly cleared. I was sure that I had found the core concept to describe these new problems, and my research finally had a focus. The following analysis seeks to give a new definition and description of the new phenomenon represented by this concept.

Immersion is a new frontier of research on the global scale. Up to now, the research on immersion has been mainly used for network navigation papers, and most of them are about network and ecosystem phenomena. Only a few papers related to media communication research have considered immersion, and most of them are about the interpretation and phenomenological research of "remote" states.

To fill this gap, I creatively put forward and developed the concept of "immersive communication," attempting to reveal its essential characteristics and rules, which I believe already exist and deeply affect our life. A key basis for this new mode of communication is the emergence of ubiquitous networks and their widespread use worldwide. Therefore, I try to expand the embryonic immersive communication theory, to develop immersion from "remote" to "ubiquitous," and to expand the concept of immersion from the original focus on virtual networks to the whole human environment.

On the basis of these breakthroughs, I began trying to give an answer to the first question mentioned earlier: what exactly is immersive communication? In the framework of my redefined immersion communication theory, I began to study the relationship between people and media in immersive communication under the integration of "remote presence" and "ubiquitous existence," and of the virtual and the physical. In this section of the study I revealed the essence of immersive communication, defined immersive communication, discussed its characteristics,

xiv *Preface to Chinese edition*

modes, and development trends, and constructed the functional schema diagram, process schema diagram, relational schema diagram, and functional schema table of immersive communication.

II. The theoretical logic and structure of this book

It is on the basis of the preceding research that the logic of this book was formed: to explore new communication modes and their characteristics, to explore the rules of communication and social development, and to deduce that immersive communication is a new communication mode based on ubiquity that leads to a new communication age— "the third media age."

Simply put, the main progression is: immersion → immersive communication → the third media age. Immersive communication takes its place as the next stage of communication characteristics, while ubiquitous mass communication succeeds previous mode of mass communication. To be specific, these two supporting systems are: (1) from the perspective of communication characteristics: primitive communication → one-way communication → interactive communication → immersive communication; (2) from the perspective of communication objects: self-communication → interpersonal communication → mass communication → focused mass communication → ubiquitous mass communication.

In this research I creatively put forward several new concepts. Here is a brief overview:

1. *Immersive communication.* In this study, immersive communication is defined as a brand new way of communicating information. It is an omnipresent and omnipotent communication with people as the center and the human environment connecting all media forms as the medium. Immersive communication brings a qualitative breakthrough to the way humans receive information, produce, and live.

2. *Ubiquitous mass communication.* This research advances the new concept of ubiquitous mass and then introduces the concept of ubiquitous mass communication, which is defined as "personalized communication based on a ubiquitous network and provided to all people, offering many-to-many and one-to-one simultaneous communication." To go from "ubiquitous" to "ubiquitous mass," the background is the e-strategy era of national rejuvenation at the beginning of the new millennium. With the development of the new, intelligent information era of ubiquity, the environment of human survival and information communication has undergone a major change. Ubiquity as a concept was first proposed by Dr. Mark Weiser, an American scientist, in 1991. The Latin word ubiquitous, meaning "God is omnipresent," is used to compare the omnipresence of communication networks and communication needs.

   Mass communication is one-to-many and one-to-all. Focused communication is one-to-a-minority and one-to-a-part-of-the-people. Ubiquitous mass communication is based on the ubiquitous network; it is both "with people" and "without people," based on the overall mass communication; and it is a personalized information service realized against the background of "with people."

3. *The third media age.* The research described earlier further confirmed my initial judgment and led me to re-evaluate Mark Poster's idea of "the second media age." Poster posits interaction and two-way communication as the main characteristics of the second media age, but this is far from enough to describe and summarize the development status of new communication and the huge social changes on which new communication depends. Therefore, I put forward the concept of "the third media age." Based on the historical process of human information communication, this book declares the arrival of the third media age and predicts the future trends of media development. In short, I define the first media age as the unidirectional mass communication age, the second media age as the interactive, focused communication age, and the third media age as the immersive and "ubiquitous mass" communication age.

Two relationships are worth mentioning here. One is the relationship between technology and communication. Technological progress is an important driving force for the development of immersive communication. Information technology promotes the speed of communication, while biological technology promotes the depth of communication. Communication and social development are all connected and permeate each other in an all-around way.

The second is the relationship between technology and human lives, which is also the basis for the prediction of future human survival. This study combines the virtual and the physical to study immersive communication in the ubiquitous communication environment. This study intends to develop "immersion" from "remote" to "ubiquitous," from the original focus on the virtual network to the whole human environment, and on this basis, to describe the production and living characteristics of immersion.

III. Revelation and prediction of real life

This book seems to be based on an academic imagination or hypothesis, but its foundation is real life. It can be said that this study was inspired by reality, benefited from the collision and stimulation of imagination and thought, and has been subjected to academic research and verification.

So, this is a purely theoretical study, but it is not a work of pure study. More than ten years of research tours in Europe and the United States, working in the communication industry at home and abroad, and even setting foot in the industry as an entrepreneur, have enabled me to constantly open my mind and expand my imagination. Among them, my intensive study and research time was particularly precious, such as my postgraduate study in Columbia University's Journalism School, the communication I established with students through lecturing at New York University, my visit and program production in Massachusetts xvi *Preface to Chinese edition*

Institute of Technology's Media Lab, and my teaching and research at Tsinghua University. At the beginning I was fascinated by movies, so I devoted myself to them, paying attention to visual presentation, to the concentrated exploration of humanity's pursuit of beauty in life and the spread of fashion, and then to the study of consumer society, to the attraction of the ubiquitous Internet and intelligent planet. These processes are constantly updating my knowledge and stimulating my creativity. What has always attracted me is the infinity of the human imagination and the changes it brings to life; what has always fascinated me is the impact of communication on life.

In the process of gradually focusing on "immersive communication" and constructing this new mode of communication, besides the traditional methods of data collection, analysis, investigation, and in-depth interviews, field research proved to be a very effective method. Mobile new media, such as microblogs, microjournals, and WeChat, are also becoming new paths for observation, acquisition of research samples, discovery patterns, and induction and verification patterns. On the one hand, I set up and published microjournals on the Internet to share the latest information from the industry with fans. On the other hand, I sought out the laws and trends behind these information phenomena. Modern communication gives people a new way and platform to communicate with each other. It is based on a new mode of communication, which constantly integrates new technology and imagination space, that is, what I have named the immersive communication mode.

Immersive communication has changed our way of social communication and further promoted a new social structure through the change of social ways, because social communication is one of the foundations of social construction. As the philosopher George Santayana once said, no matter how deeply and simply people live, they will inevitably interact with others. Social intercourse is like air. People can't live without it, but it's not enough to live on it. This new mode of communication is also changing our ways of work and entertainment, allowing our social, work, and entertainment lives to infiltrate and interact with each other anytime and anywhere.

Therefore, immersive communication and the third media age led by it are not only a theoretical study for me, but also a summary of the present life and the anticipation of the future life. I was a childhood fan of the Hollywood fantasy movie futurism, and then grew into a fan of Woody Allen's *Sleeper*, but in fact, those visions of the future in movies have become reality in recent years. Dreams have lost their fantasy element, but they show us the power of human wisdom.

How are the illusions of the past embedded in the reality of our lives? Much of this magic is created by the ubiquitous connection and location-based service described by immersive communication. Let's see what a beautiful morning we can have:

When you wake up in the morning and blink your eyes, the intelligent curtain opens and the warm sunshine comes in.

The air conditioner starts automatically and quickly reaches your preferred daytime temperature.

You get up and go for a run in the park. The electronic display on your smart-watch reminds you that your heart rate has exceeded 30% of normal.

You work up a sweat and come back for a shower. Suitable shampoo for curly hair is already in the bathroom: when you paid for your perm on your mobile phone yesterday, the salon membership management system automatically sent your regular order for shampoo.

Preparing breakfast, you find that you're out of milk. You press the button outside the refrigerator to connect to the supermarket and ask for a gallon of whole milk. The operator answers, "You'd better try our low-fat or skim milk. Medical records show that you have high cholesterol. In addition, your mother's car has just passed Haidian Park. Global Positioning System shows that she can get home in 20 minutes. She has high blood pressure and is also advised to drink low-fat milk."

Five minutes later, low-fat milk is delivered to your door.

When waiting for your mother, you think of another person, so the mobile phone on the desk automatically dials her phone.

Good Morning! Sweet greetings from your loved one come from the air. A virtual image shows her smiling face. The map next to the video shows you that she is enjoying a seaside dinner on Long Island, New York. She sends you a fresh shrimp crawling out of a 3D printer ....

So begins a beautiful day!

This is not a movie or an imaginary future world—this is a living reality that has been realized in some parts of the world. Connected sensors, hidden in every corner of life, are as ubiquitous as air, but quiet.

This human-centered world, where people integrate with their surroundings, where the physical world integrates with the virtual world, has arrived; this is what I call the third media age. The imaginings of five or ten years ago have now been transformed into reality, one by one, before our eyes. We are witnessing the arrival of this new era.

IV. Communication industrialization leads us to the future

The phenomenon described by immersive communication is rapidly becoming a universal reality in life, and I believe that the industrial applications related to immersive communication are also accelerating.

In the third media age dominated by immersive communication, people, media, and the environment are integrated; humans past, present, and future are integrated; and the virtual world and the physical world are integrated. Joshua Meyrowitz's so-called vanishing boundaries have indeed disappeared. No need to play time or space travel drama games: everything has always been around you, never far away, but the boundaries between media in different contexts, different types of audiences, private space and public space, formed by technical and cognitive limitations, have now been smoothed out in electronic media. Immersive communication, just like the fog, once isolated from sight, clears to show the flowers in the field full of beauty.

xviii *Preface to Chinese edition*

The disappearance of boundaries makes possible much that was once impossible, and the unlimited creativity that breaks the boundary promotes the emergence of various new technologies, new products, new industries, and new lifestyles. The fast pace of technology application and industrial integration is promoting the rapid integration of the mobile Internet, the Internet of Things, and ubiquitous networks on multiple levels, such as network, terminal, business, and industry. From smart cities to smart planets, from digital entertainment to smart travel, from shopping guides to telemedicine, these are the latest convergences. The U strategy is spreading around the world. The United States is pursuing the "smart planet" strategy, Singapore is building a "smart island," South Korea is building a "ubiquitous dream hall," and Europe is building a ubiquitous European information society. China has the Mobile Ubiquitous Service Environment plan for "Experience China" astride the "broadband China" strategy. In the ubiquitous era, China has a certain leading edge.

Immersive communication is the latest communication mode and product formed by the integration of communication technologies supporting a U strategy. Here, everything is a medium, including the entire living environment of human beings. In this living environment, by 2017, there were 7 trillion wireless devices connected to the Internet, serving 7 billion people. That is to say, thousands of wireless devices are embedded in the environment around us, enabling various intelligent information devices to perform magic functions. As this book is about to be printed after three years of writing, WeChat has suddenly become a powerful trend in people's lives in China. Google launched a program to keep a diary after the owner died. 3D printers are already in use, and civil society groups in the United States are using 3D printers to print parts and assemble guns that fire bullets. These seem to be just annotations to the theory of immersive communication that I have created.

Wearable devices, in particular, built from technology related to communication, aim to arm us from head to toe: Google Glass can record everything your eyes see, while Baidu Eye can send photos whenever you want. On your feet, you can have sports shoes include singing "Apple + Nike" and talking "Google + Adidas"; in your hands, there are smartwatches and affordable mobile phones. On your body, there are endless new products, including intelligent temperature-control clothes as well as women's exclusive products, such as the super "wolf-proof underwear" invented by three female students in India. It is equipped with a global positioning system and mobile communication system, can send up to 3800 kilovolts of high-voltage current to the violator when a woman is sexually assaulted, and in the meantime will immediately alarm and inform the victim's family members.

The infinite imagination of human beings and the need for survival and development promote the rapid industrialization of new communication technologies. These new products created by new technologies are also undergoing the test of the market. As the power consumption and price of new technologies are reduced, new communication means and methods brought by new technologies are becoming more and more popular, and the marketization pace of immersive

Preface to Chinese edition xix

communication is becoming faster and faster. Nowadays, low-power chips, Bluetooth, Wi-Fi, location-based service, Big Data services, etc. are making it easier and easier to own a private cloud and intelligent information platform, and immersive communication is penetrating into our daily lives with industrialization. Our workspaces, and even our private spaces, are increasingly being transformed into part of the modern panorama society. Fitbit not only keeps track of your daily steps but also monitors how well you sleep; other devices can manage your network and use e-commerce to understand your shopping habits. India's new "anti-wolf underwear" won the Gandhi youth technology award and attracted strong interest, so soon it may be included in women's daily necessities shopping list.

New worries have emerged. As U.S. senators question the legality of 3D-printed guns, there are concerns that the proliferation of similar innovations and new communications technologies may be opening Pandora's box. More people are worried about whether the modern panoramic prison, constructed by an omnipresent, omnimedia environment, will completely change the logic and ethics of people's lives. So, does an "immersive communicator" have a private life? In the environment of information transparency and immersive communication, how do the roles and destinies of people affect each other? What is the relationship between the progress of social civilization and the application of technology?

The answer given by reality is that the constructiveness and destructiveness of new technologies and innovations are often interdependent, and human society will not end up choking away because of the new communication power brought by new technologies and the impact of this power on existing systems and rules. The new business opportunities brought by new communication concepts and technologies will promote the process of relevant industrialization, magnify the benefits and value of human innovation, strengthen contributions to the future, and constantly form a renewed communication force. The industrialization of immersive communication will keep society moving forward with its own innovation.

The power of technology, the power of innovation, and the power of imagination converge into the power of communication. Only through industrialization can the power of communication truly benefit mankind in an all-around way. Immersive media has indeed become an extension of various human senses, an assistant not only to our relaxed life but also to a better understanding and management of ourselves. As the imagination of the past continues to turn into reality, the human imagination will only get bolder and bolder. I hope that my exploration in this book can attract valuable ideas, spur society to an in-depth study of immersive communication, which has influenced and will further affect our lives, and overcome the current theoretical deficiency in related fields. It is hoped that through this study, the "immersive communicators" will be prepared for the future in advance, so that they can provide theoretical support and innovative inspiration for the industry to further expand the market.

Information communication affects human survival, and human survival changes information communication. Mankind is changing from "informationization" survival to "post-informationization" survival, from localized survival to xx *Preface to Chinese edition*

ubiquitous-ized survival. Human existence is not only physical, but also virtual. The third media age is an era when immersive communication plays a leading role, and the physical world and the real world interact with each other. The power of immersive communication will take us into the future and help us survive intelligently.

Qin Li

Preface to English edition

Today, immersive communication is further integrated into our daily life. Five years after its publication in Chinese, *Immersive communication* is being published in English, which makes me feel the power of combining theory with reality.

Due to the rapid development of technology and society, some data have been adjusted and updated in the process of translation. The whole translation and revision process lasted for a year. I was very fortunate to have several excellent publisher and editor teams at various stages of the English version project. Sun Lian, publisher of Routledge China, who recognized the book at the first place and made the whole project possible. Li Yanling, president of International Department of Social Sciences Academic Press, and Lv Qiusha, editor of International Department of Social Sciences Academic Press, whose professional support and spiritual encouragement were critical to the success of the project. Jo Hardern, Senior Production Editor of the Taylor and Francis Production, Vaishnavi Ganesh, Project Manager at Deanta Global, and their teams, who made very help suggestions and accurate proofreading. I also want to thank Jiang Jingkun, Chen Wenxin, Zhang Qiuting, and Ye Ting for helping with some data collection and translation.

I sincerely thank Professor Zhao Qizheng, Dean of the School of Journalism, Renmin University of China and former Director of the Information Office of the State Council of China, for his initial foreword to this book's Chinese version, endorsing the theoretical innovation of Immersive Communication, and encouraging international academic exchanges.

In addition, I would like to take this opportunity to thank Ms. Ji Haihong, the editor responsible for the original Chinese edition by Tsinghua University Press, for her keen recognition and active promotion, which enabled the book to be published and eventually recognized by both academic and practical circles.

Finally, I would like to thank the Chinese Fund for the Humanities and Social Sciences for its support in making the foreign translation of this book a reality.

1 Introduction

Communication is an integral part of human existence. On a theoretical level, communication has developed from face-to-face interpersonal communication to mass communication, starting with the invention of printing, and finally to interactive communication in the digital age. Communication objects have moved in a rough order from interpersonal to mass communication and lastly to focused mass communication, while communication characteristics have moved from primitive to one-way to interactive communication. Accordingly, contemporary human communication has undergone qualitative changes as well as introducing emergent communication problems that cannot be explained by existing theories.

We feel that communication is becoming more and more ubiquitous and omnipresent; we are more and more closely integrated with the media, and recognize that a new mode of communication is greatly changing our way of life. It seems that we are returning to the original state of human existence, going in a circle from the end to the starting point. We have gone from direct face-to-face information and emotional communication between individuals, to using media as a communication interface, to the invisible and even disappearing interface, and now we return to the original starting point of "direct" communication. But has communication really gone back to the more direct borderless communication? Unlike earlier interpersonal communication, this "regression" is designed to meet people's comprehensive personalized needs with the help of a vanishing or invisible boundary, brought about by science and technology. So how is this borderless "space" of human communication different from the past? What is the inevitable relationship between media evolution and the real world?

1.1 Literature review: Theories on media evolution—from interpersonal communication to immersive communication

In the development of communication, media morphosis, modes of communication, the space for communication, and the environment are inseparably intertwined. The new transformation of media morphosis is tending to expand its living and communication space, while new communication modes can also change the media environment and people's lifestyles. Therefore, the study of media and communication is essential to explain the relationship between humans and media

2 *Introduction*

and to master the influence of media on humans' production and lives. Because the new media morphosis represents a new productive force, we can predict the prospects of our society from trends in media developments and forms.

According to Everett Rogers, "The history of communication is the story of 'more'" (Fidler, 1997, p. 26). This "more" refers to a wide variety of media morphoses and modes of communication. Their overall trend, in fact, is to "coexist" and coevolve (Fidler, 1997, p. 29), forming the space and environment of immersive communication that this study attempts to describe. Specifically, the analysis of immersive communication in this book mainly focuses on the developmental relationship between communication and society. This study examines not only the change of media morphosis but also the evolution of the mode of communication, and especially the development of the whole media environment and ecology. It is based on previous theories and research on these major aspects of communication.

1.1.1 The first media age and the second media age

In 1995, just 27 years after the Internet was created in 1968, American scholar Mark Poster published *The Second Media Age*. In the book, he argued that the first media age was the epoch dominated by a one-way "broadcast model of few producers and many consumers of messages" (Poster, 1995, p. 5). By contrast, the second media age was dominated by "two-way decentralized communication" (Poster, 1995, p. 18) with the integration of media producers, sellers, and consumers.

1.1.1.1 Characteristics of the first media age

Poster attributed the era dominated by the one-way broadcast model to top-down communication led by intellectuals and cultural elites, resulting in one-way communication from a few people to the public. This age took the one-way information communication mode as its basic feature, through three periods of time: the verbal society, the print society, and the television society.

In the earliest spoken-language societies, due to the limitations of oral communication and human memory, cultural development basically relied on accumulating experience and generational inheritance. After written characters were invented, human civilization entered a completely new stage. Writing allows human civilization to document its heritage and to constantly create and recreate itself. Written communication also makes it possible for cultures to break through the limitations of interpersonal communication, so people can go beyond the restrictions of "presence." Print communication does not require a physical presence. It enables people in the same space-time to understand and experience different things, and likewise allows people in different space-times to communicate with each other when reading the same book. Compared with verbal communication, print communication can spread beyond time and space, so that people can stay at home but learn of world affairs, greet each other even when separated by thousands of miles, and get to know each other even if they were born in different epochs. For example, after the Russian novelist Tolstoy read the *Analects of Confucius* written 2000 years before, he excitedly wrote down the words of "Chuan-shi" in response.

The first media age was basically a one-way communication era. Oral language is relatively simple; printed characters are relatively complicated. In the first media age, the threshold for receiving information was also usually high. Literacy is a necessary condition and a basic ability for a person to integrate into a society that spreads information through words. Later, schools began to take responsibility for people's socialization processes instead of relying on families. As it is easier to identify different social levels according to one's ability to read written texts, in the first media age, the hierarchy of information recipients was relatively distinct. The authoritativeness of printed words gave rise to a discourse authority and social class in the structure of human society.

From leaflets to books to newspapers and periodicals, print media was the main media morphosis of the first media age, when reading the same texts allowed people to form a spiritual community. American scholar Joshua Meyrowitz, one of the representatives of the School of Media Ecology, provided an example. The sense of "we" in oral societies clearly refers to the community formed through face-to-face interactions; in the print society, "we" also includes communities in different places that share the same text, thus, "traditional group bonds are weakened and traditional distinctions among groups become partially blurred" (Meyrowitz, 1985, p. 131). The text allows people in different places to establish a symbolic community that connects them to each other, thus transcending the real physical community of people formed by living together in an oral society.

From the perspective of communication research, for the first time, print communication broke the concepts of physical "space" and "time," allowing people to form networks and form virtual communities with common knowledge. However, because of the limitations of printing, the telegraph was invented to expedite the spread of words, the telephone was invented to convey sound, the radio was invented to transmit sound, the camera was invented to record images, and the video camera was invented to record and replay moving images. This in turn produced the appearance of film and, later, television communication. The basic principle of a film is to use photography to capture dynamic images as a series of still photos, while television began image signal transmission, pushing communication into the video age. Although the main function of television in its early decades of development was still one-way communication and the audiences were passive recipients, television further accelerated the pace of social integration. Particularly, in 1962, the world's first television satellite "Telstar1" was launched successfully, allowing the people under the Statue of Liberty in New York and the people at the foot of the Eiffel Tower in Paris to watch the same live broadcast at the same time, making a "Global Village" and "telepresence" possible.

4   *Introduction*

1.1.1.2 Characteristics of the second media age

Poster mainly used the term "second media age" to refer to the media era after the advent of the Internet. It can also be said to be the post-television era or the era of digital television. It is mainly characterized by interactive communication. In his book, Poster analyzed the social changes brought by the new communication technologies and their new significance from the perspectives of social theory and cultural theory. He critically considered the concepts of technology and media in cultural theory separately, rethinking the theory of social critique in the first media age and reorienting the relationship between humans and machines. At the same time, he used new media to observe and analyze the postmodern and multiculturalist theories of his predecessors, pointing out that the rapid expansion of electronic media such as the Internet and virtual reality are causing great changes in human communication habits and lifestyles, essentially readjusting people's social identity.

The characteristics of information communication in the second media age are interaction and freedom. The production and exchange of information have become the basic needs of people's lives. People are accustomed to Internet interaction and related lifestyles. The Internet information culture also shows strong technical characteristics, as Internet communication technology largely determines the future of information culture. With the great development of communication technology, a "panoramic prison" has appeared since the middle of the 20th century. Poster attempts to "expose the cultural innovations brought about by the integration of database technology into existing political, economic and social institutions" (Poster, 1995, p. 78). He has expressed the discourse characteristics of the database as follows: "Databases are discourse, in the first instance, because they effect a constitution of the subject. The database is a discourse of pure writing that directly amplifies the power of its owner/user" (Poster, 1995, p. 85).

We cannot say that there is no discourse authority on the Internet compared with printing's discursive authority in the first media age. However, due to the technical support and the audience's initiative, this authority has been greatly diminished and returned to its original state, which is timely and accurate information transmission from communicators to users. The "authority" represented by traditional media has been broken, as technology has gone so far as to openly defy the very nature of modern government power (Poster, 1995). Tencent, Sohu, and Sina are representative Internet platforms in contemporary China. There are also ubiquitous small and medium-sized websites, such as "Tianya Community," "Wangjing Group," and sites for other social or regional groups. In addition to the changes in the authority level, the media's inherent language and functions are constantly progressing. Poster evaluated the contributions of many theorists, such as Benjamin's technical culture, Baudrillard's symbolic exchange theory, and Foucault's panopticon. In his earlier monograph *The Mode of Information*, he analyzed the communication of several cultural contexts in terms of information mode with his original way of thinking, including the political ideas presented

Introduction 5

by Spike Lee in his global hit movie *Do the Right Thing*, the contradictory feminism in Wagner's classic *Ring* cycle, and the tendencies and traits of television critics in the Gulf War.

Compared with the first media age, people in the second media age have more freedom to make choices, and of course they are also faced with various virtual features of postmodernism. Modernity is often defined as the spread of instrumental behavior. Max Weber pointed out acutely that modern society institutionalized instrumental reason in the form of bureaucracy. As Poster noted,

> The paradox and the pathos of modern society (both capitalist and socialist) is that it presumes individual freedom, defined as the capacity of rational choice, thereby rejecting all forms of domination characteristic of earlier social systems. At the same time, modern society institutes a form of organization (bureaucracy) which constitutes a new type of domination.
>
> (Poster, 1990, p. 36)

Deciphering information exchange increasingly shows the social characteristics of electronic media morphosis. The electronic database code produces unambiguous language forms, and a large part of the power of bureaucratic organizations derives from this kind of linguistic form. Poster thus believes that Habermas' concept of communicative action seeks to "preserve an Enlightenment notion of reason. The conditions of the ideal speech situation are that individuals seek consensus by adhering to 'the universal validity claims' of 'truth, rightness, and truthfulness' in symmetrical or equal relationships" (Poster, 1990, p. 41).

Zhou contended that the "[m]icroblog is the most ideal state for 'the second media age,' and communicators become scattered points of communication, with the center of communication disappearing" (Zhou, 2012). Foucault held that discourse is a social group that communicates its meaning to society according to certain conventions and thus establishes its own position in society. This classical theory regards the communication process as an existence based on discourse and holds that the relationship between people and the world is a discursive relationship. As a result, changes in the means of social communication will inevitably bring about changes in the form of social discourse. Foucault also proposed three main ways of social discourse: political power, intellectual elitism, and general daily life. He believes that these three approaches represent three main social forces competing for discourse power. Microblogging, as a product of the second media age, is a communication structure that integrates posting, retweeting, commenting, and following. It can be said that it provides a platform for the peaceful coexistence of the three modes of discourse expression, showing a new kind of relationship of discourse power that is different from previous media communication. Of course, microblogging is also an outstanding representative of the second media age, and its media morphosis and mode of communication have not yet departed from the essential characteristics of this media age.

6 Introduction

1.1.2 Evolutionary trends of media morphosis: "Coevolution and Coexistence" and "Anthropotropicness"

Media morphosis research is the core of media research. The so-called media morphosis refers to the evolution of the media under the influence of many factors, such as consumer demand, market competition, political pressure, and social and technological innovation. As the American media scholar Roger Fidler put it in his classic book *MediaMorphosis*, morphosis is "[t]he transformation of communication media, usually brought about by the complex interplay of perceived need, competitive and political pressure, and social and technological innovations" (Fidler, 1997, p. xv).

Other scholars define media morphosis as "the state of existence of the media (including the external form of the media and the communication symbol as an internal structure), the basis for survival, the method of media communication (including the form and approach that the audience receive media information) and the media functions and features" (Cai & Huang, 2003). They believe that media morphosis can be divided into visual morphosis and latent morphosis. Visual morphosis refers to the external shape and hardware of the media, which is the representation of the media as a social unit displayed to the world, while latent morphosis denotes the internal form of the media, mainly referring to its internal structure and the relationship between different parts. Both types tend to integrate with one another, a consensus of the theoretical community. Many forms of media communication, including oral language, printed characters, electronic media, and new media on the Internet, follow evolutionary laws of media morphosis. Among those laws, the most relevant are "Coevolution and Coexistence," "Metamorphosis," "Propagation," "Survival," and "Opportunity and Need" (Fidler, 1997, p. 29).

"Coevolution and Coexistence" means that all media influence each other, evolve constantly, and interweave together in a developing and complex media system. Moreover, the emergence and development of each new medium will have some influence on the existing media. A typical example of this is the impact of television on the movie: movies provide television content. The Internet and media industries such as books, magazines, telephones, mobile phones, television, movies, and records all coexist. The result is a pluralistic pattern of communication channels and forms. As McLuhan pointed out, "This fact, characteristic of all media, means that the 'content' of any medium is always another medium" (McLuhan, 1994, p. 8).

Next, "Metamorphosis" indicates that the rise of the new media is not spontaneous and independent. On the contrary, they gradually evolve from the old media morphosis through continuous technological breakthroughs, sometimes through partial improvement and sometimes through revolutionary leaps and innovations. When a new media morphosis has come into being, the old one is usually adjusted and transformed in response to demand, but rarely completely disappears. A typical example is the transformation of traditional paper media. In order to adapt to the emergence of new media, newspaper websites, magazine websites, and so on have appeared.

Introduction 7

Similarly, "Propagation" emphasizes how newly developed media forms often inherit major technical characteristics from earlier ones and maintain and disseminate these features through various propagation codes, such as programming languages. For example, Windows' personal computers were developed from the design and application interface of Apple's Macintosh; Explorer was developed from the Internet browser Netscape.

Next, "Survival" traces media adaptation or demise. In an ever-changing media environment, all kinds of media need to change from time to time. If they fail to progress, they will withdraw from the stage. For this reason, the old media need to constantly adjust their positioning in the market and in meeting consumers' needs. For example, magazines develop from generality to particularity, and broadcasting changes from targeting a broad audience to a narrow one. In the United States, for example, the 40 years after the 1960s were the golden age of magazines. They were the main entertainment medium of the time, maturing in the first half of the 20th century to form a modern magazine system. Radio arose in the United States in the 1920s. It was literally the first national medium. However, by the 1950s, under the impact of television, both magazines and radio were facing a crisis, and they ultimately survived by changing their market positioning to serve specific groups. The adaptation methods of these adjustments and evolutions mainly include "personalization," "localization," and "specialization."

Finally, "Opportunity and Need" means that the recognition of a new medium by society or the market does not depend solely or primarily on its technical characteristics. Technical characteristics provide possibilities, but for technology to be truly promoted and developed, it must adapt to the corresponding social, political, and economic needs. For instance, in the video industry, VHS beat Betamax, although Betamax was a higher-quality videotape format than VHS. The reason was that Sony held Beta as a proprietary technology, while JVC shared VHS format with manufacturers. Since any manufacturer was able to produce VHS tapes, the price of VHS tapes steadily declined, and the VHS market share continued to expand.

McLuhan's Four Laws of Media model also inspires the study. McLuhan's theory is human centered, emphasizing the role of people and proposing that "the media is the extension of man" (McLuhan, 1994, pp. 77–235). His four laws or four effects of media are amplification, obsolescence, retrieval, and reversal. But, as Levinson said in *Digital McLuhan*, these four laws are only relatively clear, "and in many respects, their very open-endedness—in which a given medium, such as television, could be reversed not only into computers but into cable, VCRs, holography, and almost as many things as a mind could reasonably imagine – made them just as frustrating as the earlier formulations for people with no heart for McLuhan's daring metaphors" (Levinson, 1999, p. 188). McLuhan's model is basically a linear analysis, but his successor Levinson expanded the model by regarding the four laws as four paths. In his opinion, there is a relationship between the media and its effects, that is, a cyclic expansion and a progressive expansion. In this cyclic process, there is a real progressive movement, which is not a closed circle but a spiral expansion. This four-in-one continuity derives

8   *Introduction*

partly from the "outdated" component of "reversal" and partly from new media or new effects because it does contain certain characteristics of the earlier media.

From these different theoretical perspectives, we can also see the complexity of the changes in media morphosis. Human communication is a complex and adaptable system, influenced in its pace and progress by all kinds of forces. In terms of influences on the evolution of media morphosis, several theories consider the relations between technology and society, including technological determinism, social determinism, interactive constructivism of technology and society, and the Anthropotropic Theory. This theory was first proposed by Levinson in his 1979 doctoral dissertation *Human Replay: A Theory of the Evolution of Media*. The core concept is:

> [A]s I discuss in my "anthropotropic" theory of media evolution—tropic=towards, anthropo=human—the overall evolution of media can be seen as an attempt, first, to fulfill the yearnings of imagination by inventing media that extend communication beyond the biological boundaries of hearing and seeing (thus, hieroglyphics and the alphabet and the telegraph each in its way extends words thousands of years and/or thousands of miles), and, second, to recapture elements of the natural world lost in the initial extension (thus, photography recaptures the literal image lost in writing, and telephone, the phonograph, and radio recapture the voice).
>
> (Levinson, 1999, p. 179)

Levinson argues that his second criterion, which includes McLuhan's idea of retrieving the medium of the past, is a great step beyond that, because he specifies what medium it is possible to retrieve. He says, for example, that the invention of the telephone replaced the telegram and fulfilled the need for progress, as we need the telephone to carry out two-way interactive communication and "retrieve" the missing "sound" part of the telegram. Other similar examples are the use of color photographs instead of black-and-white photographs, because the human eye wants to see the true colors of nature, which can be achieved by optical replication technology. In the same way, films with sound replaced silent films. However, radio has not been wiped out by television, because eavesdropping—listening rather than watching—is a significant part of the natural (pre-technological) environment of communication, and radio has done that perfectly. "Each medium enhances, obsolesces, retrieves, reverses into many more than one thing or effect" (Levinson, 1999, p. 17). In all cases, the media that stand firm and flourish must have a reason: they copy, adapt, and reproduce some of the important aspects or means of biological communication without an intermediate.

This study tends to argue that technology, humanity, and society are all interactive constructions. Based on the two variables of technology and society, this study focuses on the trend of humanization and studies the formation of "immersion," its performance varying with influence, and its communication characteristics as a newly evolved medium arising from the relationship between media and humans.

Introduction 9

1.1.3 Media space, environment, and ecological theory define the relationship between media, humans, and the environment

Media space, environment, and ecological theory belong to three intersecting conceptual and theoretical systems. The study of immersive communication is based on the relationship between humans and their environment. It focuses on the overall environment and is related to media space, environment, and ecology to some extent. The environment of immersive communication can be considered as a self-organizing system. The behavior of this complex system is caused by the activities of human beings, and changes along with changes in human production and lifestyle. It is human participation that fills the environment with its great vitality. Therefore, many scholars use ecological research methods and theories related to organisms and their habitats to observe and analyze the complex interaction among media morphosis, media environment, and media communication modes. According to Cui Baoguo (2004), "The construction of media ecology mainly falls into two categories. Human-centered—the study of human and media environment; media-centered—the study of media and its survival and development environment" (Cui, 2004, p. 265). In this study, people, media, and the environment are temporarily in a state that has not been clearly defined or needs to be redefined. Therefore, it can first be defined as a study of the relationship among people, media, and the environment.

As the name suggests, media ecology has borrowed the basic ideas of ecology. The earliest proposed concept of "ecology" can be traced back to the monograph *General Morphology* published by the German scholar E. Haeckel in 1866. In this book, Haeckel interprets the morphological structure of living things from the perspective of evolution, describes the relationship between each factor and other factors in the natural environment with the concept of "ecology," and pays special attention to how the resulting events work together to produce a harmonious and healthy co-living space and environment. Some scholars regard public demand, political pressure, technological innovation, economic development, and inter-media competition faced by media morphosis as the external ecological environment for media survival and development. They believe that changes in the external environment can induce changes within the media; in particular, the thorough innovation of concepts, technologies, and systems will ultimately promote the transformation of the media's own ecological environment.

The so-called media ecology theory actually studies the media itself as an environmental structure. There are two main schools of research in media ecology. One mainly looks at the influence of media on human production and lifestyles, ways of thinking, and cultural expressions from a technical point of view. It emphasizes the significance of the media as an environment and culture. The other school rethinks technological rationality from the perspective of humanism, seeking a healthy interaction between nature and each subsystem of human society. Although their starting points of thinking are different, both schools share "human-centered" ideas and complement research on the influence of media technology on social environments. From the perspective of semiotics, a medium

10   *Introduction*

produces different symbolic environments. When we cognize the world, we need to do so within a symbolic structure. To use a certain medium is to understand and adapt to the symbolic system it constructs, and to realize that sets of composite symbol systems often coexist in a large environment where they have a compound impact on human beings. Neil Postman defines media ecology "as the study of media as environment" (Lum, 2006, p. 28). He stated in his keynote address at the inaugural annual convention of the Media Ecology Association in 2000 that "human beings live in two different kind of environments. One is the natural environment, and consists of things like air, trees, rivers, and caterpillars. The other is the media environment, which consists of language, numbers, images, holograms, and all of the other symbols, techniques, and machinery that make us what we are" (Postman, 2000, in Lum, 2006, p. 62) The media environment shapes human beings. It can be seen that the two concepts of "media environment" and "media ecology" are to some extent synonymous in the field of media research.

Media ecology focuses on the impact of technology on society and is related to the Western emphasis on technological rationality. As human civilization passed through the Renaissance, the Enlightenment, and the Industrial Revolution in the 19th century, rational cognition continued to deepen and reached a peak during the Industrial Revolution. Technological rationality brought about by the machine industry not only improved people's living conditions but also simultaneously led to alienation between humans and machines. Western media ecologists, from Mumford to Innis, from the Frankfurt school to Postman, have mostly held a technologically pessimistic position on this process. McLuhan's inheritance from Mumford promoted the further development of "technical determinism" and made him a representative of the idea that media is technology. He believed that the media has a great influence on the maintenance of sensory equilibrium in human beings; by constantly improving itself and the human environment, media has the power to push society forward. McLuhan first put forward the concept and theory of "media ecology," and Postman subsequently established a special media ecology course and research project at New York University, which really made media ecology a discipline. He also took the lead in collating and publishing a large number of relevant academic works, forming the classical theoretical basis for media ecology. Chinese scholar Shao Peiren's research on media ecology is mainly centered on the media and studies the factors that influence the survival and development of the media, including the interaction among society, politics, economy, and the audience, and puts forward the concept of "media ecological interaction." The "media environment" defined by Cui Baoguo includes two aspects: "The media environment is a kind of living environment and communication environment for human beings. It is the media's ecological environment for the survival and development of the media itself" (Cui, 2003).

In communication research, the concept of space is also a key factor, but it has long been ignored by media research institutes. Space is a polysemous concept. Media scholarship focuses on not only geographical and natural space but also social, environmental, and human psychological space. For example, on the scales of regions, cities, and countries, space is a complex and multiple environment.

Introduction 11

Therefore, space can be regarded as either a specific physical form or a virtual mental form. Especially with full access to electronic media in social production and life, mankind's sense of space has turned from reality to virtual reality and from personal experience to media experience, thus fundamentally promoting a shift in the concept of space. This has even resulted in the media, which originally manifested social status and cultural symbols through communication, becoming an object that needs society's attention and application in order to maintain the space for its survival and development. Immersive communication research explores the feasibility of constructing the concept of "large space" on the basis of the existing concepts of space.

The concept of space varies across disciplines. In media geography, space is the landscape and material in the media environment; in media sociology, media is the brain and central nervous system of society and is located at the core of the society, while the concept of space represents the whole process of social construction. In the eyes of the 18th-century German philosopher Immanuel Kant, geography represents space, while history represents time. Anthropologists argue that the concept of society and space includes two combinations of "place and no place" and "modernity and super-modernity," so places can have symbolic significance in relationships, identity, and history. One of the foundations of the construction of media "space" is text (written words). As Sigmund Freud (1930) wrote in his famous *Civilization and Its Discontents*, writing is "the voice of an absent person" (p. 38). There are two basic situations in which a voice is not present: the space is too far and the geographical distance is too large, or the time is too far away and the listener is only present before or after the speech. Of course, both situations can be present at once. But just as with life and matter (material existence), communication can only move forward in time, not backward. At least, that's what most previous studies have suggested.

How does media break through and transcend geographical space, and how does the latest media technology reconstruct the division of geographical space? Changes in international social factors have prompted the re-division of the world's "space": the United States, as Samuel P. Huntington (2011) described, has consistently promoted its global society model, establishing an economic free trade circle around the three combined forces of North America, East Asia, and the European Union, and a dividing line between the fast-growing developing countries and the poorest countries. In terms of human perception and judgment of the media space, in addition to the environment's influence on reflected reality, the concept of space that already exists in people's minds will also directly affect their interpretation of the surrounding media space. Ernest Burgess, one of the founders of the "Chicago School," proposed a theoretical construction of the city's concentric circles as early as the beginning of the 20th century. He pointed out that cities are divided into different functional areas and can be divided into material spaces composed of concentric rings, each of which can be divided into smaller subspaces. These different spatial regions feature the coexistence and interactive development of different functions, and different locations and spaces are combined to form different scenes accordingly. The combination of these

12   Introduction

multiple factors and time and space ultimately determines people's perception of urban space.

Based on these theories, space can be divided into three major concepts. Immersive communication's understanding of space is mainly constructed on these three concepts, but they are merged together without boundaries. The first space, physical space, refers to the spatial system built with the physical environment of matter. This first space is concerned with the objectivity and materiality of space. Henri Lefebvre's *The Production of Space* is an important work representing Western scholarship on social space. He reflects on the traditional Western epistemology of space and then tries to construct a new tri-dialectics of dialectical unity of history-society-space. On the one hand, space is interpreted from the perspective of history and society; on the other hand, history and society are interpreted from the perspective of space. Lefebvre discussed "various types of space" including "physical space, mental space and social space."(Lefebvre, 1991, p. 14) His space is not only a material existence but also a spiritual existence, and more importantly, presents the existence of social relations. Therefore, a city is an important part of space: whether it is an ancient Roman city-state or a modern smart city, we can build a cognitive construction from both material and spiritual aspects. The spatial meaning, from the external landscape to the internal culture, is ultimately determined by the existence of human beings.

Next is the virtual space, also called the second space. The second space is abstract and virtual compared with the first space of matter. Its key element is the construction of discourse. The imaginative and personal characteristics of human beings construct the second space through forms such as literature, philosophy, and art, and the text of media communication can also be established in it, such as the description of the psychological world in literature or the landscape reproduction of emotions by music. Furthermore, "a computer science that can dominate space in such a fashion that a computer—hooked up if need be to other image—and document—reproducing equipment—can assemble an indeterminate mass of information relating to a given physical or social space and process it at a single location, virtually at a single point" (Lefebvre, 1991, p. 355).

In the modern virtual cyber world, the construction of the life people desire takes the form of new imaginary space. The imaginary space will also have the possibility of becoming a reality, especially as the development of modern science and technology is merging imaginary space with virtual space. This merger is an important part of communication research. With the development of modern virtual and communication technologies, many things that were once mere dreams have been transformed into reality. For example, the fictional Mickey Mouse in film has become a realistic figure and is active in Disneyland resorts around the world; singing clothes and talking shoes that used to exist only in children's fairy tales are now sold in real shops. The ever-changing spiritual world is always fascinating, and it often becomes reality in the form of matter. This makes the two spaces inevitably overlap, flourishing interdependently with each other. The boundary between the first space and the second space is gradually disappearing in the age of immersive communication.

Introduction 13

Lastly, there is smart space or thirdspace. The term "thirdspace" was proposed by Edward W. Soja in his 1996 book *Thirdspace: Journeys to Los Angeles and Other Real-and-Imagined Places*. It is different from both physical and virtual space: it is a social background integrating the first two spaces and integrating the subject and the object. Soja (1996) "defined Thirdspace as an-Other way of understanding and acting to change the spatiality of human life, a distinct mode of critical spatial awareness that is appropriate to the new scope and significance being brought about in the rebalanced trialectics of spatiality-historicality-sociality" (p. 10). He argued that everything comes together, subjectivity and objectivity, the abstract and the concrete, the real and the imagined, the knowable and the unimaginable, the repetitive and the differential, structure and agency, mind and body, consciousness and the unconscious, the disciplined and the transdisciplinary, everyday life and unending history. Thirdspace is such an open space containing all things. The boundaries between reality and the imagination or between the concrete and the abstract disappear. Media is the necessary bridge and carrier for the third space to cross the first space and the second space. The Thirdspace medium, like thirdspace itself, has strong openness. The thirdspace is the interlaced zone between material and experience. In the age of immersive communication, it is also a smart space and a ubiquitous space. We live in a highly connected and intelligent world. Homes, office buildings, shopping malls, elevators, etc. are filled with screens. All kinds of smart mobile terminals and surveillance cameras occupy our living space and every corner, impacting us and watching us day and night. The space where the individual and the environment are integrated is the modern thirdspace. It is a completely open space, and it is also the spatial background that immersive communication study examines.

In summary, both the concept of space and the concept of environment and ecology, as well as the spirit of "individualism" advocated by the West for a long time, have affected the research orientation of communication studies. The resulting research has always been people centered and regards people as the most important element. As Levinson and other scholars have emphasized, "compensating media" can remedy the deficiencies of past media and make media more humanized. Immersive communication studies examine the media space and environment from the perspective of people, paying attention to the influence of technology or the technological force represented by media on the production mode, lifestyle, and thinking mode of human beings. This study argues that the two aspects of "the media's environment" and "media as the environment" (narrowly defined media ecology) are interrelated and interact with each other. At the same time, the meaningful environment created by humans and media is also a result of mutual influence, forming the interactive integration of the physical world and the virtual world. The media environment background of this study is mainly constructed in this category. In the following analysis, unless otherwise specified, "media space" will collectively refer to the media environment, media ecology, and media space, because the concept of "space" is closer to its relevant discussion on immersive communication.

14   *Introduction*

1.1.4 How ways and modes of communication evolve to "vanishing boundaries," and how communication tools and communication relations are reconstructed

Norbert Wiener, the founder of cybernetics, published *Cybernetics, or Control and Communication in the Animals and the Machines* in 1948, proposing that the operation of both biological systems and technical systems follows the paths of information communication and feedback in this groundbreaking work. The former path generally refers to the communicative relationship and its characteristics formed by certain means and channels of communication. It represents the advanced productivity and discourse performance of an era. The mode of communication is an abstract summary and refinement of these ways of communication.

The emergence of written characters has led to a qualitative leap in human communication, from simple interpersonal communication to a higher-level communication mode. As the crystallization of the continuing evolution of ideographic symbols, these characters enabled human communication to transcend the limitations of time and space for the first time. Subsequently, with the continuous development of science and technology, along with the advent of printing, human beings fully entered the era of mass communication. The advent of telegraphy, telephony, film, and other means of communication, especially the operation of television and synchronous satellites, has brought humanity into a new era of information experience. The Internet era is yet another new milestone, where interaction is the theme of this era of communication.

The history of human communication is roughly divided into several major stages, from interpersonal communication to mass communication, focused mass communication, and interactive communication. On the basis of interactive communication, media is no longer a medium but a pan-medium. As early as the 1960s, Marshall McLuhan proposed the "pan-media theory," arguing that the extension of all human communication organs can be regarded as a medium, and that the medium itself produces a lot of information. This has important implications for later studies in the academic community on "social mediatization," "media environmentalization," and "environmental mediatization."

The media morphoses and modes of communication are "the story of 'more'" (Fidler, 1997, p. 26), and media integration is an indisputable fact. With the development of electronic media, "vanishing boundaries" occur in the communication field. Joshua Meyrowitz associated McLuhan's points with sociological concepts, especially the sociologist Erving Goffman's idea of private mask and public mask, reflecting on the mode of communication and proposing the emergence of "no sense of place" in communication. Meyrowitz's *No Sense of Place* (1985) was written too early to fully grasp the digital domination of the world. However, his prediction of the development of the media was verified by later facts. Although his evaluation at that time was mainly about television rather than computers, he discussed how the differences and boundaries between various mass electronic media were weakening at an earlier and more comprehensive level. He also pointed out that the place where one lives is less and less related to

Introduction 15

one's knowledge or experience. Electronic media have changed the significance of time and space for social interaction (Meyrowitz, 1985).

Generally speaking, people's physical location and social interaction will affect their behavior patterns. However, when electronic media make physical space or space restrictions disappear or change, how will the mode of human communication be affected? Will humans' social relations and communicative behavior change as a result? How do they change? The greatest impact of the electronic media on human society may not be the information content they convey but the fact that electronic media have broken the original connection between "physical place" and "social place," causing the reconstruction of our communication logic and living environment. In the new environment and social structure, people must regain a vital identity, social role, and concept orientation. In his later reflection on the connection between people and places, Meyrowitz wrote:

> "I did what most of us do in everyday interaction: I highlighted certain aspects of my personality and experience and concealed others. ... I thought of myself as a unified 'me' who always behaved in roughly the same way. I focused, as I now realize, only on what was constant in my behavior: across situations. I concentrated on my choices within a given situation, rather than on the overall constraints" (Meyrowitz, 1985, p. 1).

Electronic media has redefined the concepts of social "place" and media "place," breaking the traditional relationship construction between media space and social space. It continuously creates new spaces or scenes, including physical scenes such as rooms and buildings, as well as "information scenes" and virtual scenes created by media. According to the human social communication and interaction scenario described by Goffman (1959), people appear in a variety of scenarios in the society, taking on constantly changing roles and statuses, so it is necessary to understand and follow various codes of conduct in order not to mess up when switching between different roles. Goffman's "social scenario" is on the surface a constantly changing "performance," but this dynamic realization requires a relatively stable social order as its basis; that is, relatively fixed individual roles, social rules, social backgrounds, and group membership. In the ongoing social drama, individuals must abide by the corresponding social traditions, earnestly rehearse their own roles, and continue to perform. Goffman believed that environmental limitations are an important factor influencing a person's behavior. These so-called environmental limitations are determined by the places of social interaction and the audience in the group. However, he ignored the point that people's social roles and status change from time to time. McLuhan also noticed that the use of electronic media has changed the social role and status of people; "even in the age of one-way television, how new media could make large areas small enough for that kind of interaction" (Levinson, 1999, p. 71). But he did not further analyze how and why these changes occur. Meyrowitz suggested that "the mechanism through which electronic media affect social behavior is not a mystical sensory balance, but a very discernible rearrangement of the social stage on which

16   *Introduction*

we play our roles and a resulting change in our sense of 'appropriate behavior'" (Meyrowitz, 1985, p. 4).

Immersive communication studies the spatial scene in which different social spaces, media scenes, or virtual scenes are combined, especially the mixed scenes produced by electronic media. Such scenes are long-lasting or even ever-present and inevitable, so they have a greater influence on social behavior. Many of the behaviors that were appropriate in the first media age and the second media age may become inappropriate in new immersive communication situations. In this regard, this is a similar description to that in *No Sense of Place*: due to the electronic media, various types of people come to the same place, and their former social roles are no longer suitable here.

Meyrowitz inferred that the impact of electronic media on us was not essentially through content, but through changing life scenes and place:

> We would have trouble projecting a very different definition of ourselves to different people when so much other information about us was available to each of our audiences. Certain behavior patterns that never existed before, therefore, would come into being. In the combined setting, some behaviors that were once kept in the "backstage" of each performance would, of necessity, emerge into the enlarged "onstage" area. We would be forced to say and do things in front of others that were once considered unseemly or rude. The behavior exhibited in this mixed setting would have many elements of behaviors from previously distinct encounters, but would involve a new synthesis, a new pattern—in effect, a new social order.
>
> (Meyrowitz, 1985, p. 6)

Therefore, Meyrowitz predicted that the restructuring of human social scenes, coupled with the transformation of communication modes, would bring about the transformation of human behavior patterns, thus promoting the reform of social norms and the reconstruction of social relations.

1.2 The origin and theoretical evolution of the concept of "immersion"

The concept of "immersion" was first proposed in the 1970s in terms of the psychological idea of "flow," (Csikszentmihalyi, 1975) so the two terms are often used simultaneously and overlap with each other. Later, virtual technology connected immersion to modern science and technology. Communication scholarship often applies immersion to studies of both virtual reality and remote interactions.

1.2.1 The origin of "immersion" concept

In Chinese, "Flow" is translated as both "Flow of Heart" and "Immersion." It explains why people fully engage in their daily activities with a high concentration of attention, filtering out all unrelated perceptions and entering an immersive state.

Introduction 17

In 1990, Csikszentmihalyi published his influential work *Flow: The Psychology of Optimal Experience* and systematically introduced the "Flow Experience." In his words, people are most happy when they are in a state of flow—a state of concentration or complete absorption with the activity at hand and the situation. It is a "state in which people are so involved in an activity that nothing else seems to matter" (Csikszentmihalyi, 1990, p. 4). Furthermore, he argued that the flow state is an optimal state of intrinsic motivation, where the person is fully immersed in what he or she is doing.

> Concentration is so intense that there is no attention left over to think about anything irrelevant, or to worry about problems. Self-consciousness disappears, and the sense of time becomes distorted. An activity that produces such experiences is so gratifying that people are willing to do it for its own sake, with little concern for what they will get out of it, even when it is difficult, or dangerous.
> (Csikszentmihalyi, 1990, p. 71)

In an interview with *Wired* magazine in 1996, Csikszentmihalyi likened immersion to a person's wholehearted state of devotion to playing jazz: "Being completely involved in an activity for its own sake. The ego falls away. Time flies. Every action, movement, and thought follows inevitably from the previous one, like playing jazz. Your whole being is involved, and you're using your skills to the utmost" (Geirland, 1996). Csikszentmihalyi likewise pointed out in *Finding Flow* that to achieve a flow state, a balance must be struck between the challenge of the task and the skill of the performer.

> "Most activities that produce flow also have clear goals, clear rules, immediate feedback—a set of external demands that focuses our attention and makes demands on our skills. ... But just free time with nothing specific to engage one's attention provides the opposite of flow: psychic entropy, where one feels listless and pathetic" (Csikszentmihalyi, 1997, p. 66).

Linda Klebe Trevino and Jane Webster developed Csikszentmihalyi's concept of flow to propose the "Flow Theory" in 1992, pointing out that "flow characterizes the perceived interaction with CMC [computer-mediated communication] technologies as more or less playful and exploratory" (Trevino & Webster, 1992). Similarly, Trevino (Trevino & Webster, 1992) wrote, "[f]low theory suggests that involvement in a playful, exploratory experience—the flow state—is self-motivating because it is pleasurable and encourages repetition. Flow is a continuous variable ranging from none to intense." The stages of this flow include "Concentration," "Control," "Interest," "Anxiety," and "Arousal" (Trevino & Webster, 1992).

The flow theory study featured several methods of data collection and measurement, including descriptive surveys, empirical sampling, and an activity survey. A descriptive survey was mainly used by the participants to describe their own flow experiences and then use survey tools to evaluate each experience. The Experience Sampling Method (ESM) uses a pager or watch alarm to remind participants to fill

18 *Introduction*

in the handbook on time. It is a research method Csikszentmihalyi founded at the University of Chicago in the early 1970s, and is now one of the most commonly used methods for measuring flow. In his book *Finding Flow*, Csikszentmihalyi specifically discusses this investigation method: participants receive calls every two hours, every day for a week, and "when the pager signaled," participants should write down where they are, what they are doing, what they are thinking, and who they are with. Then, they would use numbers to describe their current state of consciousness, such as happiness, concentration, motivation, self-esteem, etc. (Csikszentmihalyi, 1997, p. 79), and then use survey tools to evaluate their ongoing activities at the time of the call.[1]

Thomas P. Novak and Donna L. Hoffman also proposed their own methods of measuring and investigating flow experiences. In order to conduct an empirical study on their own network flow model, Novak and Hoffman designed a construal development scale in 1996. After four months of preliminary testing, they established a final survey consisting of 77 items. This questionnaire eventually received 19,970 responses, the basis for their further analysis (Novak et al., 1997). However, as the development of modern digital technology pushes humans into the environment of human–computer interaction, virtual reality, and mobile Internet, scholars have not only observed and analyzed the physical and mental state of humans but also begun to study the structure of environmental information and its influence on people. The study of immersion from the perspective of communication has just begun.

1.2.2 Immersion's application in virtual reality

Both flow and immersion are significant in the literature on human–machine interaction, resulting in several intersections of research fields. In general, immersion research focuses on the study of the environmental factors that cause immersion, while flow emphasizes the effect of immersion. In 1996, Donna L. Hoffman and Thomas P. Novak first applied the concept of a flow experience to network navigation. Hoffman mainly studied social media, while Novak was committed to the exploration of the virtual world. They collaborated on the concept of using the virtual to better understand the real world. They defined flow in network navigation as a psychosomatic state, which must include several key elements: (1) human–computer interaction leading to a series of seamless and uninterrupted reactions, (2) truly enjoying the process, (3) entering into a state of selflessness, and (4) being able to motivate oneself in the process. Hoffman and Novak also examined virtual life in settings such as Second Life and explored the connection between the virtual world and the physical world (Novak and Hoffman 2000).

---

1   In his work *Finding Flow*, Csikszentmihalyi describes the experience sampling method (ESM) and describes the time that the subjects are called every day, from early morning to 11 PM or later. At the end of the week, each person can fill out the whole 56 pages of the ESM manual and faithfully record their daily activities and experiences. Researchers can look for changes in a subject's mood when he or she was engaged in an activity or was with someone.

Introduction 19

Novak and Hoffman also jointly published "Measuring the Flow Experience among Web Users" (Novak & Hoffman, 1997), an empirical study of the state of immersion in the Internet environment. The first public presentation of the study was made at the Interval Research Corporation in 1997, followed by additions and amendments in 2000. On the basis of *Finding Flow*, they proposed the construction of skill and challenge, a pair of key elements in the flow experience. If the challenge is too high, people will feel anxious or frustrated because of lack of control. On the contrary, if the challenge is too low, people will feel bored and lose interest. The flow state mainly occurs in the balance between challenge and skill.

Novak and Hoffman expanded the concepts of flow state in the Internet environment, emphasizing nine elements: skill (people's cognition and ability to act), challenge (opportunities and difficulties given by actions), control (people's level of control over the course and outcomes), encouragement (motivating people to have interest and enthusiasm for action), focused attention (people concentrating their attention on action), telepresence (people having the feeling of being in a virtual environment), interactivity (people participating in the construction of the media environment's form and content), exploratory behavior (people pursuing their inner needs to achieve the action goals and values), and positive affect (the entertainment and positive emotional impact of the action itself). Their theory has been widely used in discussions of the behavior and psychology of netizens in Internet environments, such as Internet surfing, bulletin board systems (BBSs), online games, and online shopping, to explore the flow experience of human–computer interaction and to describe the causes and patterns (laws) of the "flow" phenomenon in network use behavior.

Immersion has also been applied in communication scholarship, mainly in terms of virtual reality (VR). VR applies to computer-simulated environments that can simulate physical presence in places in the real world and the imaginary world. As cited in Hudson, Matson-Barkat, Pallamin, and Jegou (2019), VR uses computerized and behavioral interfaces to simulate the behavior of 3D entities such as people, places, and objects in a virtual environment (VE). These entities interact with each other in real time, engaging one or more of the users' five senses (Fuchs & Moreau, 2006; Guttentag, 2010). It can be seen that virtual reality is the product of the integration of computer technology and information technology, forming a new tool and mode of communication.

The emergence of VR can be traced back to a report titled "The Ultimate Display" presented by Ivan Sutherland, director of the Advanced Research Projects Agency (ARPA) Information Processing Technology Office of the United States, at the International Federation for Information Processing (IFIP) conference in 1965. At that time, virtual reality appeared in the venue only in the form of a graphic emulator. In 1968, Sutherland successfully developed the head-mounted display "Damocles' Sword." It was the world's first head-mounted display, although it could only show 2D images, and it can be regarded as the prototype of 3D interactive technology. It was hard for the wearer to achieve the feeling of immersion because the experience was not realistic enough, but it let people see the dawn of virtual reality applications. After more than ten years of

20   *Introduction*

arduous research, American computer scientist Jaron Lanier officially proposed the concept of VR in the early 1980s; in 1992, the world's first virtual reality development system came out to high expectations. Since then, VR systems of various forms and functions have been developed. At the end of the 20th century, products that incorporated key technologies such as multimedia technology, computer graphics, human–machine interface technology, simulation technology, artificial intelligence, and sensor technology were born, one after another. They can all create a real-time, dynamic, three-dimensional image world for users through analog simulation. With almost realistic perceptions and interactive experiences such as viewing, listening, touching, and smelling, people can experience the feeling of immersion.

The perceived characteristics brought by VR with a human–computer interface are generally called the "illusion of immersion" because VR uses computer and communication technologies to impact the human body's perception system, allowing people to fully immerse themselves in the virtual environment and interact with it, creating an illusion that makes people cross the limitations of time and space. Indeed, studies on both flow and immersion argue that the immersion of virtual reality is mainly the immersion of the perception system. The first form is visual immersion. Vision is the most important factor to form the feeling of immersion, because about 90% of human perception comes from vision. VR image processing technology and stereoscopic display make people's eyes produce parallax, creating realistic stereoscopic feelings and magical visual immersion. Virtual towns and architectural designs presented in "smart cities" often use this technology. The second form is auditory immersion, as 15% of the information that humans obtain is from hearing. Hearing can also increase visual perception and enhance one's sense of environmental simulation. Finally, immersive systems use tactile immersion, behavioral system immersion, and the immersion of other sensations. Human beings have extremely sensitive perception systems and behavioral systems. For example, Japanese scientists have developed a simulator for the human olfactory system that can make the fruits in a virtual environment also emit fragrance: when people sniff a virtual orange in a virtual environment, the device associated with the virtual environment immediately emits a faint orange scent. VR technology can be confusing and even surpass things in the real world, which makes it easier for people to be completely immersed.

In addition to visual, auditory, olfactory, and tactile sensory systems, human beings also exert influence on the environment through their behaviors and languages. VR is widely used in both engineering and communication. At the same time, virtual reality in the online world has emerged, which creates the illusion of an online representation of real life and makes many people experience a sense of immersion, in both body and mind, while playing in these online virtual worlds. However, these are just the initial meanings of the concept of immersion in this study, and they belong to the concept of immersion of the "first space." Based on these previous studies, this study attempts to demonstrate that in immersive communication, media and people are fully integrated, forming a large space of immersive communication that integrates the three spaces described earlier.

1.2.3 Remote presence and immersive communication

With the development of electronic information technology, virtual reality has changed from the physical experience of entities to virtual worlds on the Internet. Internet and mobile communication enable people to enter a "remote presence" state anytime and anywhere. This concept has two basic layers. The first layer refers to the omnipresence achieved through the emerging remote presence technology. This technology makes comprehensive use of computer-generated three-dimensional imaging, virtual reality, and electronic holography to move the remote real-world environment to the vicinity and implement interventions, thereby bringing people into a wonderful and realistic three-dimensional world and reaching a realm that is not a real world, but better than the real. As for the second layer, it refers to the remote presence in the sense of mobile communication, which achieves omnipresence by means of electronic communication.

The origin of immersion as a concept was covered earlier in this chapter, but only a few fragmentary discussions have considered immersive communication specifically, so no complete theory has been established. First, it is worth mentioning that the concept of immersive communication was first proposed in research on virtual reality. It is mainly used to refer to human–computer interaction based on a combination of elements of the perceptive behavior system in virtual reality, as well as the immersive characteristics in such interactive communication. As one study put it, "Virtual reality, with its new communication technology and unique interface design, is creating an immersive communication method that has never been seen in history" (Hang & Su, 2007). Once this phenomenon is fully recognized and accepted, virtual reality will become a very influential medium, because compared with traditional media such as film and television, it can communicate beyond time and space.

After entering the field of virtual reality, especially in terms of remote presence, immersive communication began to attract research attention in some technological industries, such as the related electronics industries. For instance, the Institute of Electrical and Electronics Engineers (IEEE) is an organization of engineering and electronics experts in the United States, which also attracts a large number of members from other countries to form "the world's largest technical professional organization dedicated to advancing technology for the benefit of humanity" (IEEE, 2019). In recent years, IEEE has paid much attention to immersive communication. The 34th IEEE International Conference on Acoustics, Speech, and Signal Processing (ICASSP), held in April 2009 in Taipei, China, can be seen as the world's oldest, largest, and most comprehensive professional technology conference dedicated to signal processing and applications. "Immersive Communication" is one of its four thematic forums, chaired by Ton Kalker, Zhengyou Zhang, and representatives from Microsoft and Hewlett-Packard. The forum discussed user experience, language processing, 3D video, and multimodal processing. Its organizers introduced immersive communication in this way:

With the advent of modern communication technology, physical distance is no longer a barrier to real-time interaction. But current technologies are not

22   *Introduction*

perfect: cellular networks typically lack a video component; broadband connections hardly provide for an immersive experience; high-end remote presence solutions are expensive and constraining. Therefore, there is a strong need for research and development of advanced technologies and tools to bring immersive experience into teleconferencing so people across geographically distributed sites can interact collaboratively. This requires deep understanding of multiple disciplines.[2]

The overall theme of the 2009 ICASSP conference was "Signals over the Horizon," emphasizing that the frontiers of technology and the invention and application of various new technologies are creating a new horizon for communication. IEEE also began collecting papers from scientists and researchers around the world in 2009 to publish the "IEEE Signal Processing Magazine Special Issue on Immersive Communication." Its open letter of solicitation noted that

> The vision of immersive communication is to enable natural experiences and interactions among people, objects, and environments as if they were co-located, although they may be geographically distributed. In recent years, various research communities have been developing technologies for capturing, processing, analyzing, transmitting, and rendering remote people, objects, and environments (such as room reverberation and lighting) across space and time. For example, we are on the verge of moving from traditional teleconferencing systems to telepresence systems, which is a form of immersive communication enabling effective remote collaboration through realistic audio-visual reconstruction of participants and their environments. Additional future promising applications of immersive communication include education, entertainment, health care, and industrial design.[3]

In other technological literature, studies of immersive communication mainly examine immersive video, immersive audio, multimedia network communication for immersive communication, signal processing and rendering to expand and enhance user experience, immersive interaction interfaces and sensors, and systems for immersive communication. However, these studies are mainly in the field of electrocommunication: research from the perspective of communication studies and direct references to "immersive communication" are rather limited. Professor Xiong Chengyu of Tsinghua University once pointed out: "With the development of interactive media, the emergence of mobile media, and the innovation of the Internet of Things in the future, we will be immersed in a media-surrounding environment. New media technologies have become more and more indispensable. There will be a new type of communication—virtual telepresence and immersive communication" (Xiong, 2011). What he refers to as immersive

2   www.icassp09.com/TS-3.asp
3   www.signalprocessingsociety.org/uploads/Publications/SPM/CFP_immersive_communication. pdf

Introduction 23

communication is based on the mobile Internet and advanced portable terminals, forming a ubiquitous, all-time, and omnipotent communication platform.

The study of immersion and immersive communication, starting from virtual reality, first and foremost reflects humanity's deep dependence on media, as the human-centered nature of media penetrates almost every field of society and then pushes the environment to be completely mediated. A fully mediated natural environment and social environment have already started becoming reality and are a trend for the future. Of course, this also brings many new problems, just as McLuhan argued that all media can have some connections with the human body. When the information subject has more information choices, it will increase the risk of public opinion. In his *Playboy* interview, he said: "[The tribal will] is consensually expressed through the simultaneous interplay of all members of a community that is deeply interrelated and involved, and would thus consider the casting of a 'private' ballot in a shrouded polling booth a ludicrous anachronism." (Levinson, 1999, p. 71) In *Public Opinion*, Walter Lippmann (2010) proposed the concept of the "pseudo environment," which is the symbolic environment that the mass media provides to the public through selecting, processing, and restructuring news and information, emphasizing the traditional media's disguised control of information and its influence on social orientation. In today's media society dominated by immersive communication, the authenticity, authority, and depth of information are at risk of being further decreased. A highly developed media society may lead to the distortion of sourcing information or the unlimited expansion of the harm of misinformation.

In the study of immersion, scholars are also concerned about such things as "virtual race," a specific reality derived from the Internet that may affect ethnicity. Can people keep their regionally rooted racial identities when they are in cyberspace? On the Internet, people create a unique identity image for the purpose of communication. Will the ability of each person to dress up his or her identity with words also affect and determine his or her success in interpersonal communication? This raises the question of the new balance of power in human society brought about by the Internet.

Overall, immersion studies started with the initial psychological concept of flow and then extended to the crossover with the concepts of flow experience and the illusion of immersion that emerged from the study of virtual reality. Next, they moved to the idea of immersive communication used in the study of electronics and Internet technology, and finally to the ubiquitously immersive communication environment, which is studied in this book. Technological progress has always been an important driving force in the development of immersive communication, so this study adopts a technical orientation of "immersion" rather than following the "flow" system, although it is compatible with many flow-oriented perspectives and methods. Its goal is to give a certain normative definition and inspiration for immersive communication study, to promote the relevant technical standards, and to establish the specification and system construction for professional research on immersive communication.

24 *Introduction*

1.3 Media technology and social development: Conditions and environment for the evolution of immersive communication

In this section, we observe and analyze the changes in the environment where people live and in the media environment. When thinking about the development of communication, it is necessary to recognize the global development environment we face, the nature of the information society, and the most active new phenomena in globalization. If there is a correlation among these phenomena, what is its nature and extent? Likewise, what is the influence of media morphosis change on communication change?

Scientific and technological progress has always been a powerful driving force for the development of human society. Marx and Engels (1848) once said that "the bourgeoisie, during its rule of scarce one hundred years, has created more massive and more colossal productive forces than have all preceding generations together." Indeed, by less than 100 years after the Industrial Revolution, more productive forces had been created than all those that human beings had created in the past. The history of modern communication also clearly shows that the progress of science and technology is an important and necessary condition for the development of modern communication and the evolution of social forms.

With the advent of the Internet and the ubiquitous network, profound changes have taken place in the global media environment. Mobile phones and other mobile terminals are playing an increasingly important role in people's information lives. In 2008, the Pew Internet and American Life Project predicted that by 2020, most people in the world would access the Internet through various mobile terminals for work and life, and that a mobile social network, developed on the basis of the need to access information on mobile phones, would become an important carrier for people to establish their own social status and develop social networks (Anderson & Lee, 2008).

China has also rushed to join this unavoidable globalization process. The scale of Chinese netizens and the Internet penetration rate in China have shown rapid and steady progress in the first decade of the century. As of the end of December 2011, the total number of Chinese netizens had increased by 4 percentage points from the end of the previous year, reaching 513 million people, while the Internet penetration rate reached 38.3% (CNNIC, 2012a). After seven years of high-speed development, according to the 43rd Statistical Report on the Development of China's Internet Network published by the China Internet Network Information Center (CNNIC) in February 2019, as of December 2018, the number of Chinese Internet users was 829 million and the Internet penetration rate had reached 59.6%. Among them, 817 million people are mobile Internet users, 98.6% of whom access the Internet via mobile phones (CNNIC, 2019). Mobile Internet access is a powerful driving force for the growth of Chinese Internet use. Correspondingly, the number of users who access the Internet in a fixed manner continues to decrease as mobile users increase (CNNIC, 2013). According to CNNIC, the total number of Internet users using mobile phones to access the Internet in China surpassed that of desktop Internet users in 2012 (CNNIC, 2013). By the end of 2018, the number of people using desktop computers to access the Internet was only 48%, down about 25 percentage points from 2011 (73.40%), while the number of people using mobile phones to access the Internet was up by about 52 percentage points from 2011 (CNNIC, 2012a, 2019).

Globally, nearly 4 billion of the world's 5.5 billion adults own a smartphone and are connected to a vast array of information and services on the ubiquitous web (Strategy Analytics, 2018). Meanwhile, China's smartphone market saw its first decline in shipments in 2017, marking the end of the era of rapid smartphone development, according to a report by research firm Canalys (Sohu, 2018). The global smartphone market has also declined for four consecutive quarters, the industry's first annual decline, according to data released by Strategy Analytics at the end of 2018. Apple topped the list with a market cap of $1 trillion in the summer of 2018, but CEO Tim Cook started the New Year 2019 by lowering Apple's revenue forecast for the fourth quarter of the previous year, sending stock markets around the world into turmoil. After a decade of rapid smartphone adoption, few first-time buyers remain. As *The Economist* reported, "Apple's pain is humanity's gain. The recent slowing of smartphone sales is bad news for the industry, obviously. But for the rest of humanity it is a welcome sign that a transformative technology has become almost universal" (*The Economist*, 2019).

People's habits in accessing the media are also undergoing profound changes: "The change in the proportion of exposure time of different types of media in the total exposure time of the audience is as follows: except that the proportion of the Internet increases greatly, the proportions of the remaining four types of media all decrease to varying degrees. This means that the Internet has a stronger competition for audience time" (Cui Baoguo, 2011). Data from CNNIC also shows that the way Chinese netizens use the Internet to communicate has changed significantly in recent years, with mobile and social networking becoming important features. The usage rate of traditional communication applications, such as email and blogs, continues to decline significantly. At the same time, the user scale of online banking, online shopping, online payments, group purchases, and other e-commerce applications continues to increase steadily. The number of young and well-educated people who watch videos has overtaken the number of people who watch television, and online video has more influence than television among well-educated people.

The role of mobile phones in people's lives likewise continues to become more important, with fragmentation becoming a powerful complement to the growth of Internet use. People use in-depth Internet services and applications, prompting linkage effects based on social characteristics. Access to PCs, mobile phones, TVs, tablets, cameras, and other devices continues to improve the service content of the Internet. The commercial value of the mobile Internet is even more prominent. In 2018, Internet coverage in China further expanded, with the "last kilometer" of network infrastructure in poverty-stricken areas gradually opening up and the "digital divide" bridged at a faster pace (CNNIC, 2019). Mobile traffic charges dropped significantly, inter-provincial "roaming" became history, the threshold

26 *Introduction*

for residents to access the network was further lowered, and the efficiency of information exchange was improved.

In the past half a century or so, starting with a beautiful utopian prediction, human beings have been continuously conjecturing and demonstrating the arrival of the information society and the post-information society. With the constant innovation and development of modern information technology, dreams about an information society have become a reality. A new revolution is also driving the progress of human society: a ubiquitous communication concept, which emphasizes "anytime," "anywhere," and "omnipotent" characteristics as the latest qualities of human communication, is taking us into the post-information society. Nowadays, people live not only in the real world but also in the virtual world. In real environments there are virtual elements, while in virtual environments this is reality. This is the ideal environment for media development. Let's take a look at some of the specific communication phenomena that are emerging, and how they are related.

1.3.1 From "informational" survival to "post-information" survival

In 1995, Nicholas Negroponte presciently argued that human society had entered the post-information era: "The transition from an industrial age to a post-industrial or information age has been discussed so much and for so long that we may not have noticed that we are passing into a post-information age" (1996 p. 163). In the post-information era, people and the media blend with each other. Information becomes extremely personalized, mass communication turns from broadcasting to narrowcasting, and individual narrowcasting can be turned into broadcasting instantly through media. In fact, perhaps the concepts of the era of mass communication, such as broadcasting or narrowcasting, are insufficient to describe the relationship between human beings and information today. Human beings are entering a new era of communication.

At the end of the 1950s, the term "information society" began to appear. The American scholar Daniel Bell (1973) first proposed the idea of "post-industrial society," deeply believing that the accumulation and communication of theoretical knowledge was a direct force of social change, and implied that the post-industrial society would be an information age, where information is a powerful driving force for social development. The impact of Bell's imagination inspired other theorists to construct the future society in the following decades, and several representative figures emerged. Among them, American futurist Alvin Toffler set off the wave of the information revolution with his *Third Wave*. Toffler outlined a beautiful blueprint of the future information society and metaphorically described it as "a Third Wave phase" following "a First Wave agricultural phase" and a Second Wave industrial phase" (Toffler, 1980, p. 20). Another American futurist, John Naisbitt (1982), wrote *Megatrends: Ten New Directions Transforming Our Lives* in 1982, analyzing the pace of transition from the industrial society to the information society, and predicting the symbol and characteristics of the future

Introduction 27

information society. It also opened up a new thinking mode for analyzing social progress.

Corresponding to the expectations of the theoretical community, the technological revolution brought about a series of industrial revolutions. Since the 1990s, the rapid development of the information superhighway and the Internet worldwide has led to a new level of informatization in society, as new types of information communication modes have emerged. The human expectations of the information society have turned into a series of new technology applications and new lifestyles. As survey data published by the CNNIC shows, new mobile smart terminals have begun to replace desktop computers and become the main tools for people to send and receive information. This has happened not only in China but also globally, which is in line with the characteristics of mobility, speed, and efficiency in the post-information age. Based on upgrades to computer information processing technology, these mobile terminals integrating text, pictures, audio, video, and other information communication functions are closely associated with people, especially personal information terminals such as the iPhone. The Guinness World Records Office in 2011 identified Microsoft's Kinect motion-sensing camera as the world's "fastest selling consumer electronic device," with 8 million units sold in 60 days. However, the iPhone 4S broke this record: Apple announced that it had sold more than 37 million iPhones in the last quarter of 2011. Although there is no accurate sales data on iPhone 4S, according to a market research company, the iPhone 4S accounted for about 89% of iPhone sales, and after Apple released the iPhone 4S on October 14, 2011, more than 33 million iPhone 4S units were sold in 78 days. Apple also claimed that more than 4 million iPhone 4S units were sold within the first three days before its official release (The Video Bus, 2012). The hot sales of the iPhone's various follow-up models continued until 2018, when the Apple legend started to be replaced by newly emerged smart speakers.

With the continuous development of artificial intelligence (AI), all the intelligence in the ubiquitous connection is poised to take over human life: "The smart assistant will reach its potential anytime, anywhere, seamlessly across multiple user scenarios" (Canalys, 2019). Ubiquitous sensors will provide AI assistants with new "senses" that can act as a medium between them and their environment. Home AI assistants use smartphones and smart speakers as hubs to communicate with other smart assistants such as laptops, smartwatches, and connected cars that can carry out voice commands built into them. Nicole Peng, senior director of Canalys Mobility, said, "The adoption of smart assistants is no longer a question of price or availability." The key to 2019 is sound, and smart speakers are bringing technology to center stage. Global shipments of smart speakers were 16.8 million in the second quarter of 2018, up 187% from a year earlier. Canalys predicts that the United States will have 1.6 billion devices supporting smart assistants in 2022, with a total of 351 million smartphones and 129 million smart speakers (Canalys, 2019).

Fierce battles are heating up between global big brands over intelligent information terminals and applications. The first decade of this century focused on all

28 *Introduction*

kinds of social networking sites, Instant Messaging (IM), and personal space on the Internet, from blogs to Twitter and from YouTube to Facebook. Now, from smartphones to smart speakers, from virtual reality to artificial intelligence, terminals and applications integrate the use of multiple technologies and modes of communication. As a result, they are free to switch among various information processing methods, such as the Internet and mobile Internet, publishing and receiving information. People can enjoy the features of instant synchronization, recipients and transmitters have equal rights and can swap roles at any time, and the boundary between the virtual world and the physical world is even fuzzier. According to relevant statistics, by April 2011, the number of Twitter registered accounts had exceeded 200 million. And by the end of 2011, registered users on China's Weibo had passed 300 million (China Media Technology, 2011). WeChat, which integrates social, mobile, entertainment, and business, went online on January 21, 2011, and accumulated 100 million users in 433 days. This adoption speed is four to five times that of Twitter and Facebook, which reached more than 300 million users in two years and one billion users worldwide in 2018. Still, Weibo is only the third most active user application in the global social software sector, behind WhatsApp's 1.5 billion active users and Facebook's 1.3 billion active users.

Similarly, due to the increasing popularity of mobile terminals, network communities, and personal microblogging, location-based services (LBSs) are becoming increasingly popular and attractive. Technically speaking, an LBS or MPS (mobile position service) obtains mobile terminal users' location information (geographic coordinates) through telecommunication operators' radio communication networks (such as GSM or CDMA) or an external positioning method (such as the Global Positioning System [GPS]), relying on a geographic information system (GIS) platform to provide users with corresponding services. In short, LBS is "location + service": it first locates mobile devices or users and then conducts location-related information services. In addition to mobile phones, many wearable devices, such as smart glasses, musical running shoes, and electronic pedometers, are now equipped with LBS.

The positioning-related service system is not a new technology. The 911 system in the United States and the 110 and 120 phone system in China have long had the function of finding the current geographic location of mobile phone users. However, it was not until the development of functions such as "check in" for entertainment or social life services that LBS came into full play with the concept of commercial competition. This mode enables businesses to carry out precise marketing to consumers: Foursquare gains an average of 15,000 new users every day, a growth rate exceeding that of Twitter at the same stage of development. In 2010, China's Dianping formally introduced the Foursquare model of location-based mobile social service. The Dianping mobile app includes an LBS function, allowing users to search for nearby restaurants, movie theaters, shops, and other information through their mobile phone's GPS or assisted GPS (AGPS) functions. Under the premise of interesting interactions, Dianping's check-in function can improve the accuracy of merchants' location information and facilitate LBS precision marketing in the later stage through active user participation. The

Introduction 29

opportunity for resource interaction between merchants and users via Dianping is exactly the advantage of its Foursquare model. According to the company's data, within a year of introducing Foursquare, it had covered 700,000 businesses in more than 300 large and medium-sized cities across the country, with over 16 million monthly independent visitors and over 200 million monthly page views. Many other imitators in China, including WanzhuanSifang, LaShouSifang, Cubenet, and Streetside, also attracted VC contestants (Financial Circle, 2010). China's Ministry of Industry and Information Technology predicts that by 2020, the revenue of Big Data–related products and services will exceed 1 trillion yuan (about 145 billion U.S. dollars), with an annual compound growth rate of about 30% (Xinhua, 2017).

At the same time, the combination of traditional media and new technologies has led to the emergence of new media fields, such as smart television. On December 19, 2011, the *Wall Street Journal* quoted executives from several major media groups as saying that Apple was working on the legendary "iTV" smart TV, an unfinished project of the late Steve Jobs. The new product, they said, will stream TV shows and movies wirelessly, allowing users to watch them as they are being downloaded. The iPhone and iPad can also be used as TV remote controls to search channels and switch pictures by voice control, while AirPlay also allows users to use an Apple phone or tablet to bring unfinished TV shows on the road to continue watching. Apple was also said to be likely to integrate DVDS with its iCloud service, so that users can enjoy watching programs through multiple devices by a one-time purchase or recording the programs. In addition to Apple, a number of global high-tech giants are eyeing the smart TV market. Microsoft has upgraded the game system Xbox360, allowing users to use it to watch and order video programs, while Google launched a set-top box and partnered with Samsung and LG to develop a TV using Google software. The origins of television can be traced back to 1926. More than 80 years later, smart TV dreams such as these of Apple, Google, and Sony are changing people's traditional viewing experiences. What other functions will this information terminal with a screen carry? Or is there any function that it can't carry?

Electronic terminals are accelerating the pace of integration, and the integration of various media is also intensifying. For example, traditional online shopping for physical books, periodicals, and other publications is shifting from entity to virtual. The Dangdang electronic book platform was put into trial operation at the end of 2011, which can be regarded as an innovation of a traditional "old brand" online bookstore in China. The driving force of its innovation derives not only from digital publishing but also from the rapid spread of wireless Internet and mobile terminals. In addition, print media has shifted from predominantly "newspaper-to-Internet" interactive management mode to a user-oriented integrated platform construction. Mobile video is increasingly becoming the basic content of newspaper networks, and print media have started to build social media platforms, introducing cloud computing intelligence databases. These developments also influence print media such as newspapers, which are moving from a product-oriented mode to a new user-oriented communication mode.

30   *Introduction*

There are also more life-related changes in information communication; some are seemingly small but imply significant revolutions. A small SIM card based on the Internet of Things, which can be installed on a phone without changing the number, can utilize "swiping the phone" for shopping, taking the bus, clocking in and out of work, and so on. And then there will be face-brushing: the alphanumeric codes now in common use will be replaced by biometric indicators such as facial recognition and retinal scans. According to an annual report released by IBM at the end of 2011, five major innovations are expected to bring significant changes to human life, including the rapid development of mobile communication technology that can eliminate the "digital divide," and fields such as e-commerce and telemedicine will benefit greatly. Intelligentization will narrow the digital gap continuously so that machines can talk with people, just like Siri, the iPhone's artificial intelligence voice assistant, which has partially achieved this goal (IBM, 2011). These predictions have now been fulfilled.

In the post-information era, information transmission will be more accurate and feature personalized customization. Spam email will be extinct. This does not mean that companies will send fewer advertising messages, but that such emails will become more personalized and targeted. Mail filters will also become more and more accurate, minimizing the possibility of users receiving irrelevant information. New real-time analytics technology can tailor and deliver the information users need most, based on their web preference and their behavioral characteristics on social networking sites.

The transition from "informational" survival to "post-informational" survival is fundamentally reflected in knowledge management and information acquisition. Media has become an important channel for obtaining information. The way people access knowledge is not limited to traditional knowledge bases such as classroom lectures and libraries. Knowledge and information are scattered throughout the network and surrounding environment, presenting a decentralized and open ubiquitous knowledge environment. On the one hand, people can search for information through such ubiquitous networks. On the other hand, they can use blogs and personal spaces to publish information and establish information interaction with others. With the emergence and development of immersive communication, and the digital gap's disappearance brought about by the advancement of humanized science and technology, the media for communicating knowledge will be better integrated with people.

1.3.2   From "localized" survival to "ubiquitous" survival

The current lifestyle and developmental environment of human beings can be said to be inseparable from media at any time and in any place. In recent years, a new goal in information communication has resonated in the world: the "ubiquitous" (or simply *U*) network communication and communication mode. Compared with the previous electronic communication, ubiquitous communication is characterized by its emphasis on omnipresence.

Introduction 31

This ubiquitous network society (UNS) is entering our lives in the footsteps of the 4G and 5G era. 5G, as a fusion technology, pushes wireless communication technology to a new height, brings new breakthroughs in mobile computing technology and applications, and promotes the transformation of the mobile communication industry from technology driven to demand driven. Professor Zhang Ping, director of the Key Laboratory of Ubiquitous Wireless Communication of the Ministry of Education, Beijing University of Posts and Telecommunications, believes that "the distinction between broadband mobile communications and broadband wireless access is becoming increasingly blurred. The Internet, mobile communications and digital broadcasting networks will constantly be integrated at three levels which are services, networks, and terminals. This convergence will be reflected in the political, economic, and industrial dimensions" (Zhang Ping, 2009). "Perceive China" and "Smart Earth" emerged in this integration. Immersive communication based on ubiquity connects the world as a whole. The communication revolution triggered by ubiquitous network technology and ideas have affected all spatial dimensions of human living environments. Every day, billions of people all over the world interact in it, and communication is ubiquitous, occurring anytime and anywhere.

The concept of ubiquitous communication was first proposed by the American scientist Dr. Mark Weiser in 1991. He used the Latin word ubiquitous ("omnipresent") to illustrate the ubiquity of communication networks and communication demand. Weiser introduced the idea of "ubiquitous computing" in his article "The Computer for the 21st Century," which was first published in the *Scientific American* special issue on Communications, Computers, and Networks in September 1991. He predicted the arrival of the era of ubiquitous computing: "Ubiquitous computing names the third wave in computing, just now beginning. First were mainframes, each shared by lots of people. Now we are in the personal computing era, person and machine staring uneasily at each other across the desktop. Next comes ubiquitous computing, or the age of calm technology, when technology recedes into the background of our lives" (Weiser, 1991).

Apart from his emphasis on the ubiquitous nature of computers, Weiser pointed out that they become very quiet in places that were "invisible" to us. In a conversation, he said: "The purpose of a computer is to help you do something else," "The best computer is a quiet, invisible servant," and "Technology should create calm" (Weiser, 2012). In Weiser's description of the ubiquitous era, computers are embedded in the environment or everyday objects, and smart terminals are all around without a trace. He believes that the more invisible the technology, the more profound it is, because it integrates completely into everyday life and serves us like water and air. These are the basic conceptions of the later developed concepts of "ubiquitous network" and "ubiquitous society." Twenty years later, Weiser's ideas have mature technical support, such as embedded technology, radio-frequency identification (RFID) sensor networks, micro-power, cloud computing, and wireless communication. The key is how to construct such a ubiquitous environment with corresponding devices, and networks can achieve the "ubiquitous and invisible" communicative demands and effects.

32 *Introduction*

In 2009, the International Telecommunications Union (ITU), the UN's specialized agency in charge of information and communication technology (ICT), published the "Y. 2002 standard proposal" to delineate the blueprint of a ubiquitous network and define its key characteristics, namely "5C" and "5Any." "5C" refers to Convergence, Contents, Computing, Communication, and Connectivity, emphasizing the functional features of the network's omnipotence. "5Any" refers to AnyTime, AnyWhere, AnyService, AnyNetwork, and AnyObject, emphasizing the coverage feature of a ubiquitous network. The construction and function realization of a ubiquitous network mainly depend on the existence and interaction of three ubiquitous physical entity layers: network transmission, terminal unit, and intelligent application. U-Japan, U-Korea, and so on indicate the specific practices of the earlier ubiquitous network. The European Union and other countries recognize and follow this new goal of human information communication, believing that this goal is higher than the information society, as it represents the highest level of the upcoming comprehensive integration of modern information technology and human production and life.

When connection is satisfied as a need and participation becomes a natural way of life, then these phenomena, such as the consumption of fragmented time, the formation of fragmented culture, and the corresponding virtual communities, can all be regarded as the realization of an essentially ubiquitous network. Based on the concept of ubiquitous communication, a new wave of the construction of the UNS has emerged globally, and it is listed as a grand future development plan beyond the information society. The new information development mode focuses on U features with ultra-high speed in the "post-information era," replacing the electronic (E) rejuvenation strategy put forward on the occasion of the new millennium, namely, the development mode of E science and technology.

From a worldwide perspective, Japan and South Korea first began to reform their practices from "E" to "U," a trend that rapidly spread across the world through the national resolution of each country. According to the China Information Industry Network, Japan upgraded from the new millennium version of E-Japan to U-Japan in June 2004. The U-Japan strategy, adopted by the Japanese cabinet, was listed as a key project of the annual ICT development strategy "Heisei 17 ICT policy outline," aiming to build a "4A" environment in Japan by 2010, where "anytime, anywhere, anyone, and anything" can be connected to the Internet. South Korea upgraded its 2002 version of the E-Korea to the U-Korea strategy in March 2004. The E strategies of Japan and South Korea both focus on IT infrastructure, but they switched to U strategies after the significant improvement of communication infrastructure. A U strategy emphasizes that the development of information technology should not only meet the needs of economic growth but also promote the transformation and improvement of people's daily lives. The goal is to enable anyone to enjoy the convenience brought by modern information technology, at any location and at any time.

The ubiquitous characteristics and demands of the information society are bound to promote the comprehensive integration of various communications technologies and human production/life. In ubiquitous vanguard countries such as Japan and South Korea, two core foundations—mobile and broadband—are being built first to complete the key elements of the UNS: a machine-to-machine dialogue via the Internet of Things. South Korea is leveraging U technology in its bid to conquer the world market. The government has teamed up with telecommunications giants such as Korea Telecom (KT), SK Telecom, LG Telecom, and Samsung Electronics to create the "Ubiquitous Dream Hall," an ubiquitous demonstration application environment. Led by the Ministry of Intelligence and Communications, Korea Telecom and SK Telecom jointly promoted the country's digital home network and established the SK Association and the KT Association to integrate their respective standards. Japan's Nippon Telegraph and Telephone Corporation (NTT) DoCoMo has likewise implemented a "mobile ubiquitous" business goal and has also actively developed and launched a variety of U-shaped applications.

Singapore's "Next-Generation I-Hub" program was officially launched in 2005, but the country's informatization construction started in the early 1980s. In 1992, it put forward the IT2000 plan, a "smart island" plan to improve the quality of life, which uses ATM exchange technology as the core and the integrated HFC and ADSL network as the backbone, and connects all homes, offices, and public places through local area networks (LANs). Subsequently, Singapore successfully implemented national information construction projects such as "21st Century Information and Communication Technology Blueprint" and "Connected City." If its previous several informatization strategies were still in the E-strategy phase, then the "Next-Generation I-Hub" plan, launched by the Information and Communications Development Agency of the country in February 2005 to achieve ubiquitous connectivity through ubiquitous networks, demonstrates that the U network construction is formally incorporated into the national strategy. The goal is to build up the entire island into a truly ubiquitous network world.

In September 2006, the European Information Society Congress discussed "i2010—Creating an omnipresent European information society" and reached a strong consensus: the information society is becoming a new ubiquitous information society in which anyone can communicate with any person or anything, at any time and in any place. In 1999, Europe established the eEurope plan to seize the new economy and new opportunities on the Internet and catch up with the United States in information technology. The EU's five-year plan "i2010" for creating a ubiquitous network social information and communication policy framework was announced by the European Commission in June 2005. Its goal is to promote economic growth and employment. According to i2010, the era of digital convergence requires the integration of communication networks, content requirements, and terminal equipment to form a consistent management framework and develop market-oriented new technologies. i2010 has three priority objectives, known as "3i": to create a unified European information space, to strengthen innovation and investment in ICT, and to build an information society featuring inclusion and a better quality of life.

The United Nations plays a positive guiding and normative role in the global development strategy from E to U. In the World Summit on the Information

34 *Introduction*

Society (WSIS) held in Geneva at the end of 2003, the United Nations for the first time began to discuss the ubiquitous network. The 2006 ITU Radio Frequency Identification Symposium was also held in Geneva, which specifically put forward the concept of the Internet of Things, emphasizing that it can realize the important characteristics of ubiquitous network connectivity at any time and any place.

In 2005, China submitted to the ITU a future ubiquitous communications plan named MUSE (Mobile Ubiquitous Service Environment). MUSE is a controlled connection mode and business mode, with many terminal devices throughout the environment, and the form of network construction by terminals can vary with tasks or demands. This is a soft environment for business services supported by computing. China is indeed speeding up its ubiquitous construction. The "2011 China IT Market Index Analysis Report," issued jointly by the Ministry of Industry and Information Technology's Monitoring and Coordination Bureau and the China Electronic Chamber of Commerce, believes that "in China, cloud computing and the Internet of Things are entering the growth phase." Cloud computing is emerging as a core technology, and in the next three years it will be increasingly used in government, communications, medical care, education, and petroleum. The cloud computing market size will be increased from 16.8 billion yuan in 2010 to 117.5 billion in 2013, with an average annual growth rate of 91.5%. Similarly, the Internet of Things has major strategic potential and can effectively promote the consolidation and upgrading of the industry; its market will maintain over 30% growth in the next few years and reach 489.6 billion yuan in 2013. In the next five years, the number and scale of mobile Internet users will surpass the traditional Internet, to jointly promote the upgrading of China's information industry and the improvement of people's quality of life.

In the process of evolution from E to U, M (Mobile) is an important transitional stage, making mobile communications an indispensable part of the UNS. M refers to the use of mobile communications to achieve communication anytime and anywhere. In order to achieve ubiquitous connectivity, mobile communication terminals are crucial. From individuals to companies, and from smart cities to public management, many countries and regions around the world have introduced M as a necessary path from E to U, and they are actively promoting this process to fully enter the U era as soon as possible.

1.3.3 Human beings live not only in a physical world but also in a virtual world

We live in both the virtual and the physical world. Maybe they were originally two parts of one world. As Levinson pointed out in 2001, "[T]here can be a sense of accomplishment and relationship in the virtual realm which is illusory, or at least incomplete, until full flesh-and-blood people have shaken hands, and tangible things have been moved" (Levinson, 1999, p.14). Levinson divided the "global village" into the traditional global village and the cyberspace global village. He used three metaphors to distinguish them: the broadcasting global village

Introduction 35

is the village of children, the television global village is the village of snoopers, and the cyberspace global village is the global village of participants.

The virtual world is the media world, and vice versa. The construction of a global village on the Internet is itself a governing mechanism. In the Hollywood science fiction blockbuster *The Matrix*, the virtual world (Matrix) directly affects the central nervous system of humans, making their whole actual human body lose its existence value without having to open their eyes, mouth, or ears. McLuhan has a famous assertion that "media is the extension of man." When the human body reaches its limit, it would be the birth of biological media if it weren't for the degradation of the human body or the complete amputation of limbs.

If the *Matrix* scenario represents a future landscape of the virtual world, then can the virtual world be regarded as the ultimate media or hypermedia from the perspective of media communication? The ultimate media corresponding to the old media are all the existing media, starting with the natural media of the human body, such as touch, hearing, and taste. Then there are the artificial media created by human beings, such as spoken language, text, pictures, newspapers and periodicals, movies and television, and the Internet. Just as the virtual world is no longer only science fiction, the human migration from the real world to the virtual world is no longer limited to the imagination of the film's directors. Second Life, the famous online virtual world in the United States, became extremely popular in 2007, attracting a series of famous companies and institutions who seized the opportunity to land on and launch various business promotions and activities, which soon brought direct competition and cooperation between the virtual world and the physical world. IBM bought an island in Second Life and convened an employee conference. It also launched a 3D local area network and paid for the relocation of its technicians. Being afraid of lagging behind their competitors, Coca-Cola, Toyota, and Sony also settled in Second Life, evidently sensing another business battleground and opportunity that could actually boost real-world competitive outcomes.

The boundaries between the virtual and the physical business world are constantly blurred, and their transactions infiltrate each other. People's roles in these two worlds can also be switched freely. If a person wears Adidas in real life, he can custom-order the same style in Second Life's Adidas store. Customers who visit virtual stores in Second Life can enjoy the discount in the physical world promised by the virtual world, which has become a way for many to save money. In the virtual world, you can wander around bookstores and watch movies at will, as well as communicate with people who read the same books or watch the same movies. At the same time, you can also place orders and request that print books or DVDs be sent to your physical home to be shared with your physical family. Reuters and other large global media are transferring information between the physical and virtual worlds. Second Life's members can learn about physical-world news through a variety of pictures, texts, and videos, while physical-world readers can also log on to Reuters and other media's specialized websites to learn about housing prices, recruitment advertisements, etc. in the world of Second Life.

36 *Introduction*

What is it about Second Life that fascinates so many? Some people think that it is another massively multiplayer online role-playing game (MMORPG) like "World of Warcraft," while others say it is a 3D version of MySpace. In fact, it is a virtual world that coexists and converges with the physical world. The mode of Second Life, then, has brought Web 2.0 into a whole new realm. The virtual world it creates and the world that interacts with the physical life have become a part of many people's real lives. Users create their own virtual worlds with creativity, not only with text, videos, and pictures but also with any virtual objects or people you can imagine, including houses, cars, and girlfriends. Some of these virtual objects have counterparts in reality, and some of them exist only in the virtual world. But it is possible that they will be put into practical production soon and produce benefits in the physical world.

This raises new problems. What if an object created in the virtual world is put into production by someone else in the physical world? What if cartoon animals in the virtual world are used as trademarks by manufacturers in the physical world? How can a company compensate a physical user who encounters virtual hacking that damages his physical computer or costs him virtual property? There are also problems in the social operation of the virtual world itself. For example, what should be done if a virtual TV station violates the image rights of a virtual star? Should the virtual world adopt the logic of full realism, or should it find a different but equal mode of operation to the physical world? Solving the copyright problem of electronic products and characters in the virtual world will probably open a breakthrough for the integration of the virtual and the physical, and also become a prerequisite for virtual objects to enter the physical world. Second Life entered its breakthrough phase in 2003 by allowing users to own the virtual goods they create. In order to solve other problems related to copyright, not only does the virtual world need a whole set of self-designed virtual institutions to manage virtual economic and social operations, but also it needs to interface with regulations in the physical world.

Second Life began to have its own economic system after its recognition of property rights and copyrights, and trading is the main driving force of its activity. Players consume hundreds of thousands and even millions of dollars every day, creating a huge virtual GDP. There is also a link or barrier between the virtual world and the physical world, which is currency convertibility. Through exchange rates, the virtual economy and physical economy can be closely linked. In this regard, different countries currently have different management methods. According to China's current policy, virtual currencies and the yuan cannot be traded in virtual worlds such as Second Life. The electronic payment channel, which can directly use yuan to make small payments, is one of the practical solutions. Issuing point cards and setting up virtual accounts are also possible trading options, thus forming a customer-to-customer (C2C) trading platform in the virtual world. However, taxation and other issues that may arise from the resulting high volume of transactions still need to be regulated by the physical-world authorities. At present, this kind of trade is confined to the exchange from RMB to virtual coin only, as players cannot go in reverse: the transaction results of the virtual world cannot be directly converted into physical-world income. But they can be achieved through indirect transactions such as online channels.

In China, the combination of the virtual world and the physical world is still advancing rapidly in various fields, such as the cooperation of movies and social media. In December 2011, Xu Jinglei's Lunar New Year romance movie *Dear Enemy* initiated a cross-border cooperation with social gaming company Zynga's "Star City" and Tencent Weibo, which has over 300 million users. The players of Star City and the fans of *Dear Enemy* formed a new kind of relationship. Players got close to the film by completing a series of tasks customized for the film in the game, and intimately connected with animated images of the heroine, Amy. Through the interaction with Amy and through the interaction in games and Weibo with other players, people shared happiness and got rewards—the virtual architectures of the central scene in the film. The filmmaker hoped that players would deepen their emotional connection with *Dear Enemy* in the game and build a *Dear Enemy* commercial building in their virtual cities (Science & Technology for China's Mass Media, 2011).

The virtual world is increasingly becoming both an extension and a part of the physical world. With the Internet of Things and "smart city" and "smart earth" concepts entering everybody's lives, both the virtual and the physical are merged into a complete environmental medium, the medium on which immersion is based. When your house is built with integrated intelligent network facilities, when your city is full of multi-functional information terminals, and when you can eat, drink, and have fun with just a click or swipe, you will begin to feel the convenience brought by immersive communication, as well as the joy of the virtual and physical world crossover. Today, there are public multimedia information terminals on the streets of Beijing, with information on catering, tourism, transportation, shopping, and real estate in easy reach. Such multimedia information terminals have also entered banks, government departments, universities, parks, etc., and have even begun to be worn on our heads, wrists, and feet. Such development makes people see that the virtual world is beginning to be compatible with the physical world, although only at the primary level.

1.4 Limitations of existing theories and research significance

Whether it is the digital and multiple media in the media morphosis, the equal interaction in the mode of communication, or the "remote presence" in the immersive communication, no current models can cover and clearly explain the relationship between human beings and the media, the media environment, and the great changes that have taken place in the mode of communication. The disappearance of boundaries predicted in theoretical circles is now appearing not only among various media, between the media and the environment, and between the macroenvironment and the microenvironment, but also in the material space or in the spiritual space, as well as between these two spaces. However, most of the existing communication theories focus on the specific and material media. These theories derive from relatively separate studies in terms of media form,

38   *Introduction*

communication modes, and media environment, each with its own theoretical system, so they do not consider integrating all three variables.

In addition, the current theoretical research on immersion is only in the state of remote presence, even though ubiquity has been playing an increasingly important role. Immersion reflects both a static state and a dynamic state, as it is both physical "absence" and spiritual "existence." It is not only the realization of a virtual world but also another manifestation of virtualization of the physical world. How should academic circles respond to these trends? Similarly, how should we deal with the new problems brought about by immersive communication? The Internet prompted many societal responses in its early days. For example, in 1996 the U.S. federal government tried to control the Internet through the Communications Decency Act, but it was not successful. In the present situation, where the media environment is more complex and diverse, especially when we are discussing not just the Internet but the entire social environment as the media, existing theories are even more limited when facing the new development of reality.

1.4.1 Media morphosis breaks through traditional spatial categories

The morphosis of immersive communication media is not only the traditional forms of newspapers, radio, television, and the Internet but also some devices that appear as a result of intelligent living, such as the surveillance systems that now produce media functions. Even the environmental space where the monitoring system is located is also within the research scope of media morphosis. Modern people are under surveillance almost constantly. At a basic level, surveillance cameras are everywhere in the environments where we live. They provide information collection, records, and even communication. One example is the Little Yueyue case in Foshan, Guangdong, China. On October 13, 2011, Yueyue, a two-year-old girl, was crushed twice by a car on the roadside of Guangfo Hardware City in Huangqi, near the South China Sea. Eighteen people passed by, but not one of them offered assistance. This tragedy was faithfully recorded by the city's surveillance cameras and spread through traditional mass media such as television and the Internet, triggering shock and concern in the entire society.

Monitoring generally refers to the collection of personal information, whether the identity of the person is confirmed or not, in order to manage or exert influence on the information being collected. David Lyon, a professor of sociology and an expert on surveillance, argued that "the information society is a surveillance society." He described surveillance as "any collecting or processing of personal data, identifiable or not, for the purposes of influencing or managing those whose data have been gathered" (Lyon, 2001). When traditional monitoring is put into the environment of a ubiquitous network, it becomes a kind of media morphosis connected by that network, and its media function is further amplified. Ubiquitous connections further widen the space and environment of media. When a ubiquitous network hides all kinds of intelligent terminals in the environmental background, the entire environment becomes the media morphosis of immersive communication.

When discussing recent changes in media morphosis, Prof. Xiong Chengyu pointed out that

> The media morphosis is also a kind of productivity. This kind of productivity has led to the change of our media morphosis. That is, "ubiquitous, anytime, omnipotent." Today's media is the result of integration. It is the coexistence of multiple types of information and a variety of terminals. Media information can be received anywhere and at any time, through the modes of multi-channel communication and media platform, to achieve information exchange between users, resulting in an omnipotent situation.
>
> (Xiong, 2009)

Indeed, new technologies and their promotion by the government are greatly accelerating human communication, generating new media forms and modes of communication, while further promoting the transformation of the space of communication. The most basic condition for the establishment of ubiquitous networks is the construction of high-speed and high-quality networks. The data released by the Broadband Forum, an international non-governmental organization, shows that in 2012 the number of global broadband users exceeded 600 million, led by Chinese users. China Telecom launched the "Broadband China 'Optical Network City' Project" in February 2011, which aimed to achieve optical fiber covering all cities in China within three years, with fiber-to-the-home access bandwidth reaching 100M (Science & Technology for China's Mass Media, 2011). With the National Development and Reform Commission and the Ministry of Industry and Information Technology taking the lead, nine other ministries jointly researched and developed the "Broadband China Strategy."

According to the World Wireless Researchers Forum (WWRF), by 2017, 7 trillion wireless devices were connected to the ubiquitous network, serving 7 billion people, which means that thousands of wireless devices are embedded in our surroundings. Professor Zhang Ping believes that "[f]rom the analysis of the mode of 'ubiquitous,' its characteristics are human-centered, focusing on people's feelings and experience, the computer is embedded in the surrounding environment and actively interacts with the physical environment to provide a natural human–machine interface. From infrastructure to service, it is a comprehensive and natural interaction and service" (Zhang, 2009).

The cloud computing model of data storage and transmission has separated data storage from a single specific hardware, further breaking the interface and boundary of the media, providing important technical support for ubiquitous operation, and also promoting the reconstruction of the concept of communication space. According to the data from cloud computing surveys conducted jointly by Forester and VMware, the continuous rise of the "industry cloud" also benefits more industries, especially strategic emerging industries, including the media industry. Media cloud, radio and television cloud, publishing cloud … new concepts of clouds and programs related to the media industry are constantly being proposed, and many media are also directly involved in the field of cloud

40   *Introduction*

computing. The media is no longer merely a user of cloud computing but has gradually become a cloud computing service provider.

Cloud computing, which represents the future computing model, is given great importance by government, industry, education, and research circles around the world. But at the same time, its information security is of particular concern. For example, the leakage of network usernames and passwords is constantly happening around the world. This leakage not only causes immeasurable impact and loss but also makes cloud security a key issue for technical solutions.

1.4.2 The concept of "presence" has undergone a qualitative change

The emergence of immersive media and modes of communication has led people to become ubiquitous and ever-present. This has led to a qualitative change in the concept of presence, going from "physical presence" to "remote presence," and from there to "ubiquitous presence." These concepts have changed with the development of media morphosis and applications. The services of mobile social networks generally rely on users' permission to use their current location and share other personal information. Therefore, one of the meanings of "ubiquitous" is the sharing of locations, GPS positioning, and mobile fixed-point services provided by LBS. In addition, the spiritual and virtual existence caused by modern simulation and artificial intelligence technology also expands the connotation and extension of the concept of presence.

The change in the concept of presence also brings about the sharing of personal location and personal information, which reduces personal privacy to a certain extent, and in fact facilitates surveillance by the media operations department. Early in the Iraq War, for instance, the U.S. third mechanized infantry division relied on the Blues tracking system to successfully locate friendly and hostile troops, as well as to plot the best offensive routes. The situation of the enemy and the situation in the battle were clear in their mind. This accurate information helped them not only to effectively execute in the air but also to launch in-depth ground attacks. To do so, the U.S. military used a portable, general-purpose automated command and control system device, which determines its own position through GPS and then receives continuous terminal displays from satellite communications. Now, the technical principles for civilian use are the same as those used in the military.

Levinson noted that

> [w]e should not be surprised, then, to find in the history of information technology, and in its current configurations and future projections as well, an evolutionary dynamic in many respects very much like that of the literally natural, organic world. This complex process of media evolution, of course different from as well as similar to the evolution of living things.
>
> (Levinson, 1997, p. 1)

Building on respect for the evolution of life and the recognition of reality, this study, based on the recognition of remote presence, will develop immersive communication from electronic virtual remote presence to ubiquitous presence, expanding the research scope of the new media field—which is now mainly concentrated in theoretical circles—to the overall environment and larger space of human existence.

1.5 Summary

In terms of communication characteristics, human communication has generally experienced a development course of primitive communication → one-way communication → interactive communication. In terms of communication objects, it has generally developed from interpersonal communication to mass communication to focused mass communication. This chapter tracks the origin of both processes and gives a theoretical review of them to form a foundation for the study's primary research problems and direction.

Starting from the relationship between media evolution theory and the real world, this chapter traced the development process from interpersonal communication to immersive communication by means of a literature review. It analyzed the emergence and respective characteristics of the first media age and the second media age, explored relevant theoretical systems such as "coevolution and coexistence" and anthropotropic trends in the evolution of media morphosis, sorted out the theories of media space, media environment, and media ecology, and redefined the relationship among media, people, and environment. By demonstrating the evolution of communication methods and modes to the disappearance of boundaries and the reconfiguration of communication tools and communication relationships, this book proposes a model for the development of immersive communication: primitive communication → one-way communication → interactive communication → immersive communication. Immersive communication makes a breakthrough in space and time in this sequence.

The concept of immersion can be traced back to psychology, but it first emerged in communication theory in studies of virtual reality. Its research on communication mode is currently mainly in the remote presence stage. As for the concept of immersive communication, there are only scattered discussions in existing Chinese and foreign theoretical literature and no complete theory. This is a new research area in the early stages of construction. Thus, the main research significance of this book is to make media morphosis break through the category of traditional concepts of space and presence, develop immersive research from remote to ubiquitous, and expand space to the whole environment of human existence.

Media technology and social development have created the conditions and environment for the evolution of immersive communication. Human beings are changing from information survival to post-information survival, and from localized survival to ubiquitous survival. They exist not only in the physical world but also in the virtual world, as mankind moves from the E age to the U age. China-based WeChat reached 1 billion users worldwide in 2018, but still trails behind WhatsApp (1.5 billion) and Facebook (1.3 billion). Mobile Internet access is a powerful driving force for the growth of the number of netizens worldwide.

42   *Introduction*

In Mark Poster's famous book *The Second Media Age* (1995), he argued that the first media age was the epoch dominated by a one-way "broadcast model of few producers and many consumers of messages"(Poster, 1995, p. 5). By contrast, the second media age was dominated by "two-way decentralized communication" (Poster, 1995, p. 18) with the integration of media producers, sellers, and consumers. This study proposes that a new immersive communication mode based on the ubiquitous network, along with a third media age dominated by ubiquitous immersive communication, is on the horizon.

2 The definition of immersive communication

Based on the previous literature review, this chapter, following the trends of the theories of technological determinism and humanization, extends media, the research object, to the entire human living environment and constructs a definition for "immersive communication."

2.1 Logic of the new definition

The first chapter has elaborated on the trend of the theories of technological determinism and humanization. Using these two theories as its main framework, this chapter will analyze the inevitable existence of immersive communication and its connotations.

2.1.1 "Technological determinism" "decides" immersive communication as a new mode of communication

Marshall McLuhan once said that "outmoded technologies become art forms" (Levinson, 1999, p. 13) and "new technologies do not so much bury their predecessors as bump them upstairs to a position from which they can be admired, if no longer used" (Levinson, 1999, p. 145). When a form of technology is at its peak, it is basically invisible to us, because all technologies are "like the blades of whirring fans, upon which the unwary might well cut their fingers" (Levinson, 1999, p. 13). He described how new technology replaced some of the functions of old technology and began to play behind the scenes. The mechanism of technical operation suddenly becomes clear, as if it is pushed to the center of the stage. "Media is the message" means that old media become new media's high-definition content: "If novels have become the content of film, the film the content of television, then novels and film seem hardly outmoded or replaced" (Levinson, 1999, p. 146). "Motion pictures (along with elements of radio, including serials, news and the network structure) became the content of the Internet, the medium of media" (Levinson, 1999, p. 42). Following Internet technology, significant technological breakthroughs with virtual reality (VR) and ubiquitous networking technology are now being pushed to the "center of the stage." These new technologies are supported by a media form containing all the old media. "Ubiquitous

44   The definition of immersive communication

networking" and its connection to the media system can be seen as the master of all media forms, containing not only all previous texts, pictures, audio, podcasts, interactive videos, and other content, but also virtual and physical people who are both online content and a part of the media network itself.

According to McLuhan's four laws of media, the four patterns in the evolution of media forms are represented by "amplification," "obsolescence," "retrieval," and "reversal" (Levinson, 1999, p. 188). As the current highest-level form of medium development, immersive communication contains all media forms, including the "amplification" of video, where video is an important content of almost all kinds of media; the "retrieval" of phones, where cellphones are the main terminal through which human beings and machines communicate; the "obsolescence" of interactive communication, with the super-authoritative one-way communication of surveillance video monitoring; and the "reversal" of texting, where mobile phones are used to "read" text rather than to talk, and more and more display terminals around us have text that needs to be read.

Taking the development of the phone as an example, broadcasting existed before the invention of wireless radio. The original broadcasting was "broadcasted" through the telephone, and that's why it was called "telephone newspaper," the prototype for the later wireless radio broadcasting. In 1861, a German named Philipp Reis made the first phone that could transmit only sounds. In 1875, an American named Alexander Graham Bell invented a phone that could transmit real conversation. To date, the phone is still one of the more important communication tools. With the development of the Internet of Things, ubiquitous networking cloud computing, and so on, all media are cleverly connected into a large environment to meet humans' high demand for information services that can be provided anytime and anywhere. Immersive communication, the master of all media forms and the new communication paradigm, is one of the more recent products of this technological development.

2.1.1.1   Virtual reality technology enables mankind to go beyond body and physical limits, becoming completely "immersive"

When this book previously mentioned the concepts of a "virtual world" and "virtual reality," it was mainly from the point of view of a combination of computer technology and information technology. Continuing with the prior chapter's discussion of the nature of virtual reality as a meaning and a way of communication, this chapter will analyze the implementation of virtual reality technology and its development as a technological support to "immersive communication." The virtual world is completed with the aid of electronic equipment, and the developing reality indicates that we can go further to achieve a comprehensive integration of the virtual and reality, which means that humans' media experience will begin to evolve from the separation of human and machine to the full integration of human and machine. VR technology transforms complex, abstract electronic data space into almost anything from the physical world so that people can flow freely inside, resulting in a sense of immersion. At the World Electronics Annual Conference

The definition of immersive communication   45

in 1993, Grigore Burdea and Philippe Coiffet presented the "3I" characteristics of VR technology: interactivity, immersion, and imagination. "Immersion" refers to using VR technology to simulate a three-dimensional virtual environment that can arouse people's senses to see, listen, smell, and touch, so that they cannot help but feel themselves totally immersed in the multi-dimensional information environment and enter a state of ecstasy or "flow." From the aspects of both hardware and software, VR technology is building a 3D virtual vision of the multi-dimensional information space. When VR technology was at an early stage, most of the time the user needed to wear a special helmet, data gloves, and other sensatory equipment—or to have the help of a keyboard, mouse, and other auxiliaries—to enter the virtual space, to have a surreal experience combined with a visual sense, an auditory sense, and other bodily and mental feelings, and thus be immersed inside a surreal fantasy. But with the newly developed "augmented reality" (AR) of technology, the visual information, including computer-generated graphics and people overlying objects and people in the physical world, combines to produce a new, augmented physical world. Its ultimate goal is to let people immerse themselves inside this new, enhanced world while not feeling or being able to tell the difference between physical objects and virtual objects; the visually enhanced information becomes part of the physical information and finally makes the virtual become real. And, as mentioned in the previous chapter, there is another virtual world more strongly changing our lives: virtual life on the Internet, such as Second Life. This is the major referent for this study when discussing the coexistence of the real and virtual worlds through crossing borders and merging. We now have our own identities and ways of living in both these worlds. For many people, these two worlds are indispensable and are our physical and spiritual sustenance, allowing us to go beyond the physical limits of the body and geography, and making us call the virtual world a "home" that we can immerse ourselves in.

2.1.1.2 *Ubiquitous technology enables human beings '"presence" anytime and anywhere and extends immersive communication from "remote" to "ubiquitous"*

Ubiquitous networking is the basis of the so-called intelligent city and smart planet. Ubiquitous technology makes it possible to form a combination of humankind and the environment and to make the dreams of intelligent living a reality. The global ubiquitous network has realized the true meaning of "global village." The ubiquitous network is very powerful; not only can it provide services such as information dissemination and remote information exchange, but also, it can make it possible for all surroundings to intelligently connect and interact. Both ubiquitous networks and traditional media function as information communication. But, although the information content they communicate is similar, there are essential differences in their ways of communication. With the development of interactive media, mobile media, and the innovation of the Internet of Things, we have become immersed in an enormous media environment, which is expanding endlessly without boundaries. It is this ultimate "realized" large space, made from

46   *The definition of immersive communication*

fully integrating virtual and physical media into a whole, that lets people enjoy the realization of cross–time and space "presence" in information exchange with the help of more intangible tools, and to enjoy the unique experience and fun made possible by "borderless" communications.

2.1.1.3 Biological communication technology fully integrates people with the environment

Biological communication technology has just begun to be used in the communication industry, and it is too early to qualitatively define it. But it is foreseeable that it will be fully integrated with the environment and human beings will be able to use their minds to give orders directly to surrounding sensors, to communicate without boundaries or obstacles, and to easily complete all kinds of work for a living. People seem to have returned to the ancient time before the invention and use of tools, and this return "back" to the new "no tool" era can be called the "invisible tool era," because in fact most of the modern "tools" are invisible or even part of the human body. From the point of view that "media is the extension of the human body," clothes are an extension of the skin, television is an extension of the eye, and so on, and the whole environment should be the extension of the human body. This book will further present how the whole environment is part of the human body. The human body, as a biological media ontology, integrates with the environment as its own "bodily extension" and merges into a larger whole. In Chapter 8 on "Immersive communicators," there will be more discussion on the integration of human beings and the environment.

2.1.2 The "anthropotropic" trend leads people to choose the most suitable things in order to survive

Paul Levinson believes that there is a pattern in media evolution that applies to everything, and he calls it "a pattern of 'human replay." "Media are evolving towards an increasing replication of pre-technological or human communication environments" (p. 16). That is, their ways of dealing with information are increasingly "natural," like those of a real human being, and increasingly better than any existing media, and thus, the convenience of communication continues to improve. Levinson's anthropotropic theory of the evolution of media "sees media increasingly selected for their support of 'pre-technological', human communication patterns in form and function" (Levinson, 1999, p. 41). He believes that human beings basically control the process of media evolution. Moreover, the emergence of immersive communication is to some extent also a testimonial.

Specifically, as Levinson (1997) predicts in his monograph *Soft Edge: The Natural History and the Future of the Information Revolution*, the first reason for these old forms of media development, such as telegrams, black and white photographs, and prints, can be attributed to their ability to provide a huge extension that broke through time and space, beyond human physiological ability. We are

The definition of immersive communication 47

able to tolerate the compromise of their sacrificing essential elements of human communication simply because we cannot pass through such a wide area by other ways of communication.

> If the information revolution is insufficient, in the absence of tangible, direct human presence, as a generator and even conveyor of formal knowledge—if we need more than cyberspace and robots for knowledge and exploration of deep space—how do transactions in information fare in the digital world?
>
> (p. 228)

Levinson believes that the media that realized these extensions have crossed human physical barriers to a certain degree, but new new media, which are outstanding in both the natural world and the human world, will continue to break the surface slowly. This is the inevitable result of media's evolution toward humanization, as addressed in Levinson's anthropotropic theory. On the other hand, the evolution of media content follows the law of "more and more": "We might say that not only are prior media the content of the Internet, but so too is the human user who, unlike the consumer of other mass media, creates content online with almost every use" (Levinson, 1999, p. 39).

According to these media development trends, including the humanization evolution and the content development trend, it can be inferred that new media formed after the Internet will be a "full media" space, humanized, human centered, combining tangible and intangible networks, and containing all information content and all media forms, including the old media, new media, and the people themselves, and including both the physical world and the virtual world. It can be said that the media humanization trend calls for "immersive" communication because immersive communication is a completely human-centered, comprehensive, and personalized service, as well as the most humanized communication. As a medium or form of communication, immersive communication itself is a way of being closest to human nature, because it "naturally" puts people at the center of every media environment and naturally disseminates the information that is most needed. Since the Internet is the medium of all media, and ubiquitous networking includes the Internet, then immersive communication, with ubiquitous networking as its technological basis, is the inclusion of all media, including the Internet. Humans in immersive communication are also the content of immersive communication. Immersive communication is a new way of communication—a ubiquitous, ever-present, omnipotent communication space. And, because of the impact of technical variables, people are able to see themselves and others from a new perspective via immersive communication. Don't people and media together become art? People often appreciate old technology that has been replaced by new technology and feel the fun. McLuhan's favorite example is the earth itself. When the first satellite revolved around the earth, we were able to see the earth from the outside for the first time. Thus, the earth became an artistic form, a stunning object of beauty, and a valuable thing

48   *The definition of immersive communication*

that must be protected as a whole. "But will this increase in art a la McLuhan—this shift in many older technologies from our unthinking use to our critical appreciation of them— result in a net improvement of society?" (Levinson, 1999, p. 14).

Following this reflection, let us look at changes that have been made to the definition of "human communication."

2.2 Definition of immersive communication

Based on the preceding analysis, this study attempts to define "immersive communication" as follows: Immersive communication is a new means of information communication. It is a human-centered, ubiquitous, and omnipotent communication occurring anywhere and at any time and having the infinite human environment as its medium, while being created by connecting all media forms. It is a process of communication that enables a person to be fully focused on the dynamic customization of their individual information needs. Immersive communication is a ubiquitous experience beyond the boundaries of time and space with the "3I" effects: invisible, intangible, and insensible.

This definition includes several aspects of meaning:

1. All media and technology are turned into the background, embedded in our surrounding environment, and connected together.
2. The environment or space is their medium. This environment is the whole environment where humans live. In other words, it can be said that everything is media.
3. The contents include all previous media, as well as all future media. Immersive communication is an open system that includes everything.
4. Media space is the coexistence and integration of the material and spiritual, the physical world and the virtual world. Media interface has disappeared; media is invisible, without boundaries; media and the environment are integrated.
5. Media is people-centered with people completely inside it. From the "invisible man" to intangible people, humans and media have merged into each other. People are the communication subject but also the contents of communication.
6. People can be materialized as a medium; the media can also be humanized, become the humanized media with humankind merged into a whole new media—thus, a "biological media" occurs.
7. Immersive communication is a dynamic process of communication, including constantly positioning the object (a person or a sensor) by making real-time adjustments of the content of information, such as by using location-based services (LBS), Global Positioning System (GPS), and other location methods, first to locate objects and then to search the information database and issue instant new messages back to the object.

The definition of immersive communication   49

8. Cloud computing makes it possible for information to be communicated anywhere and anytime, because cloud computing data is stored at places that are not bound to a single specific hardware, thus further breaking down the boundaries between object and space, space and space.

9. The virtual world is a part of the physical world, and the physical world is a part of the virtual world.

10. It completes the development process of users in communication: "interpersonal communication—mass communication—focused mass communication—ubiquitous mass communication." This book has come up with the new term "ubiquitous mass communication" to describe users in immersive communication. Compared with mass communication, which means communication with the public, there is "no public" in the definition of "ubiquitous mass communication," but in a different way than there is "no public" in direct interpersonal communications. "ubiquitous mass communication" is a comprehensive, personalized, ultra-precisely customized information service based on a "ubiquitous" connection. In "ubiquitous mass communication," "I," an individual, is at the center of all information services, so it is unlike the focus of communication that focuses on a group of people. ubiquitous mass communication is a complete one-on-one personalized information service.

In short, immersive communication is a revolutionary new way of communication. It can only emerge when media forms are greatly enriched; communication technology is highly developed; the integration of the virtual world and physical world ultimately amplifies the media environment; and humans, media, and the environment are fully integrated into each other, resulting in a new mode of communication and status that engages the full participation of material aspects and spiritual aspects. With cloud computing–supported ubiquitous networking, virtual reality, and other technologies, media forms have evolved from the "soft edge" to "no edge" communication, where a "remote" presence and "ubiquitous" presence coexist, so that immersive communication can finally achieve infinite space, anytime communication, and infinite development of communication, and result in the final development of biological media where people become the media ontology, embedding both human nature and a digital personality. Immersive communication profoundly subverts humans' means of information communication and inherent subsistence.

2.3 The breakthroughs of the new definition compared with existing definitions of communication

The theoretical breakthrough of the new definition of this study is mainly the expansion of the concept of "immersive communication" into the whole environment, thus redefining the connotation and extensions of "media" when the whole environment is seen as integrated with humans and media. The new definition extends former concepts of media into the whole category of human living space,

50   *The definition of immersive communication*

which embodies human communication from the "soft edge" to "no edge" and opens up the whole space of the human media environment into an infinite space and time without boundaries.

2.3.1 Immersive communication reconstructs the three "spaces"

In this definition of immersive communication, we can see that the human, media, and environment can become each other, and all of them are connected to form an infinite media space. This space contains three spaces: physical, spiritual, and intelligent. Altogether, it is a ubiquitously connected infinite space.

First, the physical space of immersive communication includes all media and all substances that can send and receive information through the ubiquitous network. Second, the spiritual space of immersive communication is the entire virtual space that includes the medium's content and the physical real world inside the virtual world. Finally, the intelligent space of immersive communication is the entire human living space, which includes the first two large spaces. Unlike previous definitions of the third space, the intelligent space of immersive communication is first extended to the entire environment without an interface or boundaries, along with the infinite extending physical connections of the ubiquitous network; then, it brings new meaning to the first two spaces through the integration of physical space and spiritual space.

The changeability and ambiguity of space was also a point of interest for McLuhan, who predicted the advent of an environment that exists anywhere and anytime. From his book The *Mechanical Bride*, published in 1951, to his articles published in *Explorations* magazine in the 1950s, to his book *The Gutenberg Galaxy*, published in 1962, he has seen increasingly clearly that an ubiquitous electronic environment is forming that allows instant communication: "The new electronic interdependence recreates the world in the image of a global village" (McLuhan, 1962, p. 85). This environment existed in the old telegram, which evolved to the voice over the telephone and then to the sound on the TV screen. McLuhan finally named this environment "acoustic space," indicating that the sound encompasses us in the same way that electronic media does. When McLuhan talked about acoustic space, he actually meant cyberspace, as the Internet was just unfolding. Paul Levinson later discovered the importance of the cellphone, and he predicted in his book *Cellphone: The Story of the World's Most Mobile Medium and How It Has Transformed Everything!* that the Internet would become a vassal of the cellphone, because the cellphone accommodates the various functions of cyberspace. Cellphones, on the one hand, allow us to step out of our houses and offices and return to the outside world; on the other hand, they keep us on standby all the time, damaging our freedom of travel. Cellphones may also turn the entire world into a huge office (Levinson, 2004). This is also a testament to media's ability to change the function and significance of space.

The definition of immersive communication   51

Immersive communication contains the functions of all previous media, such as the mobile phone and the Internet, in order to tear down the walls of all previous media spaces and build a polysemous, fully featured new space. Space no longer represents the concept of location but different symbolic meanings of information. The French scholar Armand Mattelart (2000) argued that a characteristic of contemporary society is the ambiguity of locations: the flow of space (e.g., highways, air routes), consumption space (e.g., large supermarkets), and communication space (e.g., telephone, telex, television, and the Internet). In these no-place spaces, people coexist and cohabitate but do not live together. The position of a consumer or a lonely walker is determined by his or her contractual relationship with society. People with different mental attitudes and the "no place" status of different types of social relations are all categories of "super-modernity." Super-modernity is defined in relation to modernity. Because the current metropolis is represented as "a central point" that forms the "contact points that receive and send information in the world's huge networks," it is located at the intersection where the "place" of modernity and the "no place" of super-modernity overlap (p. 218).

When the concept of the "global village" was invented by McLuhan in 1962, these two images of "earth" and "village" had not yet been fully developed. It was a TV-dominant communication era, but television was only the domestic medium of each country rather than an international medium, and people could not communicate through a TV screen. In the 1980s, with the arrival of cable television, the "village" began to become a global community, but what made the "village" really interact was the Internet and the mobile phone. The best example comes from the Iraq War, where American journalists were embedded with phone and videophone connections for live TV news broadcasting. This new media with video cameras made the "global village," the concept of the new space, known worldwide overnight.

If the concept of the "global village" mainly existed on a spiritual level at that time, ubiquitous networking has now made the "global village" exist in reality and turned it into the "intelligent earth," as the media space changes into intelligent space. Joshua Meyrowitz (1986) believed that media's influence on space could change humans' behavior and the roles they play. He was concerned about television recombining social scenes into electronic scenes and the original backstage turning into the front stage. The vanishing boundary leads to a reconstruction of social relations. When immersive communication eliminates the boundaries of space, spatial context rules that were originally necessary are also broken. Of course, the integration of the front stage and the backstage in immersive communication will bring new social problems as well. McLuhan (1976) discussed the telephone's inherent disadvantages in his article "Inside on the Outside, or the Spaced-Out American," published in the *Journal of Communication*: "Whereas we accept the phone as an invader of our homes ... The North American car is designed and used for privacy ... the motor car then,

52   *The definition of immersive communication*

for us is not only a means of transportation but a way of achieving a deeply needed privacy." This article was written in 1976, at a time when car phones and mobile phones had not yet arrived to break our privacy's hard shell, had not yet opened up the spaces of indoors and outdoors, personal and social. Now, no matter whether we are under the sun or incandescent lighting, we no longer have a private space to which we can escape.

According to de Souza e Silva (2011), previous studies have assumed that "cell phones allowed people to inhabit two places at the same time: their own physical space and the remote place of the other speaking person." However, "contrary to this approach, Michel Serres suggested that telephone conversations take place nowhere—they actually happen in a virtual place."

Unlike the previous theories, according to the logical framework of immersive communication proposed in this study, now two separate or independent spaces exist; the boundary between virtual space and physical space is broken and vanishing, and so is the boundary between spiritual and intelligent space. Immersive communication is occurring in the infinite human environment anywhere and anytime. This environment's core is the modern intelligent city and the spatial form created by modern science and technology and instrumental rationality. It is also the main public domain in humankind's future, and the corresponding social–generation relationship will be produced. Especially with the use of cloud computing to support the ubiquitous connection, the ways in which and the places where a database is stored and computers are operated have changed fundamentally, freeing people from their original dependence on their personal computers. Thus, the human brain space can be unlimitedly amplified via cloud computing, and the intelligent city can unlimitedly amplify the social space and natural space supported by media data. The "immersive" space this study focuses on is also an infinite immersive communication space that is mainly a combination of media space, human brain space, and urban space. Immersive communication not only contains outdoor advertising, surveillance cameras, and television screens in the communication environment, but also takes the city itself as media forming the entire communication space. This is also a reflection of the space reconstruction mainly based on the third space. Immersive communication has its own unique means of narration and rules of existence. As the third space of both material and spiritual space, media is not only a carrier but also has cultural significance, and because immersive communication merges media into the environment, it is impossible for media itself to stay out of the affair. Immersive media, while displaying the space landscape, is inevitably becoming part of the landscape space and will be marked by the cultural imprint of the entire space.

People are living at the center of immersive communication's intelligent space and using various means of media to communicate and create, anywhere and anytime. There is no doubt that their behavior is essential for the reconstruction and characterization of space. The process through which everyone blends with space itself creates a new mental space, and one should have a central position in every

The definition of immersive communication   53

space. These small spaces are also constantly breaking the original space open to a broader imagination and eventually converging into the entire large infinite space of human physical and spiritual coexistence. Therefore, the spatial meaning of immersive communication exists in a dynamic state of instant adjustment, anytime and anywhere.

2.3.2 Immersive communication reconstructs the relationship between media and the human being. It's the hottest and the coolest medium

In accordance with the definition of human and media constructed in this study, "immersive communication" reconstructs the relationship between media and human beings. In immersive communication, human beings are both active participants and passive and ignorant recipients; they are not only a media subject but also a thinking object—both a real person in the real world and a virtual human being in the virtual environment.

Immersive media is the hottest medium, because immersive communication is active. Interaction is not a major feature of immersion; actually, it is essentially counter-interactive. This interaction is characterized by the fact that it requires the active participation of people, while immersive communication can make all information dissemination and absorption proceed quietly under a default preset unknown even to the people involved.

Immersive communication is different from the new media Internet interactions. According to Levinson (1999),

> Online communication—email, group discussions, digital text in cyberspace—is by all standards the most fully interactive medium in history and much more ephemeral, sketchy, wide-ranging, fast-moving than print fixed on any paper. Online text thus seems cool to the point of approaching Kelvin's zero. ... Because the coolness of a medium, its invitation to fill in the details, comes not from the number of senses it engages, but from the degree of intensity of its engagements.
>
> (Levinson, 1999, p. 107)

Immersion is also the coolest medium, because in this structure, the human has been set as the center of immersive communication, as the commander and leader. Immersive communication reconstructs the virtual environment and thinking objects, not limited to the definition by Aukstakalnis, Blatner, and Roth (1992): A virtual environment is a computer-generated, interactive, and three-dimensional environment that enables people to immerse themselves in the sense of immersion. Immersive communication allows people who are in the three-dimensional and multi-channel space not only to use the physical world in the customary way to manipulate virtual things in a virtual environment in real time, but also to let virtual world people control things in the physical world. No matter in which

54   *The definition of immersive communication*

world they are, people can feel immersed, and each environment is both real and unreal. Immersive communication allows former media, such as television, to be resurrected in it, as well as allowing its features and characteristics to flow through the immersive space. And the environmental conditions in which "viral marketing" and "viral videos" can survive also secretly correspond to what Edmund Snow Carpenter (1974, p. 3) clearly declared as the relationship of "discarnate man" and "omni-centrality." In *"Oh, What a Blow That Phantom Gave Me!,"* he says, "Nixon on TV is everywhere at once ... That is the Neo-Platonic definition of God." "He went on to say that God is "a Being whose center is everywhere, whose borders are nowhere." American broadcasting critic Lowell Thomasalso said, "On the air, you're everywhere"(McLuhan & Powers, 1989, p. 70). Television allows people to be less engaged, so the noisy pictures represent cool media characteristics. With the old media, for example, the phone often beat other media, not only because telephone information is the closest to reality but also because it calls for a positive response from both ends of the phone. Of course, a more primitive knock on the door is more compelling and enthusiastic than a ringtone. Levinson (1999) said:

> Cool connotes a profound, effortless synchronicity with the universe as it actually is and will likely be, speaks softly of deep pools, of being in tune with the future. Hot is fast cars indeed, fast food, life in the fast lane, encounters quick, overwhelming, intense—hot buns, hot abs, hot babes and hunks, embrassez-moi, run me over and leave me senseless. (p. 110) ... But what happens when a medium issues a soft invitation to interaction that can be accommodated more, pursued as never before? What happens when the participational possibilities are hardwired into the very system that tempts us with its low-profile, incomplete presentation? We get electronic text and its consequences. (p. 113)

People who use online chat rooms often feel that online synchronous chat is more sensational than face-to-face conversations. Because of the "cool," people chatting online can only rely on written words to test each other and to make requests. As a result, when fingers move on the keyboard, the usual inhibitions are removed. Therefore, strangers may demand excessive pornography because they want the hypothesized relationships in this space also to exist in real life. Text in a phone conversation is cooler and more appealing than face-to-face discussion. Some people are addicted to online chatting, a kind of psychological addiction, because the manner of chatting online cannot fully satisfy their needs.

Which trait and which temperature will eventually dominate? "The answer hinges on how media perform as the content of other media ... [E]very medium is like a Chinese box or a nesting doll—a medium within a medium within a medium, going back to thought itself"(Levinson, 1999, p. 109). What kind of media can make us notice all the old media that it contains and let us forget the existence of all media, including the existence of the self, entering the realm of complete self-absorption? It is immersion, the hottest and coolest medium.

2.4 Summary

This chapter takes the two major theories of technological determinism and the humanization trend as its main framework and analyzes the inevitability and connotations of the emergence of immersive communication. The logical thinking of the new definition is that "technical determinism" "decided" on immersive communication as a new way of communication; media evolution theory lets people choose the most suitable things needed for survival.

Based on this logic, this study develops the following definition of immersive communication: Immersive communication is a new way of information communication. It is a human-centered, ubiquitous, and omnipotent communication taking place anywhere and at any time, with the infinite human environment as its medium, which is created by connecting all media forms. It is a process of communication that enables a person to be fully focused on the dynamic customization of their individual information needs. Immersive communication is a ubiquitous experience beyond the boundaries of time and space and with "3I" effects: invisibility, intangibility, and insensibility.

The breakthroughs of new definition, compared with existing definitions of communication, can be summed up by the following two points:

1. Immersive communication reconstructs the three "spaces" and extends the concept of communication space into the whole environment. Media and the environment can become each other and be connected with each other to form a large, infinite media space. This space contains the three major spaces: physical, spiritual, and intellectual. This definition extends the former concept of media to the category of human living space, which reflects how human communication has developed from the "soft edge" to the "no edge," opening up each space of the human media environment and forming a large space via an ubiquitous connection.
2. Immersive communication reconstructs the relationship between media and people. It also demonstrates the formation and characteristics of immersive communication as both the hottest and the coolest medium.

3 Morphological characteristics of immersive communication

In what form does immersive communication take place? Why have the previous means of communication, such as self-communication, interpersonal communication, group communication, organizational communication, mass communication, and interactive communication, not developed immersive characteristics? Borrowing from the related themes of poststructuralism, the subject is constituted of communicative action and communicative structure. Changes in communication patterns cause changes in the subject. So, how did this change happen? What is the concrete manifestation of the change?

The world is being revolutionized by the new immersive communication technologies. Immersive communication technologies are becoming an indispensable tool, extending people's visual, auditory, tactile, and olfactory senses. As McLuhan (1994) said, "Media is the extension of man." Media is not only the extension of human senses, but also the extension of the central nervous system. Glasses can be an extension of people's eyes, just as mobile phones can be an extension of people's ears. The virtual world is the common extension of people and media, which combine to form super-media. This is very likely to be the future media, meeting people's maximum demand for information.

Immersive communication actually contains all previous communication forms. But in the course of the new reconstruction, it has its own unique morphological features. Based on the definition of "immersive communication" in the previous chapter, this chapter summarizes and analyzes the morphological characteristics of immersive communication.

3.1 Immersive communication is human centered: Everything is media, and humans are also a media form

Immersive communication is a human-centered, open media form. It contains all the old and new, tangible or intangible media that can produce, transmit, display, and receive information. It includes the environment and humans as media forms. Immersive communication is a comprehensive "aggregation" of all forms of media.

Human communication history has passed through the stages of "cross media, whole media, and pan media" and then entered into a comprehensive integration of "media convergence." The concept of media convergence was first put forward by Ithiel De Sola Pool at the Massachusetts Institute of Technology in the United States. In his book *Technologies of Freedom*, published in 1984, he discussed "the convergence of modes." Pool believed that the development of electronic digital technology had led to the convergence of communication modes that used to be quite distinct from each other. Media convergence is the developing mode that presents the integrated multi-functions of all media forms. The new converged communication technology and its functions are greater than the sum of its original parts (Pool, 1984). We can infer that the result of media convergence is that digital technology and ubiquitous Internet communication will lead to the formation of a new communication mode: immersive communication.

Immersive communication enables "media humanization" to be fully realized, and its communication is entirely human centered; the combination of communication patterns and methods changes with different people and their needs. According to Levinson's anthropotropic theory of the humanization tendency, the choice of media in the process of evolution, in both form and function, increasingly supports the pre-technological human communication model. People are active masters of media—not the ones presented by the media, but the ones who give orders and create media content. People have an unprecedented ability to make choices about the content created by others. In immersive communication, the role of human play has evolved further: humans are not only the active controllers of media but also a body of media that has entered the center stage. Humans are the ultimate state of media, the real super-medium, and the subject of future biological media.

The "human-centered" concept of immersive communication determines that it is a dynamic, fully personalized, customized communication. "Human centered" here means each individual as the center. Thus, each process of immersive communication is actually in a circle of "positioning, communication, feedback, re-positioning, communication and feedback" (the book will address this "location-based service" in more detail in the following chapters). McLuhan's judgment that "centers are everywhere and margins are nowhere" (Levinson, 1999, p. 7) is appropriate to describe the relationship between humans and media and the change in humans' status of immersive communication.

Humans, as the center of communication, are passive information receivers and active information senders, as well as passive information senders at the same time. So-called passive information senders occur in immersive communication because information is no longer the center of communication. Instead, humans are the center, with their surroundings, which could be another person, a group of people, or a mobile terminal, able to communicate, to provide services, or to send demands for information, especially requests for private information about the person at the center, such as location information. Many such communications are preset and are processed automatically.

So, the technological revolution brought by immersive communication is not only the change in the traditional information communications chain or the conceptual subversion of the traditional concept of the "audience," but also the

58 *Morphological characteristics*

comprehensive reconstruction of the concept of the human and the media. In immersive communication, people are not only passive receivers of information but also active and passive communicators. They can also be the media themselves and part of the environment. And the environment here is itself a medium. In immersive communication, the media has no interface, and media and the environment merge into one another. It can also be said that human beings are in harmony with media and the environment. The interface disappears at both the psychological and the physical level.

The person who is at the center of immersive communication is an "invisible man," formless, intangible, and invisible, with the characteristics of electronic communication and electronic human nature. Of course, his physical body is not really in the ubiquitous cyberspace. When we make phone calls, watch TV, or surf the Internet, we produce the effect of what McLuhan called "invisible man." But during communication on the phone, both parties are "sent" out, while their bodies remain where they are. When watching TV, the people on TV are "invisible," but the people watching TV are not. In the ubiquitous network connection in immersive communication, people are the same as when they are on the phone, having lost their physical bodies like an "invisible man." But the "invisible man" here is different from the man watching TV, as is mainly reflected in the constant changes in "invisible man" that can happen all the time, and the communication relationship that "invisible man" can build is dynamic. Unlike people watching TV, who cannot immediately exchange places with the people on TV, in immersive communication, this kind of exchange is always possible. It can be said that, as a form of communication that embraces all forms of media, human beings play the ultimate role in their media subjectivity, and their passivity is also played to the extreme.

3.2 Immersive communication is instant and anytime: The present, past, and future are integrated, and the virtual world and physical world coexist as integrated, instantaneous, and long-lasting

In immersive communication, communication is instant and anytime. Communication can pass through time and space and bring the past, present, and future together. Communication can occur between the virtual world and the physical world without a boundary, so that people can roam freely in the two worlds at all times. Therefore, immersive communication has both a past form and a present form, a virtual form and a physical form. "Media by appointment" is the characteristic of all the old media (Levinson, 2014, p. 7). The immersive medium distinguishes itself from the old medium by its "anytime" form.

Immersive communication connects all types of media to work together to meet human society's increasing information needs. All media, including those that are intentionally invented to be media and those that hit the market through a fluke (such as surveillance cameras), indispensably service the same goal: to provide information services "anytime."

Morphological characteristics 59

We often use the term "pseudo environment" to refer to the media environment created by language, text, video, and so on. From the American critic Walter Lippmann (2006), who first proposed this concept in the *New York Times*, to the Japanese socialist Fujitake Akira, who proposed that the "pseudo environment is becoming the real environment," many scholars have believed that pseudo environment–created media will affect the real world and become a part of the real world. Now, virtual reality, supported by the ubiquitous Internet, is permeating the physical real world, launching an attack on all fronts, and forcing the comprehensive fusion of the physical world with the virtual world in both cognitive styles and lifestyles.

One characteristic of immersive communication is the integration of virtuality and reality. Nicola Negroponte's *Being Digital* was mainly a forecast when it was published in 1996. At that time, the futurist confidently predicted that "virtual reality can make artificial things as real as real things, or even more real than real things" (Negroponte, 1996, p. 116). It was a prophecy, but now it is a reality. Immersive communication really brings together people from the physical real world and the virtual world. In the second media era, Facebook, Kaixin.com, and renren.com showed that people long for relationships based on real life. The main feature of all of these is that most people are registered in their real names, and they want to find enthusiasts with the same interests or hobbies and receive their own social acknowledgment. Although this kind of identity unification might sometimes occur with game players, such as in the virtual reality game Second Life, game players have the faces of avatars. But virtual reality has indeed stepped into reality, and people living in physical reality sometimes think in the logic of the virtual world, just as described in some American TV drama series. In 2007, the crime scene investigation show *CSI* had an episode on people living in the real world who carry out criminal investigations through Second Life. Another TV series, *Lost*, opened up a real website for Oceanic Airlines, a virtual airline, with the itinerary of the flight that was lost on the show. A large number of game players also launched operations on the website to search for "other" airlines. These are just some examples of millions of similar stories happening simultaneously in the real world and the virtual world.

Another thing that makes the virtual world appealing in the real world is that the virtual world is infinite. For example, a physical clothing store has space constraints, but the space for hangers in a virtual clothing store is unlimited. Stores in the physical world have business hours, but virtual stores are always open online. In the physical world, a person's time and energy to make money are limited, while in the virtual world, people have more opportunities to earn money. That is why an increasing number of people have opened virtual stores and keep themselves busy but happy every day. People seek the dreams that they cannot fulfill in the real world, but the pleasure and the satisfaction they derive from the virtual world are real.

The break in the boundary between the real and virtual brought about by immersive communication is also a breakthrough between the present and historical time and space. Will these breakthroughs impact the public interest and the

60 *Morphological characteristics*

social responsibility that people bear? Is the expression of "immersive communication" an objective reflection of reality? In what sense does immersive communication move beyond morality? Will the people in the virtual world also lose their identity and personality or commit urban violence? The popularity of online games and the illusion of virtual human relationships have attracted a lot of theoretical attention. Either one or both sides initiate, virtual interpersonal illusion in interpersonal communications already existed far earlier with the invention of the telegraph and telephone, or modern private letters via email and blogs. As long as the two sides have not met, there will be fictitious imaginings, which are more easily led to Plato's love. Because what we fell in love with was the word (text), the sound, or the picture, we use our imagination to fill in the unknown parts, and this virtual image stays with us all the time. If two people who communicate in the virtual world finally get to meet each other face to face, perhaps disappointment is inevitable. So, the best thing to do is either never to expect to make virtuality a reality or just to merge the virtual and the physical at the beginning. It can be said that immersive communication provides the greatest opportunity to find and achieve these answers, because the customization of immersive communication lets us have more freedom of choice. On the other hand, the two worlds of the virtual and the physical have already been regarded as one common space in immersive communication.

Due to the fusion of space and time and of virtual and physical presence, in the context of immersive communication, a person may have already disappeared from the real physical world, but the virtual life he or she created will keep going in accordance with the game as set, to go to work and study and also affect the lives of others. For example, he or she will continue to appear in an online virtual "restaurant" and order his or her favorite food. If we can create the agenda setting of the human mind's DNA model in the future, people will probably continue to exercise civil rights, such as giving opinions and voting. Of course, this kind of passage through time tunnels will bring new problems to human ethics and social structures.

3.3 Immersive communication is pervasive anywhere and everywhere: In "remote" presence and "ubiquitous" presence, fixed, mobile, and virtual coexistence converge

As mentioned earlier, immersive communication reconstructs the third space of communication and opens up lines between the three large spaces, so that all of these spaces, the material space and spiritual space, psychological space and emotional space, physical space and virtual space, and real space and imaginary space, merge into one infinite space. All forms of immersive communication are carried out in this large space or environment after this enormous fusion and thus are characterized by the traits of all these spaces.

Technology and imagination provide infinite possibilities for immersive communication in terms of morphological changes and locations of existence. Daniel Bell (1976), an American futurist, once said that technology is destructive, which

Morphological characteristics 61

sounds like a critique of technology, but actually he emphasized the essentially inherent nature of technology, namely, that it is beyond the status quo, like the emerging electronic interdependence in the form of the "global village" or "smart planet," reshaping the world of human existence. Immersive communication, via the Internet, ubiquitous network, and virtual reality, and via the fusion of "remote" and "ubiquitous" presence, not only make the global village a reality but also let the people in the village enjoy communication everywhere and at all times.

From the perspective of the space of immersive communication, the environment is the media, and the media is the environment. On the one hand, as we have already discussed, the form of immersive media as various terminals has been embedded into our surrounding environment. On the other hand, it is because media and people are connected via an ubiquitous network to constitute the space environment, such as all sizes of intelligent spaces with immersive environments, that our whole environment, including the "smart planet" itself, is becoming the media. Today, despite the variety of human living environments, the value of urban space as a medium is obviously crucial. The concept of "city" includes various factors related to urban space and external images, including cultural factors such as virtual survival, information transmission, and value inheritance in the city. As early as the 1950s and 1960s, Western countries had already launched thorough and extensive specialized research on the city.

At the same time, the technical realization of ubiquitous communication lets people surrounded by information anytime, anywhere, and "unconsciously" access instant information. The process of information communication is not only replaced by immediacy and interactivity, but also has a "latent" and intangible quality that quietly "erodes" our lives. Joshua Meyrowitz (1986) explored the "electronic erosion," but what he studied was how television acts as a major enabling agent. In his research, he found that television erodes basic differences between the public and the private and between adults and children. For example, children who cannot read can watch TV with their parents. In the online virtual world "Happy City," the person who serves as the director of the marriage registration office in my city, according to the data, is a five-year-old girl.

Immersion is an open communication space that absorbs all information from the surroundings and spreads information to various surrounding terminals (including people). The instant and constant information exchange becomes an important force affecting humans' social life. We can see that, via human-centeredness and openness, immersive communication completely breaks the "center of power" of traditional mass communication to let immersive communication form new dynamic, multi-polar information communication forms and new space, containing everything, as well as to immerse people completely within it.

The ability of humans to control the world depends largely on the ability to communicate at any time, at any place, and to any object. It is another great advancement of the ability to communicate to evolve from "remote" communication to "ubiquitous" communication. From a technical point of view, the evolution of the network has entered a higher stage of collaboration, with terminals moving not only from a single mode to a multi-mode but also to a deeper reconfiguration

62 *Morphological characteristics*

in accordance with the needs of information communication. The terminals "hidden" in the surrounding environment can be aggregated at any time to readapt to the needs of the network, and when demand is met, the network will disintegrate, waiting for the next polymerization.

Real life has become an increasingly intelligent world, and virtual reality is part of real life. Mobile phones, the Internet, TV, and cities (including elevator advertising, video monitoring), as well as convergence media—a fusion of individual media with mobile Internet as the core and a re-fusion with intelligent city space—enhance functions as well as instantly achieving all communication possibilities. From buying lottery tickets directly on the TV screen to a key sharing function connecting various media, from electronic magazines and individual microblogs to the personal space of the virtual world, information is everywhere and "you" is everywhere, whether it is "telepresence" or "ubiquitous presence."

The large space of immersive communication contains McLuhan's visual space. Visual space is the content of artificial media. McLuhan's "acoustics" space concept makes his position on visual space very clear. As described by Levinson (1999), "[I]t is the world viewed through pre-literate eyes, a world of no boundaries in which information emerges not from fixed positions but anywhere and everywhere. It is the world of music, myth, total immersion" (p. 45); "[T]he world that comes to us after the alphabet, in the form mostly of television, mythic, immersive, and unlike the book and the newspaper, lacks perspective or distance from its subjects" (p. 46). The immersive world contains a world of television, but it is a world embracing all kinds of colorful things, and it also needs us to fully immerse ourselves in it.

In the age of immersive communication, information is open to infinity. Anything can become an information source. Anything can become a target. Whether fixed or mobile, through the ubiquitous video screen terminals that are virtual or physical, people are always engaged in dialogues "remotely" and "ubiquitously."

3.4 Immersive communication is all-powerful: Boundaries between entertainment, work, and life vanish; cloud computing integrates everything

Immersive communication makes the boundaries separating entertainment, work, and life disappear, enabling the functioning of omnipotent communication. "One of the signs of all the new media is that anyone can join, whether games or work" (Levinson, 2014, p. 13).

Immersive communication breaks the boundaries separating entertainment, work, and life, especially when cloud computing frees us from the physical personal computer we used to depend on; the ubiquitous Internet provides a unified, continuously working electric mind connected to all media, so that we can bring both work and life with us on walks because the cloud in the sky lets everything move easily.

Morphological characteristics 63

As early as, or even before, the phone era, work already could be done in an entertaining way. Levinson's (1999) "toy, mirror, and art" theory talks about the role media play in entertainment and work: media swaggers onto the horizon, mostly in the form of toys, but mostly as a type of gadget. People like them because they are fun, not because they can do something. A famous example comes from the year 1881, when chairman William Orton of the Western Union Telegraph Company advised his friend Chauncy Depew not to spend 10,000 dollars to buy one-sixth of the stock of the Baer Telephone company because he thought the newly invented telephone was "a kind of toy" that had "no possibility of business development." Similarly, the use of the telephone in Britain was delayed for ten years because the British people always regarded it as a "scientific toy." In fact, later, the phone entered into family rooms. When people picked up the telephone in their bedrooms, the phone started to break down the wall between work and life.

However, not until the Internet and the virtual world were the boundaries between work and entertainment further blurred. In immersive communication, most of the time, entertainment and work have been designed together: games are work and work is a game. This has also begun to become many people's work and lifestyle; sometimes it improves work efficiency and brings spiritual joy. When people play games, rational detachment occurs, together with happiness; that is what we call flow, a psychological immersion. Immersive communication brings the duality of work and recreation. Is it a virtual world tour or work? That is the human choice. The idea of doing work online was a paradox, because the Internet itself is fun. Now, more and more people are combining work with games, immersing themselves in work and life, which provides new ways of and opportunities for human emotional expression and psychological satisfaction.

Of course, when the electronic machine and the ubiquitous connection are fully connected with life and work, this can also to a certain extent trample on people's aesthetic tastes and judgment of entertainment. This has existed ever since the Romantic era, from the first wave of protest in the industrial age. Of course, all-powerful immersive communication will combine each side of art with the whole and then merge into our daily lives, which is the inevitable road of art becoming living, working becoming life, and life becoming media.

3.5 Summary

Electronic technology, launched 100 years ago, captured humanity's attention through interaction and focus. But do "interaction" and "focus" accurately describe the status of human communication today? What is the next logical phase of "interaction"? The answer is "immersion." Immersion is a new concept in communication and describes people having a remote presence in virtual reality and a ubiquitous flow experience in the cyber world. In the last decade, immersive communication took root globally with the development of mobile Internet, the Internet of Things, the ubiquitous network, biological communication technologies, and the development of the "smart city" and "intelligent earth."

64 *Morphological characteristics*

This is a world revolutionized by immersive communication. Immersive communication technology extends people's vision, hearing, and touch and smell, and it is becoming an indispensable tool.

On the basis of the definition of "immersive communication" in the previous chapter, this chapter summarizes and concretely explains the morphological characteristics of "immersive communication":

Immersive communication is human centered: everything is media, and humans are also a media form. It is an open media form containing all the new and old media, including all media forms that can produce, transmit, display, and receive information, comprising tangible and intangible forms, the environment itself, and human beings as a kind of media form. Immersive communication is the comprehensive general form of all media.

Immersive communication is instant and anytime: it is the present. Immersive communication can pass through time and space and bring the past, present, and future together. Communication can be conducted between the virtual world and the physical world without boundaries, so that people can roam freely within the two worlds at all times. Therefore, immersive communication has both a past form and a present form, a virtual form and a physical form. With the integration of space and time of virtual presence and physical presence, in immersive communication, a person can keep living a virtual life after having disappeared from the physical world, can still communicate with others and affect the lives of others, and perhaps continue to exercise civil rights, such as offering opinions and voting. This newly coming digital people phenomenon, will challenge the human ethics and demand the reform of social structures.

Immersive communication is pervasive anywhere and everywhere: the "remote" and "ubiquitous" converge, and the fixed, mobile, and virtual coexist. The form of immersive media is various terminals embedded into our surrounding environment. On the other hand, it is because media and people are connected via the ubiquitous network that the space environment is constituted in all sizes of highly intelligent spaces within the immersive environment, and our whole environment, including the "smart planet," becomes media. At the same time, the technical realization of ubiquitous communication lets people surrounded by information anytime, anywhere, and "unconsciously" access information instantly. The process of information communication is not only replaced by immediacy and interactivity but also has a "latent" and intangible quality that quietly "erodes" our lives. Immersion is an open communication space that absorbs all the surrounding information and spreads information to various surrounding terminals (including people). This instant and constant information exchange becomes an important force affecting humans' social lives. We can see that via its human-centeredness and openness, immersive communication completely breaks the "center of power" of traditional mass communication, allowing immersive communication to comprise new dynamic, multi-polar information communication forms and new space, with everything contained.

Immersive communication is all-powerful: boundaries separating entertainment, work, and life are vanishing; cloud computing integrates everything. In immersive communication, entertainment and work are designed to be indistinguishable and inseparable. This new way of working and lifestyle, mostly beings work efficiency and spiritual joy in the same time. When people play games, rational detachment occurs, together with happiness, and this what we call flow, a psychological immersion.

4 The information content and movement mode of immersive communication

As Mark Poster argued in his book *The Mode of Information: Poststructuralism and Social Context*,

> In a sense all signs are now considered information, as in cybernetics and often in popular parlance, where "information" is contrasted with "noise" or non-meaning. Information has become a privileged term in our culture. TV ads for information services warn consumers and corporate executives alike that they and their children will fall behind in the race for success if they do not keep up with current information. Information is presented as the key to contemporary living and society is divided between the information rich and information poor. The "informed" individual is a new social ideal, particularly for the middle class.
>
> (Poster, 1990, p. 7)

At the same time, he explained,

> What the mode of information puts into question, however, is not simply the sensory apparatus but the very shape of subjectivity: its relation to the world of objects, its perspective on that world, its location in that world. We are confronted not so much by a change from a "hot" to a "cool" communications medium, or by a reshuffling of the sensoria, as McLuhn thought, but by a generalized destabilization of the subject.
>
> (Poster, 1990, p. 15)

McLuhan's famous judgment "the medium is the message" (McLuhan, 1964, p. 7) also revealed that any media use, such as watching TV, has influence that goes far beyond the specific content that the media spreads.

McLuhan sought to shift people's attention from the content to the media, because he believed that the content takes away our attention and damages our understanding and perception of both the media and its surroundings. "The 'content' of a medium is like the juicy piece of meat," McLuhan observed in a frequently quoted metaphor (1964, p. 32), "carried by the burglar to distract the watchdog of the mind." His later work used wordplay to reinforce this point: he co-authored *The Medium Is the Massage* with Quentin Fiore (McLuhan, Fiore & Agel, 1967), while *Counterblast* included the phrase "the medium is the mess-age" (McLuhan & Parker, 1969, p. 23), and "mess-age" became "mass-age" in *Take Today: The Executive as Dropout* (McLuhan & Nevitt, 1972, p. 63).

The communication itself may be more important than the content, but that doesn't mean that we should pay less attention to the "message" in the study of the communication process. One reason that media content is important is that another medium becomes its "content." As we discussed earlier, the content of a movie may be a novel, while the content of the Internet encompasses all or at least most media that have come before it. So not only is the content significant, but it may be the best way of examining a medium and its impact. In short, the analysis of information content and movement mode is an essential part of the study of immersive communication.

4.1 Language form

Immersive communication is a comprehensive "aggregation" containing all the forms of communication language recognized by communication academics: oral language, graphic language, written language, electronic language, scene lan-guage, pseudo language, and outdoor advertisements. It also includes some new forms of media yet to be included in communication theories, such as surveillance cameras.

4.1.1 Previous media languages

Immersive communication contains all the old and new media—traditional media such as newspaper and television; mobile media such as mobile phones, mobile television, blogs, and podcasts; and environmental media such as outdoor adver-tisements, building advertisements, and interactive screens on vending machines. All of these media belong to a large media space, connected via the ubiquitous network, so they can interact with each other at any time. For example, infor-mation communication can occur between mobile phones and outdoor vending machines. Various terminals such as Internet screens have been embedded into our surrounding environment, continuously transferring data to people. In fact, immersive communication actually contains all the contents of communication forms such as mobile communication, individual communication, and interac-tive communication, making such content pervasive anywhere and everywhere. Content from a podcast on a mobile phone could be spread anywhere at any time with a ubiquitous network. We speak directly to the terminals in our environment, just as we did in primitive times, and our fingers walk on the keyboard.

Levinson (1999) noted: "not only do old media become the content of new media, but in so doing retain the older media that served as their content, which in turn retain their even older media as content, going back and back ... to the oldest medium of all" (p. 41). Immersive communication not only integrates

68   *Information content and movement mode*

the communication forms and content of various media, but also eliminates the boundaries between media, between people and media, and to the greatest extent, the differences between content and media.

4.1.2 The pan-media language of the whole environment: The monitoring camera and environmental advertisements in the intelligent city

One of the core information carriers of immersive communication is the intelligent city. With the support of the Internet, the Internet of Things, and ubiquitous networks, the modern intelligent city (UCity) merges media functions into almost every corner of the city, including building walls, the ground, elevators, and public transportation. An intelligent city is a huge carrier of media content. Meanwhile, its space landscape and culture could also be the content of that media.

The city participates in constructing the information content of immersive communication with its large-space form and function. New terms such as "environmental media" and "environmental advertisement" have emerged as the whole environment where we live has gradually become a medium. These terms emphasize the relationship between advertisements and their surrounding environment. Based on their specific communication environments, the advertising ideas commonly achieve unique visual impacts and communication effects through effective use of space or environmental elements, which has become a new fashion in the global advertising industry. Moreover, there is a growing trend combining environmental advertisement with unconventional thinking and various means of mobile new media, creatively developing the plasticity of the environment. Royal Swedish Opera's advertising campaign for its new work *Orpheus in the Underworld* was a classic case of environmental advertisement. Surprisingly, advertisements were posted on busy sidewalks. People walking with their heads down would suddenly stop in surprise, because a person had appeared in front of them, seemingly crawling out of the ground! What they saw was a 3D artistic advertisement, which vividly recorded the key plots of the opera's "escape from hell."

In addition to these 3D artistic advertisements, handle advertisements on buses and subways, large-scale outdoor billboards, interactive LED screens and building advertisements, and urban smart monitoring systems consisting of all-weather city surveillance cameras are also worth mentioning. All of these together create a "stereo-phantom" in urban space. Meanwhile, the collection and communication of information, along with the production and analysis of information, can be done anytime and anywhere.

The production and dissemination of a recent news story of heroic self-sacrifice also demonstrates the function of the city as a medium to some degree. According to Xinhua News, Guo Xiaoqi, a 15-year-old junior high school student from Mishan City, Heilongjiang Province, was on her way home from school with her classmates when suddenly a car rushed toward them at high speed. Facing an emergency, Guo Xiaoqi pulled her classmates behind her, a split second before

Information content and movement mode 69

the car hit her. This scene was captured by the roadside monitoring equipment. Thousands of netizens were touched by the video and called her "the most beautiful junior high school student" (Xiong Lin, 2012). Guo Xiaoqi's story caused a big stir in the local area. The video of the roadside monitoring equipment was spread to the Internet and TV. Many citizens went to the hospital to visit her. City leaders recognized Guo Xiaoqi's brave behavior by giving her a cash reward and an opportunity to study at the best local high school. Meanwhile, local citizens were called on to learn from Guo Xiaoqi. Like the Xiao Yueyue event mentioned in Chapter 1, this story is another small example of information generation and circulation in immersive communication.

4.1.3 Humans as the source of media language and information content

Continuing the previous discussion of humans as the ontology of media, this chapter will analyze how humans form media content. As Paul Levinson wrote, "the user is the content of the Internet—which, it turns out, is much what McLuhan went on to say, in a metaphoric sense, about media in general" (Levinson, 1999, p. 39). McLuhan's notion of the user as content goes back at least as far as the literary criticism of I.A. Richards (1929), who argued that the meaning of a text resided not in its author's intentions but in its reader's legitimate interpretations. Starting from Richards' theory, McLuhan moved reasonably from the user interpreting the text to determining the text to being the text. But McLuhan's examples of users as content are mainly electronic media such as telephone and television.

To extend McLuhan's model, Levinson proposed a three-part hierarchy in which (a) humans serve as the determiners of content of all media by virtue of our inextricable interpretation of all that comes before us, (b) the human perceiver travels through one-way electronic media such as radio and television, therein becoming their content, and (c) humans as interlocutors literally created all the content for old interactive media such as the telephone, and much of the content for the Internet. Further, after the emergence of the Internet, when it does not transmit information by means of human conversation, it introduces images by means of television or words by means of printing. The Internet can be seen as a collection of all the media of the past in which content was determined by people, so it encompasses all three levels of Levinson's hierarchical system. The present study also advances this line of thought, because ubiquitous networking, the technological basis of immersive communication, encompasses the Internet, so it can be inferred that immersive communication itself at least encompasses all aspects of the hierarchy.

Not only all past media but also their users form the content of immersive communication. No matter what they are doing, people in the space of immersive communication are creating content all the time. In immersive environments such as smart cities, the ever-expanding information collection terminals are collecting and exchanging information with the human body at any time via touch sensors. Later chapters will discuss these "immersive communicators" in further detail.

70 *Information content and movement mode*

4.1.4 The language of the virtual world

Virtual reality can be seen as part of the online world, but it also has its own unique information language features. As mentioned earlier, the Internet is the medium of all media. The all-embracing Internet has the ambition to liberate all past media and use them as its own means, eventually turning all media into its own content. In the virtual world, distance is no longer a buffer. You are "you" and it is "you" at this moment: "Electronic mediation complicates the transmission of language and subverts the subject who would limit language to the role of a simple medium of expressions. ... To copy an original means, in the mode of information, to create simulacra" (Poster, 1990, p. 10).

New forms of language wrapping in the virtual world impose significant changes in both the virtual world and the social field. Drawing on poststructuralist theory, changes in the configuration or wrapping of language alter the process by which the subject converts symbols into meanings, a sensitive part of cultural production. When oral or print-wrapped language is transformed to electronically wrapped language, the subject's relation to the world will also be reconfigured.

The languages of the virtual world in immersive communication also have something in common. Beyond a certain point, increased distance between the transmitter and the receiver allows a reconfiguration of the relation between them, and between the message and its context, generating new forms of language wrapping. These reconfigurations will also impose new relations on the relevant aspects of the society and the system of relationships, which includes relations between states and citizens, individuals and groups, etc. The revolutionary characteristic of immersive communication, which can extend across the virtual world and the physical world, will powerfully boost the reconstruction of relationships.

Electronic media tends to distance the relation of communicators. It doesn't have the palpable material relationship between the ancient reader and the printed text. Instead, it may disrupt the relation of the subject to the symbols it emits or receives and then reconstitute this relation in brand new forms. In Poster's words,

> For the subject in electronically mediated communication, the object tends to become not the material world as represented in language but the flow of signifiers itself. In the mode of information it becomes increasingly difficult, or even pointless, for the subject to distinguish a "real" existing "behind" the flow of signifiers, and as a consequence social life in part becomes a practice of positioning subjects to receive and interpret messages.
>
> (Poster, 1990, pp. 14–15)

The virtual world's content, form, and language are compatible with the physical world, but it has its own electronic character. Technology or other innovative powers make virtual worlds such as Second Life and Kaixin.com more and more appealing, attracting a growing amount of people to live there. On the one hand, they ingeniously convert some old media into new content in the virtual world, just as movies were adapted from plays and TV dramas were adapted from

Information content and movement mode　71

movies. On the other hand, people in the virtual world are constantly creating their own new content, such as building their own virtual homes and cities, while creating virtual relationships, personal status, and social culture.

4.2　The linguistic hegemony of immersive media

The language of immersive communication exists anywhere and anytime. Language produces meaning, so it is not only the presentation and representation of material reality, but also the carrier of ideas and ideology. For example, when English is disseminated globally, it also unconsciously transmits the lifestyle, values, and ideology of English-speaking countries, especially the United States and the United Kingdom. American scholar Joseph Nye defined this process as "soft power" (Nye, 2004). Pierre Bourdieu, the French socialist, compared this strong trend of English symbols to symbolic violence. In his view, symbolic violence is essentially a privilege, a wide-reaching peremptory norm established and strengthened within a certain range (Bourdieu, 1997).

4.2.1　*Presenting ideas in immersive communication:*
Moistens everything softly and silently

According to Mattelart (2000), "[t]he invention of communication as an ideal occurred at a time when the prevailing ideas were those of modernity and the perfectibility of human societies. It was thus the product of a belief in the future" (p. 3). Historically, language revolutions often led to "one country, one law, one language." Of course, they were sometimes accompanied by symbolic pollution, non-standard usage, etc. Compared with the characteristics of interpersonal communication and mass communication, immersive communication presents a unique style, as described in ancient Chinese poetry: "sneaking into the night with wind, moistening everything softly and silently."

(1) Wrapping into personalized services and demands

As discussed before, immersive communication is a human-centered and fully personalized communication. The thoughts it communicates were embedded into personalized service. After one-to-one precise positioning, then collecting and analyzing the clear requirements of a particular object, immersive communication determines the specific mode and content in constant adaptation. This process is just like an instant flash in electronic brains such as cloud computing, and it often occurs without "human" awareness. Because all the media functions of immersive communication are hidden in the environment around us, we naturally breathe them like air.

"The self" is the service center of immersive communication. Where oral communication is concerned, the "self" is embedded in the face-to-face relationship of direct communication; in print communication, the "self" is constructed as an actor and is located in the center of self-discipline; and in electronic

72 *Information content and movement mode*

communication, the "self" is continuously uncertain in a decentralized state. But in immersive communication, each "self" is situated in an unambiguously central position, so the information and ideas can emerge not only in the form of issuing orders but also in the form of demands that must be satisfied.

(2) Wrapping into entertainment and games

As mentioned earlier, immersive communication breaks the boundaries separating entertainment, work, and life. Thus, it is quite natural to spread ideas in the form of games. The technological foundation of immersive communication makes the shape of information ideas ever-changing, so it could be integrated into any communication node without worrying about extending it. Because it occurs anytime and anywhere and includes the dynamic process of personalized real-time adjustment, immersive communication could transform work into entertainment, or life into work, in an instant.

Because the boundary between virtual space and physical space has been broken, the spatial function of immersive communication can be expanded indefinitely. The human work and entertainment spaces have become an infinitely extended carnival paradise in which people feel a natural realization of personal satisfaction and pleasure.

4.2.2 Media advertisement and the social discourse power of immersive communication

Advertisements exist everywhere in immersive communication. The segmentation of advertising and discourse power is translated from lingering to instant. "Individuals receive their identity in relation to others not primarily from their type of work but from the signs and meanings they display and consume" (Poster, 1995, p. 106). *1999: Victory Without War*, written by former U.S. president Richard Nixon (1989), revealed that the shift of discursive power brought about the shift of international power. Nowadays, the largest export product of the United States is no longer crops and industrial products, or even Coca-Cola and McDonald's, but the mass-produced pop culture: Hollywood blockbusters, TV shows, online games, books, music, software, etc. They comprise the American global "soft power" and discourse power, becoming the best advertisements of the U.S. culture.

Advertising communication was also initially the communication of symbols. About 15 years after the telegraph was invented, the application of telegraphy regarded symbolic language as the basis of "universal harmony" and led to the invention of the "Dream Transmission," using Mercury as a relay station that could link London and India in four hours. As a fruit of such labor, the symbol has become a new kind of intangible asset while increasing social value and generating "symbolic value." In a commodity society, people begin to pursue the value of social information contained in goods that can be transmitted to users. This kind of behavior is called "symbolic consumption." Comparing symbolic consumption

Information content and movement mode   73

results in the popularity of "symbol worship" in our daily life and may be intensified in the era of immersive communication. As communication occurs anywhere and anytime, the spread of popular symbols can immediately reach every corner of the "smart earth." No place will be spared.

French philosopher Guy Debord defined the globalization of commodities and commercialization of the world as "spectacles": "In society dominated by modern conditions of production, life is presented as an immense accumulation of spectacles. Everything that was directly lived has receded into a representation" (Debord, 2007, p. 3). "Spectacles" refers to a social life completely colonized by the commodity. It consists of commodities, images, and spectacle consumption and is therefore closely related to media and social consumption. This spectacle, Best and Kellner (2002) argued, spreads its narcotics mainly through the cultural mechanisms of leisure and consumption, services and entertainment, as ruled by the dictates of advertising and a commercialized media culture (Best & Kellner, 2002,p. 117). In the virtual world dominated by symbolic values, commodities are produced, distributed, and exchanged due to their apparent social significance.

Assisted by a ubiquitous network and a powerful real-time database, immersive communication could enable advertisements to accurately target everyone, integrate into smart cities, and function subtly in the environment. This has undoubtedly improved the quality of the discursive power of advertisements, achieving a qualitative change. Of course, the "personalized" positioning of immersive communication and its culture of absolute self-aggrandizement will exert a strong counterbalance to the language hegemony of communication.

4.3 Information presentation

Immersive communication completely liberates people from the restrictions of time and space. The spread of information occurs instantly at any time and place. Web 2.0 transformed the original human–computer interaction into a human–human interaction. The Internet of Things and the ubiquitous network further build human-to-thing, thing-to-thing, and human-to-human communication anywhere and at any time. The single communication path has been replaced by a composite pattern. This fully opened immersive communication space, with intelligent and ubiquitous features, has overturned the traditional presentation and path of information communication.

With the development of mobile media and interactive media and the revolutionary breakthrough of ubiquitous networks, coupled with the high integration of traditional media and smart cities, humanity is immersed in a ubiquitous, ever-present, omnipotent communication space. In the spectacle of the postmodern world, and "(I)n electronically mediated communications, subjects now float, suspended between points of objectivity, being constituted and reconstituted in different configurations in relation to the discursive arrangement of the occasion" (Poster, 1990, p.11). The late 20th century featured the reterritorialization of the relationship between man and machine. However, the appearance of cybernetic information machines and the cyclic, reversible man–machine relationship

74 *Information content and movement mode*

replaced the irreversible conquest relationship between the two in the industrial machine era, which was reflected in the fact that people were enslaved by TV as human machines and TV viewers became the subject of "being made" (Deleuze & Guattari, 1987). Human-centered immersive communication redefines the space consisting of media as media itself. In such a symbolic system of perception and communication, the presentation of information is also necessarily centralized, dynamic, and personalized. This brought a revolutionary correction to the so-called cybernetic relationship in the era of cybernetic information machines.

The "More-Is-Better" communication theory has severely inhibited the connection between language and society, limiting post-industrial social theory to an economic metaphor. The new immersive communication of information has, to some extent, supplemented or even replaced the existing forms of social interaction. New modes for the immersive communication of information are also taking shape, which are likely to fundamentally affect human political and economic life.

Immersive communication contains almost all ways of communication, such as interpersonal communication, group communication, organizational communication, and mass communication. Its information presentation features great flexibility and inclusiveness. Compared with traditional media, the characteristics of immersive communication may be both its strength and its weakness. Changes in the ways of communication lead to changes in communication effects. How can we maximize the potential of technology to achieve maximum information validity and communication effect? What kind of changes will the central function of humans, the "immediacy," and the personalized feedback mechanisms of immersive communication bring to the concept of media communication? We will further discuss these issues in the following chapters.

4.4 The paths and characteristics of information movement in immersive communication

Since immersive communication can adopt any media and method of information communication under the premise of human-centeredness, if needed, this study draws on a "humanized" perspective and focuses on human-centered communication. Meanwhile, the information movement of immersive communication also exhibits an open pattern. The difference in information movement between traditional media and immersive communication is not in "point to surface" or "surface to point." Instead, immersive communication does not merely transmit information between one or more environments but views the entire human environment as a space for its information movement.

The information movement started in the spoken language era, with text appearing later. However, once printing was invented, all media had the characteristic of a small number of messages flowing to the majority, except for telegraphs and telephones. The communication mode of traditional media such as newspapers, radio, and television is "point to surface." Reporters and editors acting as the "point" deliver information unilaterally to the audience acting as the "surface." However, when media such as text and television became the content

Information content and movement mode 75

of the Internet, a profound democracy was born. The movement path along which a few messages flow to a mainly passive audience has been changed, and a bidirectional flow of information has become its main feature.

In contrast, the mode of immersive ubiquitous network communication is both "point to point" and a "surface to point" cycling, helical, and dynamic path. In terms of "point to point," the transmitters and receivers in immersive communication are dispersed in cyberspace based on ubiquitous connections. Moreover, the spread of information is both unidirectional and stereoscopic. The immersive communication also has a "point to surface" mode. In the space of immersive communication, environmental advertisements seem to send information to all. But more often, the mode of immersive communication is "point to point," with specific information serving a specific individual.

So, the freedom of obtaining information increased as focused communication evolved into immersive communication. When you send out your demand in the form you need, you will get personalized information, with "you" as the absolute goal, instead of information wrapped in a traditional form. "Positioning" comes first. Traditional information that people often use in their lives is constantly being digitized, such as entering personal information from a business card into a mobile phone and establishing basic electronic files of personal and social relationships. Likewise, when you want to send your specific demand to a media terminal, such as finding nearby restaurants without giving specific information about your location, a cellphone app will search through a GSM network, CDMA network, or GPS to locate you and then provide the search results of related information with your consent. This human-centered, location-based service (LBS) model is a basic information movement model for immersive communication.

The communication modes underwent fundamental changes, moving beyond simple circulation, when they transformed from "point to point" to "point to surface" and then back to "point to point." Immersive communication combines the two modes in one space. In a ubiquitous and intelligent society of immersive communication, the collection and management of information can be realized intelligently, such as achieving clothes information management through an IC (integrated circuit) chip in the tag on each garment. This chip can serve anti-counterfeiting, logistics management, inventory management, and other functions. When a customer tries on the clothing, the reader information terminals hidden in the wall or in the surrounding shopping environment can learn which clothing is currently missing in the store, which kinds of design are most popular, etc., and then quickly send that information to the relevant department. By the time the customer checks out, a replacement garment is already en route to the store or even already in stock.

In 2007, for example, the U-Japan Best Business Award, issued by Japan's Ministry of Internal Affairs and Communications, was won by a management checkout information system that automatically recognizes the freshness of food. As long as the IC tag is placed on the bottom of the plate and the reading machine is placed somewhere on the conveyor belt, the kitchen can tell which sushi is the most popular of the day without looking at the conveyor belt. If a dish of sushi

76 *Information content and movement mode*

that has been on the pan for 50 minutes is still on the turntable, the robot arm will automatically withdraw it to ensure that customers get the freshest sushi. During checkout, the antenna induction in the stacked dishes calculates the total automatically, and the consumption amount can be known in about one second.

In summary, as an open system that embraces all existing and future communications, immersive communication includes the "point to point," "point to surface," and "surface to surface" information movement paths and models. Further, its demand model is mainly based on "human-centered" logic. Therefore, this study mainly observes how the entire environment provides customized information and comprehensive services to individuals, describes the movement path of its information, and tries to create an immersive information communication model.

4.5 Summary

As an open system that embraces all existing and future e-communications, immersive communication is mainly based on human-centered logic. The entire environment provides customized information and comprehensive services to each individual inside. This chapter discusses the unique information content and movement patterns of immersive communication. There are four major language forms of immersive communication: (1) including all previous media languages, (2) pan-media languages in the whole environment, such as surveillance cameras in smart cities and environmental advertisements, (3) humans as media languages and information content, and (4) the language of the virtual world.

The linguistic hegemony of immersive communication is reflected in its ways of presenting ideas. It is a kind of personalized customization without any trace that is mainly reflected in wrapping the information ideas into personalized services, audience demands, and entertainment games. The media advertisements and the power of social discourse in immersive communication also show a corresponding uniqueness.

In terms of information presentation, the methods of immersive ubiquitous network communication are not only "point to point" but also follow a "point to surface" circular, helical, dynamic path. From the perspective of "point to point," the transmitters and receivers of immersive information are scattered in the immersive network space, and the communication is not only unidirectional but also three-dimensional. Meanwhile, immersive communication can also accomplish "point to surface." In the immersive space, environmental advertisements seem to send information to everyone. But more often, the form of immersive communication is "point to point," with specific information serving specific individuals. A human-centered LBS model is a basic information movement pattern for immersive communication.

Immersive communication likewise contains all the "point to point," "point to surface," "surface to point," and "point to surface" information movement paths and patterns. The difference between immersive communication and traditional ways of media information movement is not just between "point to surface"

Information content and movement mode 77

and "surface to point." Instead, their fundamental difference is that immersive communication regards the entire human environment instead of one or more smaller environments as its space for information movement, forming a dynamic, multi-polar, all-encompassing information structure, as well as new forms of movement.

5 The model of immersive communication and its graphic forms

The model of immersive communication mainly refers to the various ways and paths of information generation, communication, acceptance, production, and re-communication that take place between remote and ubiquitous space, that is, physical and virtual space. It is the regular presentation of information interaction that occurs between humans and the large environment consisting of many small spaces, and those intertwined new spaces. This model is formed against the background of an open pattern in which the entire human environment is the space of its information movement.

This study attempts to avoid the limitations of the previous media research on models of communication. Meyrowitz argued that the research on television has been severely limited to the extent that it views electronic media merely as new links among pre-existing environments. Such research ignores the possibility that, once widely used, electronic media may create new social environments that reshape behavior in ways that go beyond the specific products delivered (Meyrowitz, 1997). Harold Adams Innis, originally a political economist, extended the economic monopoly principle to the research field of information monopolies. He saw the control of the media as a means of implementing social and political control, while the new media can break the old monopoly (Innis, 1999). Based on the understanding of the nature of media and its relationship with society, communication model diagrams show the flow path and relationship structure of information.

5.1 The main communication models in communication studies

Model research plays an important role in the study of communication, as models can make complex regulations clear. A model of communication represents a formula for studying the process, nature, and effects of communication. The sociological model is an intuitive and concise description of social laws. It is generally an abstraction of reality and a simplified form of the theory that reproduces reality. A given communication model can not only represent the communication elements, their mutual relations and structure, and the communication process and function but also describe the spatial structure and time sequence specific to the communication activities. It is an auxiliary tool that helps people recognize and grasp the characteristics and laws of communication.

Models can be divided into structural models and functional models based on their structure and form. A structural model is mainly used to describe the structure of the research object, while functional models of communication describe the relationship and interaction between the communication system and the communication elements from the perspective of communication function, energy, and information flow. A good model should have the functions of constructing, interpreting, simplifying, guiding, and predicting, and should clearly show the integrity of the relationship among elements. For work and research, it has practical value as well as advanced theoretical applications.

Model studies have evolved with the development of human social communication activities. Since the 1920s, there have been many models in Western communication studies, representing different perspectives and research methods. However, none of them has been widely accepted. As a way to study the process, nature, and effects of communication, the representative communication model in early research was the one-way linear model. After the 1950s, a two-way cycle and interaction model became the new representative, followed by a social system model and a network communication model.

Specifically, the earliest communication process model was developed by American political scientist Harold Dwight Lasswell (1948), who proposed five questions to describe an act of communication: *Who*, *Says What*, *In Which Channel*, *To Whom*, and *With What Effect*. The five questions correspond to five basic elements of the communication process—communicator, message, medium, receiver, and effect—and Lasswell's "5W" or political model of communication became highly influential. With its highly abstract generality, the 5W Model greatly promoted the development of mass communication studies. However, this model also has certain limitations. Lasswell took it for granted that the communicator has some intention of influencing the receiver and omitted the element of feedback; therefore, he assumed that communication should be treated as a persuasive process (Figure 5.1).

In 1949, just one year after the 5W Model was proposed, Claude Shannon and Warren Weaver, two American scholars of informatics, put forward a communication process model from the perspective of information theory in their book *The Mathematical Theory of Communication*. Known as the "Mathematical Model" or "Shannon–Weaver Model," this model describes communication as a linear, one-way process and presents five positive functions and a dysfunctional factor:

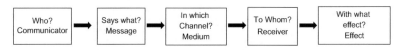

Figure 5.1 The Lasswell formula (Lasswell, 1948)

80 The model of immersive communication

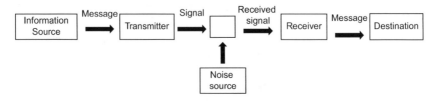

Figure 5.2 Shannon–Weaver model (Shannon & Weaver, 1949)

"noise." The presence of noise emphasized the complexity of the communication process (Figure 5.2).

Next, in 1970, DeFleur extended the Shannon–Weaver Model to develop the Bi-circulating Model of Mass Communication. This model is a closed-cycle communication system, in which people are both receivers and communicators of information. Meanwhile, noise appears in all parts of the communication process. Underlining the bidirectionality of communication, this model was generally considered a relatively complete way to describe the process of mass communication (Figure 5.3).

The Osgood and Schramm circular model, presented by Wilbur Schramm in the 1950s and originating with C.E. Osgood, is useful in describing the process of interpersonal communication. This model emphasizes the identity of the transmitter and the receiver, highlighting the role of symbolic interaction in communication. It also indicates that the communication process is bidirectional with "feedback." The downside is that the model assumes that communication is a complete cycle and returns to its original starting point intact (Figure 5.4).

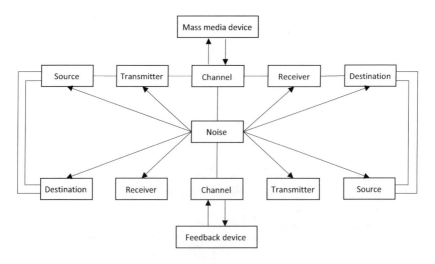

Figure 5.3 DeFleur model (DeFleur, 1970)

The model of immersive communication 81

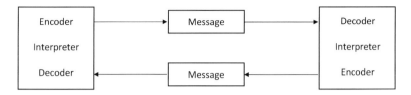

Figure 5.4 Osgood and Schramm circular model (Schramm, 1954)

Dance's helical model (1967), seen as a development of the Osgood and Schramm circular model, underlines the dynamic nature of communication and describes how different parts of the process change over time (Figure 5.5).

Maletzke's Model of Mass Communication serves as a summing-up of a couple of decades of psychological interest in mass communication and shows mass communication as "a process which is, in social psychological terms, very complex" (McQuail & Windahl, 2008, p. 42). It contains a series of factors and relationships that still have guiding value (Figure 5.6).

McQuail put forward the attention/display model in 1987. Considering that the total amount of attention is always limited at any given moment and place, communication as display is, in a way, a competition for attention (Figure 5.7).

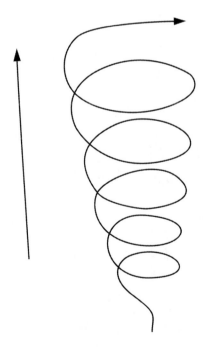

Figure 5.5 Dance's helical model (Dance, 1967)

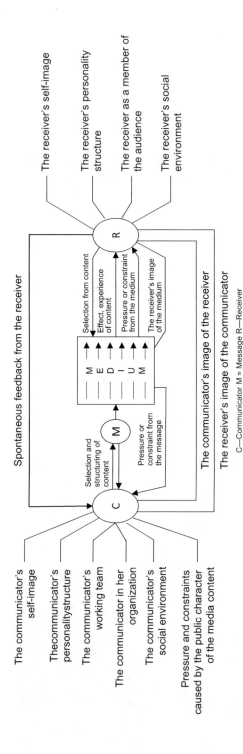

Figure 5.6 Maletzke's model (Maletzke, 1963)

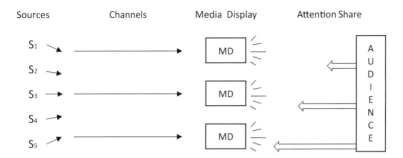

Figure 5.7 The display/attention model (McQuail, 1987)

During communication, information flows from the transmitter to the receiver. Accordingly, the historical development of communication models can shed light on people's cognitive development in terms of the relationship between the transmitter and the receiver. More than 100 types of communication model diagrams have been published, all aimed at abstracting the elements, structures, processes, and variable relations of communication. In general, these models try to capture either the process and structure of communication or the relationship between the elements of communication. The former type tries to grasp the essence of communication as a whole by the basic mode. The latter focuses on communication effect, influence, audience, and media modes. They also represent two perspectives of communication research, namely, the structure view and process view, both of which take the Laswell formula as their core framework.

Based on the existing media communication models, this study attempts to construct a human-centered immersive communication model, embodying the basic elements of immersive communication, communication process, communication relations, and communication effects.

5.2 The model of immersive communication

The immersive communication model and model diagram use simplified forms to reproduce the immersive communication phenomenon. This model is used to explore the immersive communication process and conduct detailed and systematic research on its phenomena, further discussing the effects of communication, various elements of the communication process, and their relationships. Accordingly, the model contains communication elements, relationships and structures, communication processes, and communication functions. Graphical features such as frames, lines, and flowcharts are used to describe immersive communication.

After the emergence of the Internet, human communication technology went through the stage of the Internet of Things (IOT) and the stage of ubiquitous networks. After more than ten years of development, with the Internet still in the

84 The model of immersive communication

virtual world, the Internet of Things, which incorporates Internet and sensor technology, will realize the connection between "things," making the Internet move into reality from virtual reality. The emergence of the ubiquitous network once again links the "human" with the "things," truly blending the virtual and reality together and realizing human-centered immersive communication.

Here, we use diagrams and formulas to describe and construct a human-centered immersive communication model, embodying the basic elements, functions, processes, relations, and effects of immersive communication. Among them, the matrix of the immersive communication function model reflects the communication elements and their relations. The stereo-helical model of immersive communication process is a description of the constantly positioning and stereo rising process. The schematic of immersive communication relationships shows the relationships between a large communication environment and a small one. Virtual reality is a part of real life. Mobile phones, networks, televisions, urban media, surveillance cameras, and other media are all connected to form a large environment. The technical support provided by cloud computing databases and ubiquitous networks combines information dissemination with intelligent survival. The Communication Immersion Index (CII) is also conceived in the immersive communication effect model.

5.2.1 The communication process: Comprehensive connectivity based on modern information technology

One of the key technical supports of immersive communication is the realization of a ubiquitous network. The core of the ubiquitous network is the connection of sensors. The second circle represents the connection of objects and objects. The outer circle identifies the form of the ubiquitous connection (Figure 5.8).

We can clearly identify the relationship among the ubiquitous network, the Internet of Things, and the Internet of sensors from this figure. A ubiquitous network can be considered the high-level goal for the development of an ICT (information and communication technology) society. The Internet of Things is the

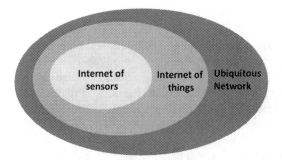

Figure 5.8 The relationships between ubiquitous network, Internet of Things, and Internet of sensors

The model of immersive communication   85

primary stage of the ubiquitous network, and it is also an inevitable development stage. The sensor network is the foundation for the application and development of the Internet of Things.

The concept of the "Internet of Things" became popular in 1999 through the Auto-ID Labs at MIT and related market-analysis publications. The initial idea is that all things are connected to the Internet via sensing devices such as radio-frequency identification (RFID) to achieve intelligent identification and management. Thus, the Internet of Things deploys physical entities with certain awareness, computing capacity, or the ability to execute all kinds of information sensing (such as sensors, RFID, QR codes, mobile communication modules, etc.), through the network infrastructure, to realize information transmission, synergy, and processing, and ultimately to capture a wide range of information exchange and demands between people and things, and between things and things. In the sensor network, a variety of sensors capable of collecting temperature, optical, electrical, and other information are utilized, supplemented by an independent network composed of medium–low-speed, short-range wireless communication technologies, along with a network system composed of tiny sensor nodes with wired or wireless communication and computing capacity to form information exchange between local objects.

To recognize this change, the International Telecommunication Union (ITU) titled its 2005 annual report "The Internet of Things," expanding the concept of the Internet of Things to the connection of Any Things at Anytime and Anyplace, and put forward the vision of ubiquitous networks and ubiquitous computing. It predicted that in addition to RFID, wireless sensor technologies, smart technologies, nanotechnology, and other similar technologies would be more widely used (ITU, 2005). In January 2009, IBM proposed the concept of "Smart Planet," to which the Internet of Things is an indispensable key. Barack Obama, then the president of the United States, responded positively to this proposal and promoted it as a national development strategy, obtaining global attention.

The Internet of Things has been defined in Recommendation ITU-T Y.2060 (June 2012) as a global infrastructure for the information society, enabling advanced services by interconnecting (physical and virtual) things based on existing and evolving interoperable information and communication technologies. The ITU's 2015 IOT report defines a sensor as "an electronic device, which detects, senses or measures physical stimuli—for instance, motion, heat or pressure—and responds in a specific way. It converts signals from stimuli into an analogue or digital form, so that the raw data about detected parameters are readable by machines and humans" (ITU, 2015).

The first chapter of this book traced these ideas back to Mark Weiser and the origins of ubiquitous networking. Based on communication and network technology, ubiquitous networks enable anyone to connect to the Internet anytime and anywhere via terminal devices to obtain personalized information services. Simply put, a ubiquitous network refers to the realization of the information acquisition, delivery, storage, recognition, decision-making, utilization, and other services that are needed between humans, humans and things, and things themselves based

86   *The model of immersive communication*

on individual and social needs. A network with great environmental awareness, content awareness, and intelligence provides ubiquitous and omnipresent information services and applications for individuals and society (Pan, 2011).

The Internet of Things and ubiquitous networks are key technologies that enable immersive communication to be realized. The ITU has listed RFID, sensor technology, intelligent embedded technology, and nanotechnology as the key technologies of the Internet of Things, among which RFID has been recognized as the foundation and core of the construction of the Internet of Things. According to the draft recommendation Y.2002 released by the ITU's Telecommunication Standardization Sector (ITU-T) in 2009, "5C+5Any" are key features of ubiquitous networks. 5C stands for convergence, content, computation, communication, and connection, while 5Any denotes anytime, anywhere, any service, any network, and any object. These features emphasize the omnipresent coverage of ubiquitous networks' communication, a fully connected and intelligent network at the sublayer, and the inclusion of integrated information and IT technology. Its communication services extend into fields such as intelligent buildings, transport, finance, supply chains, education, safety services, health care, and disaster management, and provide people with accurate information transmission services and applications anywhere, anytime.

The "ubiquitous" part of the "ubiquitous network" means that ubiquitous computing is omnipotent and cloud computing is the key. Essentially, cloud computing eliminates people's physical reliance on personal computers, making communication possible anytime, anywhere.

5.2.2 Communication relations: Human-centered communication structure

The fundamental goal of achieving a thing-to-thing, human-to-thing, and human-to-human ubiquitous connection is to satisfy people's information requirements. Beginning in the late 1960s and early 1970s, the audience has been studied as a subject. In immersive communication, people are not only the audience but also the source of information. The two are highly integrated. The construction of the ubiquitous network is based on the existence and interaction of three physical layers: ubiquitous terminal units, ubiquitous network transmissions, and ubiquitous smart applications. The core object of these services is humanity.

For the future development of a ubiquitous network that includes the Internet of Things, global consensus has been reached that ubiquitous network infrastructure should be used to help humans achieve "4A" communications: anyone or anything can unimpededly send and receive information anytime and anywhere.

5.2.3 Communication goals and effects: The Communication Immersive Index

On the basis of the research described, this book proposes several goals and effects of immersive communication. Among them, the goal of immersive

The model of immersive communication 87

communication is summarized as "4Any": Anyone, Anytime, Anywhere, and Any service. The ideal effect of immersive communication is summarized as "3In": Invisible, Intangible, and Insensible. Based on both goals, the CII was conceived to represent the extent to which "any" can be reached in terms of time, place, service, and object.

Specifically, this "4Any" corresponds to the four key factors of immersive communication, allowing human-centered omnipotent communication to take place anywhere and anytime:

Anyone means that a human can be either a transmitter or a receiver. The primary premise and ultimate goal of immersive communication is to realize human-centered communication.

Anytime represents that immersive communication, integrating the physical world with the virtual world, has both immediacy and permanence.

Anywhere represents that immersive communication, by regarding the human being's large living space as its medium, is both remote and ubiquitous.

Any service emphasizes omnipotence, stressing that immersive communication breaks the boundaries between work, life, and entertainment, maximizing information communication.

Once "4Any" is satisfied, immersive communication will show the communication effect of "3In" (Invisible, Intangible, Insensible). When Mark Weiser, known as "The Father of Ubiquitous Computing," described the ubiquitous network, he stressed that embedding computers in the environment or in common tools or objects in everyday life makes smart devices ubiquitous in the surrounding environment "without trace." Those devices stay very quiet in our "invisible" places, like air and water, serving us "invisibly." Weiser argued that "the best computer is a quiet, invisible servant," as "technology should create calm." He also emphasized that "the more you can do by intuition the smarter you are; the computer should extend your unconscious." Mark Weiser and John Seely Brown described what they expect as a "calm technology" as "that which informs but doesn't demand our focus or attention" (Weiser, 2012).

While Weiser's original reference to being "invisible" and "insensible" was basically a speculation or illusion, immersive communication has made it real. Because of the maturity and wide application of embedded technology, RFID sensor networks, and micro-power, immersive communication means that people don't have to wait or issue instructions: everything is under control, and the communication just occurs naturally. Although the ubiquitous network has everything connected and programmed well, because of the invisibility and disappearance of the media, people can't see or touch it, just as the air melts into the environment. Sensors and various types of terminals are everywhere in the surrounding environment, even on people, but we do not feel them. All this corresponds to what David Gauntlett described in the last chapter of *Web Studies*, entitled "The Future": technology is "all aboard," offering "instant everything" so "the Internet vanished." He argued that the Internet would "disappear" into a multitude of devices. It is becoming integrated into some of these already, such as mobile phones and video game consoles. But it will also be connected to other household appliances, walls,

88 *The model of immersive communication*

cars, security systems, watches, clothes, and other everyday items. This means it will be more, not less, prevalent in everyday life.

He also predicted "the vanishing wires, missing gadgets" by which cheap wireless communications allow devices in your home or workplace to communicate with each other through radio waves. These devices will get smaller and smaller, until people complain that they are much too fiddly, and then they will get a bit bigger again. Such spaces of human life are instant-on and always-on … the implication of "The internet vanishes" (see earlier) is that all the electrical devices and appliances in a home or organization will be connected to the net. Your computer would be able to get your washing machine, heating, and lighting to do exactly what you wanted at certain times of day. You would be able to monitor what was going on at home from your computer at work, or from your mobile phone (Gauntlett, 2000).

Immersive communication has realized the communication goals of "anytime, anywhere, and omnipotent," achieving an immersive effect that makes people enjoy information services in a state that is "invisible," "intangible," and "insensible" at the same time. This study uses the CII to measure immersive communication's goals and effects, that is, to track the values of "any" in 4Any. The value of "any" is the total degree of achievement in "any object," "anytime," "anywhere," and "any service." Focusing on the 4Any goals of immersive communication, this study attempts to construct the function, process, and relationship models of immersive communication.

5.3 The model of immersive communication function: IC matrix

On the basis of this technical concept analysis, we can see how the function of immersion communication is realized. Modern communication is based on technology, but the realization of communication has its own logic. Immersive communication also includes information sources, communication relations, communication channels, communication functions, communication processes, and communication effects. The following matrix diagram shows the relationship between the elements of communication, communication capabilities, and communication effects.

5.3.1 The IC matrix: Basic features

1. "5C" represents five communication capabilities (including communication technologies): C1—Contents, C2—Communication, C3—Computing, C4—Connectivity, and C5—Convergence.
2. "5W" represents five communication elements, which are W1—Want, W2—When, W3—Web, W4—Where, and W5—Who. To update Laswell's "5W" model in journalism and communication, this model changes the original "What" to "Want" to emphasize that the focus of immersive communication is what the recipient needs instead of what to send to him or her. In addition,

The model of immersive communication 89

changing the original "In Which Channel" to "Web" highlights the significance of the emergence of "the Internet" as a specific form of channel in the history of communication. This is the watershed between the first media era and the second media era, and the key factor to realize the degree of the "any" value in communication immersion.

3. There are 25 intersections in this matrix, and each intersection represents the convergence of the communication capabilities provided by the communication technology. The more intersections, the more mature the capabilities, and the stronger the immersion of the communication elements.

4. The intersection of communication ability and communication element reflects the degree of "any." That is, the variable of the "any" degree of CII develops from low to medium to high, corresponding to the low–medium–high level of immersion of communication.

5.3.2 The meaning of the 25 intersections in the IC matrix

The 25 intersection points of this matrix represent different rendezvous of the communication capabilities provided by communication technologies. The intersections are divided into low-intensity intersections, medium-intensity intersections, and high-intensity intersections, producing corresponding media forms and communication modes. Several representative media forms or communication modes are listed in Table 5.1.

The 25 intersections listed here are just a two-dimensional description of these points, because when a factor intersects with two or more factors at the same time, new forms of media and models of communication emerge. For example, network television appears at the intersection of "content," "Web," and "when." Later chapters will further explain specific illustrations of the three media ages. It should be noted that this table is only an exemplary list, so it may not be very accurate and complete. At the same time, it is necessary to use mathematical formulas to exhaust all possible intersections, crossover levels, and their media meanings.

5.3.3 The theoretical breakthrough and research contribution of the IC matrix

Models are generally divided into descriptive models and explanatory models. The model shown here is mainly an explanatory model. Its main significance lies in three contributions:

(1) The Immersive Communication (IC) matrix diagram uses a brief model diagram in the field of communication theory, proposing an explanatory model for the realization of the immersive communication function.

(2) Compared with existing models of communication, the innovation of this model is introducing the "computing" function to communication. Compared with previous communication technologies and constructions, cloud computing is also the core technology of immersive communication.

Table 5.1 Representative intersections in the function model matrix of immersive communication

	Intersection	Low-intensity intersection	Mid-intensity intersection	High-intensity intersection
1	C1W1content&want	Leaflet	Newspaper	Multimedia
2	C1W2content&when	Broadcasting	Television	Online media
3	C1W3content&web	Wire broadcasting	Email	Ubiquitous media
4	C1W4content&where	Customized mail	Outdoor advertisement	Mobile terminal
5	C1W5content&who	Mass communication	Focused communication	Focused communication
6	C2W1communication&want	Mail	Telegraph	Email
7	C2W2communication&when	Letter	Telegraph	Telephone
8	C2W3communication&web		VOIP	Smartphone
9	C2W4communication&when	Letter	Email	Push mail
10	C2W5communication&who		Customized email	Twitter/WeChat
11	C3W1computing&want	Telegraph	e-Paper	
12	C3W2computing&when		Television	Computer
13	C3W3computing&web		Internet	Ubiquitous media
14	C3W4computing&where			Cloud computing
15	C3W5computing&who	PC	Mobile social network	Personal cloud
16	C4W1connectivity&want	Online requirement	Web portal	Personal space
17	C4W2connectivity&when	Dial-up Internet	Broadband Internet	Ubiquitous connection
18	C4W3connectivity&web		Online community	Ubiquitous media
19	C4W4connectivity&where	Television	Mobile television	Environmental video
20	C4W5connectivity&who	Telephone	Mobile phone	Twitter/WeChat
21	C5W1convergence&want		Online community	IIOT
22	C5W2convergence&when	Timing service	Instant service	Anytime
23	C5W3convergence&web	Web portal	Microblog	Ubiquitous network
24	C5W4convergence&where	Video monitoring	Smart monitoring	Mobile monitoring
25	C5W5convergence&who	One-way communication	Interactive communication	Immersive communication

VOIP: Voice over Internet Protocol.
IIOT: Intelligent Internet of Things

The model of immersive communication   91

(3) The IC matrix emphasizes the importance of "places"; environmental factors have become important. This is another new development of the previous model diagram. When he referred to "a transmission model of news learning" in *Communication Models for the Study of Mass Communications*, Denis McQuail stated that "the context of reception plays [a] more minor part" (McQuail & Windahl, 2008, pp. 78–79).

5.4 The model of immersive communication process: The IC stereo helix

This stereo-helical model is a description of the unique process of immersive communication. The process of immersive communication is a dynamic process with constant positioning and spiraling.

5.4.1 The explanation of the IC stereo helix

Through positioning, communication, feedback, re-positioning, re-communication, and re-feedback, the whole process constantly collects your information and adjusts the content for communication. This process is not a cycle but a spiraling process, a reaction to the joint effects of people and media. It is also a four-dimensional stereogram: three-dimensional space + one-dimensional time.

5.4.2 The significance of the IC stereo helix

(1) The helix develops Dance's helical model, adding the "positioning" process and emphasizing the constant adjustment of the helix's starting point. Radio communication networks (such as GSM and Code Division Multiple Access (CDMA) networks) or external positioning methods (such as GPS and BeiDou satellite navigation) allow the center of communication to follow people. In the era of TV, it is the communicators under the spotlight who transmit information to you, but when it comes to the era of immersive communication, an Location Based Service (LBS) with the capability to sense your position will transmit information to you.

(2) It reflects the ultra-precision of immersive communication. Maletzke's model, mentioned earlier, reflected feedback from the audiences. Unlike the vague feedback of mass communication, however, the arrival and feedback of immersive communication information can achieve one-to-one precision.

(3) This schematic helps us study the effectiveness of communication. Just as the human eye may generate an illusion about a painting, people will continue to change or deviate in their process of receiving information. The IC stereo-helical model reflects a process of constant adjustment to improve the effectiveness of communication.

92 *The model of immersive communication*

5.5 The model of immersive communication relationship: The IC schematic

This study also introduces a "human-centered" schematic diagram describing the information movement path of immersive communication and the general environment of the communication relationship model (Figure 5.12).

5.5.1 The explanation of the IC schematic

The IC schematic is illustrated as follows:

(1) A big circle represents the entire environment.
(2) The big circle contains many small circles representing the remote, ubiquitous, physical, and virtual space; the intersections of small circles represent the integration of spaces.
(3) A human is in the center of each small circle, which represents the human-centered communication model.
(4) The cloud at the top represents the database of cloud computing.
(5) The surrounding terminals represent that the whole environment is an ubiquitous cyberspace with smart wireless connections.

5.5.2 The meaning of the IC schematic

(1) It describes the essential characteristic of immersive communication: human-centeredness and personally customized information. By contrast, the information in previous mass communication was "'made available' for attention by many individuals, not directed to particular persons" (McQuail, 2008, p. 54).
(2) It emphasizes the integration of the virtual world and the physical world in immersive communication.
(3) It emphasizes the existence and role of cloud computing in immersive communication.

5.6 Summary

This chapter first summarizes and analyzes the existing major models of communication, and on this basis proposes the model of immersive communication. This model mainly includes the propagation process, with all-round connections based on modern information technology, a communication relationship with a human-centered communication structure, and communication goals and effects measured by the CII.

Based on the summary of the immersive communication model, this study further proposes three model diagrams and a table of immersive communication (3+1).

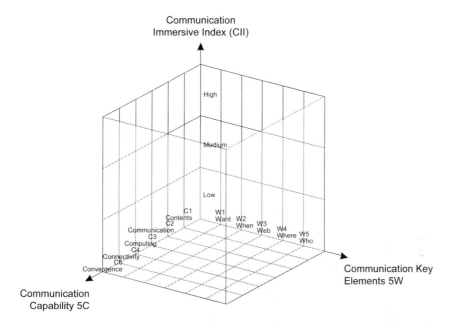

Figure 5.9 The function model matrix of immersive communication (media diagram)

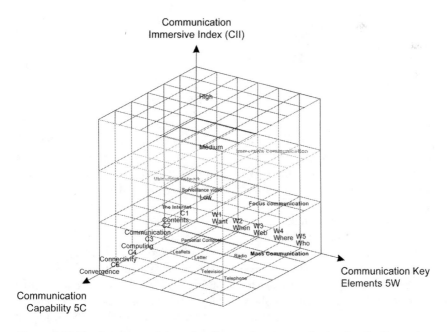

Figure 5.10 The function model matrix of immersive communication (media diagram)

94 The model of immersive communication

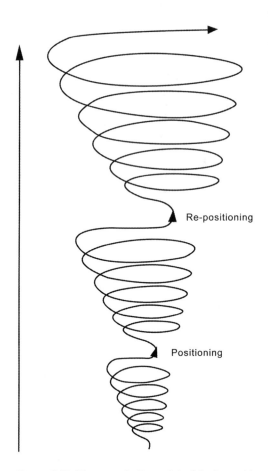

Figure 5.11 The stereo helix model of the immersive communication process

First, the model of immersive communication functions gives the matrix of the communication function model (Figure 5.9). The generation of immersive communication function was analyzed from the intersection of immersive communication elements ("5W") and communication capacity ("5C"). 5C emphasizes communication capability (including communication technology), specifically C1 (Contents), C2 (Communication), C3 (Computing), C4 (Connectivity), and C5 (Convergence). 5W stands for communication elements, which are W1 (Want), W2 (When), W3 (Web), W4 (Where), and W5 (Who). This model makes two significant updates to the earlier Lasswell 5W model. The original "message" has become "Want," emphasizing that the focus of immersive communication is what the receiver needs. In addition, the original "In Which Channel" was changed to "Web," highlighting the significance of "the Internet" emerging in the history of

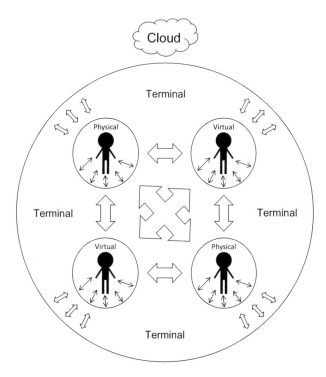

Figure 5.12 The schematic of the immersive communication relationship model

communication as a specific form of "channel," evolving from the first media age to the second media age.

Second, the model illustrates the stereo helix of the immersive communication process (Figure 5.10). It emphasizes that immersive communication is a dynamic process with constant positioning and spiraling. This extends Dance's helical model, adding "positioning" and emphasizing the constant adjustment of the helix's starting point.

Third, the IC schematic presents a model of immersive communication relationships (Figure 5.11). In the schematic, the big circle represents the entire environment; smaller internal circles represent distant, ubiquitous, physical, and virtual spaces. The schematic highlights the essential characteristic of immersive communication: it is human-centered and customizes information to individuals. The schematic also emphasizes the integration of the virtual and the physical world, as well as the existence and role of cloud computing in immersive communication.

Finally, Table 5.1 demonstrates selected intersections in the immersive communication function model in terms of media forms and communication modes. The matrix of the immersive communication model has a total of 25 intersection points, each of which represents the convergence of communication capabilities

96 *The model of immersive communication*

provided by communication technologies. The intersection points are divided into low-intensity, medium-intensity, and high-intensity intersections, generating corresponding media forms and models of communication. Table 5.1 lists the corresponding media forms and models of communication that emerged when these intersections were formed.

6 Application and verification of the immersive communication models

Based on the process, models, path characteristics, and communication effects of immersive communication, Chapter 5 proposed immersive communication models to illustrate the function, process, and relationships of immersive communication. This chapter presents illustrations of how to apply and verify those models, drawing on the history of communication development and real-world media.

6.1 Application of the immersive communication models

The immersive communication models, as proposed and illustrated in the previous chapter, can be used to investigate the communication process, describe function realization, and solve other problems of immersive communication. Through the investigation and analysis of the intersection points on this diagram, we can identify why a given effect has not been achieved or why it is only partly achieved. The immersive communication models can also be used to analyze and classify the characteristics of the communication mode.

6.1.1 General application of the immersive communication models

There are at least two dimensions to investigate in the application of the immersive communication models: the technical dimension (hardware and software) and the communication dimension (time and place, etc.). The relative degree of immersion, reflected by the intersections in the matrix of the communication function model (Figure 5.9), represents the improvement of communication technologies and communication abilities. When all points reach the high-intensity intersection points, that is, when the Communication Immersion Index (CII) reaches the highest value, it is the full realization of immersive communication. Table 5.1 presents 25 intersection points and the media communication forms and communication effects they represent. The degree and strength of the intersection's realization produce the degree of immersion index. Here are some specific comparisons.

98 *Application and verification of the models*

1. Differences in "connectivity"

When comparing the Internet model with the immersive communication model, the first thing we see is a difference in connection ability. One of the core technological advances of immersive communication, compared with other forms, is its comprehensive ability to connect people with people, people with things, and things with things. The emergence of the Internet of Things (IOT), which is a combination of Internet and induction technology, has made the Internet, after more than 10 years, finally step into reality from the virtual world.

The IOT, the technology that immersive communication leans on, plays a key role in its communication effects. The relevant experts estimate that IOT will be popularized on a large scale in 10 years and extensively applied in various fields of human life and production, such as intelligent transformation, government affairs, industrial monitoring, public security, home security, elder care, personal health, and so on. Out of 7 billion people globally in 2012, approximately 2.3 billion are netizens; meanwhile, the objects connected via IOT surpass 1 trillion. These "things" or objects can be anything, including vehicles, traffic lanes, cameras, and other devices.

Whether it is in a "smart earth" or a "smart city," without the interconnection between things, the digitalized "thing" is no more than an isolated information island. The key to realizing intelligence is a more extensive interconnection, the high-intensity intersection achieved by crossover "connectivity" (C4) with each of the respective "5W" elements, as shown in Figure 5.9.

These intersections can be individually verified with existing data. The users of mobile phones in the world exceeded 3.3 billion in 2007. According to the prediction by Forrester, an authoritative American consulting institution, the ratio of IOT business to the business of interpersonal communication will reach 30 to 1 by 2020. Therefore, IOT has been called the next trillion-level communication business (Pan, 2011). All that we imagine in science fiction movies will turn into reality based on "connectivity," as the IOT and ubiquitous network become the revolutionary products that connect everything.

The high-intensity intersections of "connectivity" with "web" in this model diagram present the ubiquity of future network technology. Computer and communication applications are changing every field of human life, and a "human body domain network" is likely to occur in the near future. New modes of communication appear not only between people and people or people and machines but even between machines and machines. Anything can be connected: these devices, carriers, or terminals cover everything from computers to iPhones, from air conditioners to curtains, and from jewelry to dogs. The terminals are all connected and operate like computers, forming machine-to-machine communications. This also shows the difference in the communication effect of low-intensity and high-intensity intersections of connectivity in the model. A high-intensity crossover connection allows everything on the web to be connected, by which people can perceive the existence of the web anytime and anywhere and enjoy the accessibility brought by ubiquitous hyperconnection. Everything is connected and under control.

2. Differences in "computing"

In the IC matrix diagram, computing can be seen as the boundary between the first media age and the second media age, while cloud computing can be seen as the one between the second media age and the third media age. Since the 1980s, as the mainframe computer evolved into the personal computer, computing has penetrated media communication. In this matrix diagram, the emergence of cloud computing, an outcome combining traditional computer technology with network technology, includes grid computing, parallel computing, distributed computing, utility computing, network storage technologies, virtualization, load balance, and so forth. It is another radical change similar to the mainframe computer, a comparatively strong mode.

Mell and Grance defined cloud computing as

> a model for enabling ubiquitous, convenient, on-demand network access to a shared pool of configurable computing resources (e.g., networks, servers, storage, applications, and services) that can be rapidly provisioned and released with minimal management effort or service provider interaction. This cloud model is composed of five essential characteristics, three service models, and four deployment models.
>
> (Mell & Grance, 2011)

One of the pivotal drivers of immersive communication's development is the rapid advancement of "Big Data" technology. Big Data represents information assets characterized by such a high volume, velocity, and variety as to require specific technology and analytical methods for its transformation into value (De Mauro, Greco, & Grimaldi, 2016). Alvin Toffler hailed Big Data as bringing about "the third wave's cadenza" in his 1980 book *The Third Wave*. But Big Data wasn't popular in the Internet information technology (IT) industry until 2009. Big Data represents the frontier technology in data analysis, possessing the ability to promptly obtain valuable information among voluminous, various data. Big Data is characterized by four Vs: Volume, Velocity, Variety, and Veracity.

The ubiquitous network that the immersive communication leans on connects various terminals, generating voluminous data in real time. This data includes that on the Internet, as well as all the information collected and sent by all the sensors connecting objects with objects and people with people. What supports Big Data in immersive communication is strong cloud computing ability. Analyzing the five intersection points of "computing" and the respective 5A element in the model diagram, it is clear that the low-intensity intersection belongs to the earlier media. By contrast, the high-intensity intersection enables communication to happen in any time, at any place, and on any network, since all the data is stored in the cloud. All the web-accessing devices and terminals connected to the ubiquitous network can receive data from and send it to the cloud. The Web browser is not the only channel, as data can also be pushed via push mail, etc.

100 *Application and verification of the models*

When "computing" and "demand" reach a high-intensity intersection, the communication structure of ubiquitous society comes into being. Zhu Peisheng, a senior engineer at the Institute of Acoustics of the Chinese Academy of Sciences, and Duan Shihui, a senior engineer at the Institute of Communications Standards of the Ministry of Industry and Information Technology, point out in their study *Development Analysis of Ubiquitous Network* that the concepts of pervasive computing, ubiquitous computing, ambient intelligence, calm computing, and Zen computing have sprung into existence successively. Despite their different terms, they share the same essence, the next-generation communication structure, based on which our future society will become a ubiquitous network society (UNS). Ambient intelligence emphasizes integration, with micro-computing, user interface design, and ubiquitous network communication as its critical technological innovations (Zhu & Duan, 2009).

3. Differences in "place" and space

In the function model diagram presented in the last chapter, the intersections of "where" with "5C" show that whether the communication reaches "any place" depends on whether high-intensity intersections can be achieved between it and "communication," "computing," and "connectivity," along with other technical factors. It's a positive correlation that works in reality. Practically, the developmental level of communication, computing, and connectivity determines the place it reaches and the effects and strength it obtains.

Guan Lu and Zhang Manling did a study on the communication effects of elevator leaflets. They treated the Olympic leaflets in China as media and distributed them both inside a closed elevator and in the open space outside, to collect the audience's different reactions and compare the communication effects. According to their report, the research environment is a closed passenger elevator under natural conditions, while the qualitative methodology is the participatory observational method, drawing samples for observations with cluster sampling. Researchers selected two typical shopping centers in Beijing: Jinyuan Business Center and Contemporary Shopping Mall. The sample population consisted of all the individuals in the closed elevators and the pedestrians in the open space outside the malls. The sampling survey was conducted in a sample box, composed of a sample of each valid elevator passenger during the experimental period.

In this case, the communication model was delivering the leaflets from person to person. The elevator, as a closed space, was used as a reference environmental carrier in comparison with the open space. The authors' model of reading parameters is most relevant to the current research: perusing rate, reading rate, and skimming rate. The researchers defined the perusing rate as the proportion of receivers who read leaflets for more than 30 seconds out of the total number of people who accepted them, the reading rate as the proportion of receivers who read leaflets for 15–30 seconds, and the skimming rate as the proportion of receivers who read leaflets for less than 15 seconds. Overall, they found that "in the closed elevator, the perusing rate and skimming rate are higher, while

Application and verification of the models 101

the reading rate is lower" (Guan & Zhang, 2010). If we assume that the recipient accepting and reading the flyer is the desired result, and we recognize the potential of the perusing readers to conduct secondary transmissions, then "in enclosed elevators, not only the ratio of the communication effect (perusing rate + reading rate + skimming rate), but also the perusing rate with secondary communication potential are greater than those of the outdoor open space" (Guan & Zhang, 2010). The perusing rate represents the degree of concentration of the audience. The degree of attention, in a sense, is also the level of immersion. Of course, the "immersion" here and the definition of "immersive communication" in this article are not exactly the same concept.

The elevator flyer model is a one-way transmission with one-to-one distribution, using a traditional medium—leaflets. This study provides an illustration of the intersection of "where" and "content" in the immersive communication diagram. Its empirical findings show that the effect of communication in a closed space is indeed better than that in an open space, which also proves that place has an influence on the acceptance of content. The difference in this "where" actually represents the difference between environment and space.

Let's take the development of Chinese TV as another example of how changes in places affect the spread of content. China initially established radio and television stations according to administrative levels and administrative divisions. In 1982, there were only 47 television stations in the country. At the "Eleventh National Radio and Television Working Conference" in 1983, officials proposed the policy of "fourth-tier broadcasting, four-tier television, and four-tier mixed coverage." As a result, the number of national television stations increased to 366 by 1987 and to 923 during the later peak period in the earlier 1990s. After the "three-in-one," "four-in-one," and "combination of office and bureau" policies were launched in 1996, the number of TV stations then dropped to 300 or so. Despite the increasing influence of Internet-based media and online videos, television is still the most influential mass medium in China's current domestic and international communications. In 2017, China's television population had a national comprehensive coverage rate of more than 99.07%, and it broadcasts more than 18 million hours of programming annually. It is currently the world's largest electronic medium, covering the largest population (Chyxx, 2018). The development of China's television in the late 20th century was driven by the four-tiered policies, which expanded television networks and sent content to millions of households, especially in remote mountainous areas. This shows the significance of "place" in communication.

Of course, in television communication, due to different technological influences, the concept of place is also changing. The four-tiered policies are suitable for cable television, but since satellite television has emerged, more people throughout the country can watch the same program at different places. In China, both in rural areas and in cities, cable television and satellite television can reach more places, from homes to buses to subways, from one-way viewing to playback on-demand, and from Internet protocol TV (IPTV) to mobile phone—not to mention webcasts and online videos of TV content.

102 *Application and verification of the models*

The intersections of place with "anytime" and "anyone" are also relevant, and there are studies on the changes in the viewer availability of presence. For TV, "'presence infuses choice behavior with considerable variation that has nothing to do with specific television content' and it is the 'single factor which is most responsible for the absence of content-based patterns of viewing'" (McQuail, 2008, p. 137). Watching television programs is directly related to the viewer's presence at the time.

Changes in places bring about changes in the space of communication. When "connectivity" and "any place" form a high-intensity intersection, it is the full realization of a mobile ubiquitous network, where communication can be achieved in any open space. This will be detailed in later case studies.

4. Differences in the ability to meet the "want"

The immersive communication model uses "want" as the first entry in 5W, because user desires and preferences emerged with the advent of communication, but their levels are stupendously different. The intersection of "want" with "content," "communication," "computing," and "connectivity" directly corresponds to the level of the immersive index CII.

The "display/attention model" proposed by McQuail in 1987 focused on how "the attention potential of the available audience is limited, and one channel or display's gain must be another's loss" (McQuail, 2008, p. 52). From the ancient "information closure" to the modern "information surplus," the ability of communication to meet the want, in modern times, is the ability to effectively deliver information. Advertising communication is a good opportunity to analyze the correlation of the strength of the intersection between "want" and "5C" with the difference in communication effectiveness, and with people's active choices or passive acceptance of system choices.

In China, Chen Tianqiao, the founder of "Shengda Network," was one of the early adopters of the web to achieve advertising want. When most Internet companies were still struggling to find a profit model, Chen Tianqiao came up with the idea of creating a cartoon character that can live in the virtual world, making people like it, making it a brand, and eventually selling the cartoon characters and derivatives. Chen Tianqiao used a higher-intensity intersection between advertising want and the new technology of the Internet, realizing the improvement of want. This also proves that the effect of communication is directly related to the ability to satisfy wants.

Jiang Nanchun, who advertised for "Shengda Network," was inspired by this innovative spirit, so he also intersected "want" with a new place and launched elevator advertising in China. Would elevator advertising produce novel advertising benefits? Nokia wanted to do a market test for a new mobile phone, so it made two versions of the advertisement. Shanghai's TV stations broadcast the version where a robot is the main character, while the other version, tested on elevator television, featured a samurai with a sword on his back as the main character. It was found that the proportion of people who came to buy "the mobile phone with

Application and verification of the models 103

the sword ad" was significantly higher than the proportion of people who came to buy the "robot mobile phone" (Wang, 2008). The effect of elevator advertising was thus recognized by the market.

Similar intersections apply to research on intentional communication and unintentional communication. Those between "want" and "network" can be used to see the influence on people's communication desires of the rapid development of broadband and Fiber to the Home, or in conveying neutral concepts that do not necessarily involve any meaning. Likewise, they can be used in research on the thoroughness of communication and direct point-to-point communication studies.

5. Differences in "convergence"

Convergence is a core issue of modern communication. The difference in integration determines the level of communication ability as well as the ability to solve the synchronous problem of communication. Maletzke's Model of Mass Communication Process considers the time difference (i.e., degree of synchronism) between the audience's exposure to the information about certain events (McQuail, 2008, p. 43). The immersive communication model puts forward a cognitive angle to this time difference problem: the degree of convergence reflects the degree of synchronicity in a certain sense. Convergence itself can be a fusion of "content" and technology, a fusion of "web" and "connectivity," or a combination of "computing" and "want." In the model diagram, the intersections of convergence and 5W at various intensity levels reflect different communication forms and degrees of immersion.

Chinese radio and TV offer helpful examples here as well. The development of communication technology has brought about major changes in the functions of the television network. China's implementation of the integration of three networks, along with the construction of next-generation radio and television networks, seeks to upgrade the old segmented cable television network into fully digitalized, fully integrated national television networks through technological upgrades and market competition. This is fairly difficult, because the advantage of the four-tiered TV in the 1980s was turned into a disadvantage. The four-tiered policy had formed a situation of regional monopolies and disconnected networks in China's radio and television industry, resulting in technological backwardness that seriously affected communication ability. The next-generation radio and television network, after the three networks are integrated, will change its production and broadcasting mode from traditional simulation, linear, and one-way to digital, network, two-way, and diversified, forming a new form of communication and an innovative format.

According to research data provided by Fusion Network, by January 2012 the number of cable digital TV subscribers in China exceeded 100 million, while IPTV subscribers numbered approximately 12 million to 15 million. With the promotion of the pilot network integration program, there was competitive pressure from various new communication modes and channels, such as Internet TV manufacturers and IPTV manufacturers. The increase in the number of cable

104 *Application and verification of the models*

TV subscribers nationwide has slowed down, and the number has even begun to decrease. Compared with the three major telecom operators, radio and television have a great disparity in power. For radio and TV to directly build a hugely expensive physical network, the difficulty is beyond words. However, one author noted, "[t]he advantages of cloud computing, such as on-demand access, resource pooling, scalability, and low cost, can help radio and TV to build a low-cost, management-optimized information system network in a short period of time to compete with telecommunications" (Min, 2012).

The high intensity of cloud computing technology in terms of "computing" and the "Web" can speed up the process of the three-networks integration in China's broadcast and television field, optimize media resources, and more rapidly achieve communication at "any time" in "any place" to "anyone." These differences prove that by examining all the intersection points, we have a lot of common sense and research evidence to support the phenomena and meanings described in the model diagram.

6.1.2 Dividing the three media ages with the immersive communication model

Let us now use the immersive communication model diagram to verify and classify the first media age, the second media age, and the third media age, to see if we can form a clear division and better understand the dividing lines among them. Figure 6.1 is a division map of the three media ages based on the immersive communication model.

This diagram has several significant elements:

1. In the first media age, content was communicated based on technical support, and the communication abilities met certain needs and reached certain places. The main forms of media were newspapers, telegrams, etc.
2. The second media age is distinguished by the emergence of computing and the web. The pre-computing era was the first media age.
3. The third media age is characterized by computing at any time and with any object, featuring cloud computing and ubiquitous computing.
4. The presence of computing can be regarded as the dividing point between the first media age and the second media age, while full use of cloud computing can be seen as the dividing point between the second media age and the third media age.
5. The intersections of "connectivity," "convergence," and "who" are also the intersections between and the fusion of reality and virtual reality.
6. "Where" distinguishes the media age attributes of the telegram, magazine, telephone, etc. The infinite expansion of space is an important feature of the third media age that distinguishes it from the first two media ages.
7. When everything in technology has converged, communication can meet the needs of any object at any place, at any time, or through any network. This is

Application and verification of the models 105

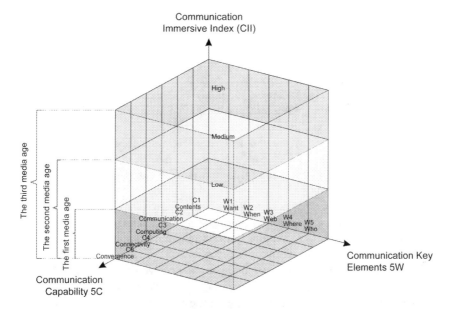

Figure 6.1 The function model matrix of immersive communication (three media ages)

the realization of immersive communication, which displays the features of the third media age.
8. There is mass communication in all three media ages, but the need for complete personalization can only be realized in the third media age.
9. This graph is downwardly compatible, and the third media age simultaneously satisfies all the intersections.

6.2 Case verification of the immersive communication model

Common sense tells us that the maximal achievement of the "4Any" goal of the immersive communication model lies in the realization of all intersections of 5C and 5W. In general, the greater the technical support, the stronger the ability to communicate, and the more effective the communication will be. So, is this the case? Here, we take the development of advertising in China and related media as an extended example to examine and validate the immersive communication model.

Advertising campaigns have a long history in China, but advertisements with modern awareness can be said to have started after the invention of printing in the Song Dynasty. Modern advertising has entered a period of rapid development in the past decade, with outdoor media advertising being a great growth highlight. With the continuous expansion of outdoor advertising, the value of outdoor media

106 *Application and verification of the models*

resources continues to increase. China's outdoor advertising resources have generated several rounds of frenzied mergers and acquisitions, and its development model is also evolving. For example, Focus Media entered the LCD (liquid crystal display) video media industry in 2003, and since then has successively acquired Framedia and Target Media to expand the scale of its outdoor media networks in China and enhance market competition. Around the same time, JCO of France, the second-largest group of global outdoor advertising companies, merged Media Nation and Media Partner International in 2005 and obtained resource advantages in subway and bus body media. Viacom, the world's largest media group, acquired China's Magic Media company, thus controlling the Beijing bus body media resources. Going back several more years, Clear Channel, the world's largest outdoor advertising company, acquired another outdoor advertising giant, White Horse Outdoor.

From the early distribution of leaflets in the foyers, to the elevator television of Focus Media, and at last to panoramic intelligent monitoring and information dissemination in open spaces, these recurring reorganizations of media resources at the intersections of "where," "web," and "want" reflect the developing characteristics of Chinese media and trends in outdoor advertising markets. That is, media companies are continuously expanding their scale in order to obtain greater market share and stronger market competitiveness. With the development of communication technology and communication concepts, these approaches and practices show different forms and characteristics. In the following sections, we take samples of representative media and use the communication concepts of the three media ages to analyze the communication situations of relevant media and further verify the application of the IC communication mode.

6.2.1 The first media age: Lobby leaflets and unidirectional transmission

The English word "lobby" literally means "foreground" and "hall," forming the root for "lobbying." The development of this word suggests that such communication was first carried out in the front hall. Lobbying is basically human communication, but it is often accompanied by the distribution of leaflets. The leaflets can be said to be the prototype of the early newspapers and are the more primitive forms of media in the first media age. As Xiong Wuyi noted, the so-called flyer is a type of promotional material distributed to the outside world. Its contents are generally groups or individuals who express their opinions or raise their own requirements on the current situation, on someone, on something, on a certain issue, etc. (1988).

In the immersive communication model, the communication behavior of the lobby leaflet at least occupies the intersection of "content + place," which of course is far from the ubiquitous level of "any place." The leaflet distributor must choose a "place," and it is usually a point-to-point, one-on-one distribution. The space in the hall is crowded with people, who generally leave the area quickly and may not focus on specific information. Therefore, the effect of communication is similar to the fairy maiden scattering flowers, whereby communicators often do

Application and verification of the models   107

not know who will receive their flowers. This widespread mode of communication cannot be very precise.

Of course, there will be a communication effect. In Wuhan, Hubei Province, there was a migrant worker named Fu Cairong, who later became the chairman of the "Yurtangtang" chain group with annual sales of tens of millions. According to reports, she started by distributing flyers on early education at the door of the provincial maternity hospital (Li, Cai, & Huang, 2007). Through her own flyers, she passed on ideas and practices about scientific infant raising. Finally, more and more pregnant women spent money to purchase her consulting services and related products.

To a certain degree, communication is lobbying, and it must achieve the effect of persuading others to adopt one's opinions. In the Warring States Period in ancient China, counselors traveled across the countries to persuade the monarchs to adopt their political ideas. It can be said that they were pursuing ancient communication activities. In *The Historical Records·Biography of Zhang Yi*, it is recorded that Zhang Yi has studied stupendously and is lobbying the feudal princes. Likewise, in *Chanting History*, written by Zuo Si during the Jin Dynasty, it is said that Su Qin lobbies in the north, and Li Si presents petitions in the west. The political strategists represented by Su Qin and Zhang Yi were listed in the Nine Schools. From this point of view, the first media age reached a small climax when Chinese policy makers traveled around the world. They presented different contents in different places to different audiences. They measured the earth with their feet and were masters of interpersonal communication; they proposed ideas in the Imperial Palace, just like handing out leaflets at the entrance of a hall.

In general, the distribution of leaflets in the foyer is basically a one-way communication in fixed places. Thus, lobbyists rely mainly on verbal debate yet do not use computing, the Web, or other modern functions.

6.2.2 *The second media age: Elevator television and focus awareness*

An elevator, as a communication space, is similar to a hallway: it is still a fixed place, but it is enclosed. Both print advertisements and television advertisements began in the first media age, but the communication method of focus awareness is mainly a characteristic of the second media age. According to authoritative statistics, China currently operates more than 200,000 elevators. Since 2000, the number of new elevators has grown at an annual rate of over 10% (Chyxx, 2015). The target audiences that can be reached by commercial office elevators are mainly the white-collar workers and managers between 24 and 55 years old, with high income, high education, and high social status. They are both important creators of social wealth and its active consumers.

For example, elevator advertisements began to appear in Beijing in 1995. At first, they only took the form of elevator car posters. By 1998, Beijing Conghui Advertising Co., Ltd. was fully involved in competition and established the communication method of a PVC mosaic and public service announcement, and their

108 *Application and verification of the models*

advertisements were quickly expanded to more than 300 communities, more than 500,000 households, and more than 1.5 million people (Chen, 2004). In China, when it comes to elevator advertising, the most representative firm is Framedia, later acquired by Focus Media. They jointly created Chinese elevator advertising communication. This study takes their work as an example to see whether the immersive communication model can be verified.

1. Focus Media reflects the realization of some intersections

In elevator advertising, the significance of the intersection between "place" and "content" is more fully expressed than in leaflets in the lobby. Unlike the foyer leaflets discussed earlier, the enclosed space here creates "mandatory reading." This mandatory reading in a closed environment is also the greatest advantage of the elevator media. According to research data from the CTR Research Company, in April 2006 the effective reach rate of the Framedia ads was 84% in seven first-tier cities. From the perspective of the acceptance of media patterns, more than 90% of the respondents stated that they were acceptable, and more than half of the audiences expressed a preference (Chen, 2006).

The connectivity function is stronger. In February 2005, nine media companies, including the original Framedia and LangMedia, established a strategic alliance in more than 30 cities such as Beijing and Shanghai, forming a strong basis for medium–high-end community media resources in the country and possessing more than 90% of the city's elevator graphic media resources in major Chinese cities. The company's overall value increased nearly ten times, as the changing market environment increased the value of integration considerably. In October 2005, Focus Media acquired Framedia, which already controlled 90% of the nation's elevator media market. For a time, Focus Media's commercial building network covered nearly 35,000 LCD screens in 54 cities across the country. The CTR research report stated that Focus Media had already secured more than 70% market share. "The acquisition of Framedia is a strategy," Jiang Nanchun, the founder of Focus Media, said: "M&A has enabled Focus Media to add high-end apartment media resources to the original network" (Chen, 2006).

2. Focus Media also lacks some intersections

Compared with the first media age, in the elevator advertising campaigns used by Focus Media, the advertisements are seen in more places, but it is still a low-intensity intersection rather than an immersive "any place." It lacks high-intensity intersections, as its connectivity is fundamentally different from the immersive ubiquitous connectivity.

1. The replacement of information is not "any time," nor is it immediate, but it is changed by humans. It mainly relies on thousands of employees of Focus Media riding bikes with advertisements on a U disk and changing the advertising content in various communities.

Application and verification of the models 109

2. It is not individualized, just focused, although this focus does reach a lot of high-income consumers. High-income people in Beijing, Shanghai, and other major cities only account for about 15% of the total population, mainly living in high-end apartments, which are covered by elevator print ads.

3. Generally speaking, it is still the merger of similar resources, that is, the homogeneity of "connectivity" or "channel," but not a qualitative mutation. Still, after being acquired by Focus Media, Framedia's average number of signed bills increased by several times, because Focus Media's office TV advertising network and Framedia's elevator print media complement each other, satisfying Focus Media in creating the "life circle media" framework.

4. Compared with the direct delivery of leaflets, there are more audience choices. Of course, leaflets can also be discarded without being read. When we focus on the degree of intersection between "where" and "content," the "unavoidable" advertising effect of the closed space can provide some evidence on the effect of intentional and unintentional communication, and on the advantages of niche advertisements such as bus and subway advertisements.

5. Media communication carries and releases content in the communication environment. In the immersive communication model, to maximize the effect of content communication, it is necessary to form a high-intensity intersection with "want," "when," "Web," and "who," and to select a communication method and implement it strategically. The media market in China is facing tremendous changes. Channels have been continuously subdivided and re-integrated. Even the bidding period of CCTV-1, the most authoritative television medium in China, has been continuously subdivided. As a media product of the Chinese market, where the mass market is transformed from mass marketing to focused marketing, elevator advertisements have appeared in the era of continuous fragmentation of products and consumption. This has inevitable effects.

Elevator TV is a medium based on the community marketing and focus communication theory, and it is a developing form of outdoor advertising media in the second media age. Therefore, the developing history of China's elevator media is a good setting to assess the immersive communication model's description of media development. Unlike in the developed countries in Europe and America, China's living environment mainly features aggregation and community service. An advertising company envisages that sales facilities will be placed directly in elevators, and that elevator operators will be sales and advertising agents. However, most of the elevators now have little space, and their management cannot keep up. While elevator television has gained the attention advantage of closed space, it also confines the space that the communication reaches. The trend of modern communication is constantly entering an increasingly larger open space.

110   *Application and verification of the models*

6.2.3   The third media age: Panoramic monitoring and personalized service

Compared with the first media age and the second media age, which privilege defined places, the third media age loves open space more. Because of its comprehensive connectivity, the communication range of the third media age is expanded, reaching any time, any place, and anybody. This also makes people in the third media age subject to panoramic monitoring. Michel Foucault features the operation of the panopticon as follows:

> By means of surveillance, disciplinary power became an integrated system ... it also organized as a multiple, automatic and anonymous power; for although surveillance rests on the individual, its functioning is that of a network of relations from top to bottom ... this network holds the whole together and traverses it in its entirety with effects of power that derive from one another: supervisor perpetually supervised.
>
> (Foucault, 1977, p. 177)

This panoramic monitoring may be similar in form to a modern panopticon, but functionally, it can achieve a full range of personalized services. In 1989, Lenkstorf stated in "Social Action Model Used by the Media" that people can be motivated or unmotivated in their media use (McQuail, 2008, p. 127). The immersive communication model proposed in this study attempts to achieve intersections from low intensity to high intensity through relevant factors, reflecting active and passive users as well as motivated and unmotivated ones. This is also a manifestation of the personalized services of immersive communication.

1. High-intensity intersection of "connectivity" and "Web"

An important manifestation of the "ubiquitous network" in the third media age is the super-connectivity. As mentioned earlier, the IOT included in the ubiquitous network has three major features. First, it uses radio-frequency identification (RFID), sensors, two-dimensional codes, etc. to obtain information anywhere and anytime; second, it realizes accurate information delivery in real time through the integration of various communication networks and the Internet; third, with the help of cloud computing, fuzzy identification, and other computing technologies, intelligent processing of massive information is carried out to achieve intelligent control of objects. All this is achieved through several methods of connectivity.

Connecting with the Internet: The IOT, in short, is IOT-connected. The IOT is built on the basis of the computer Internet, using technologies such as RFID and wireless data communication to form a network that connects everything. The Internet is the core and foundation of the IOT, and the IOT is an extension of the Internet. The user terminal extends to anything and everything and achieves information exchange.

Application and verification of the models 111

Connecting with the communication network: The communication network is an important part of the IOT, and it is also the basis for its large-scale application and management. On the one hand, the communication network is a channel through which the IOT implements the interaction of information between objects and people. On the other hand, its base stations and mobile phones can serve as sensing nodes for sensor networks, as well as integrating infrastructures for the IOT and mobile communication networks, to realize the integration of business. As it is fully integrated, a converged network of people and objects is formed.

Connecting with the real world: The IOT connects the virtual digital world with the physical world, and its terminals can spread over every object and fully enter every corner and every aspect of human life. Through Figure 6.2, we will explain the principle of composition of the IOT, along with its relevance to the real physical world and the information world.

2. High-intensity intersection of "connectivity" and "where"

The communication location of the third media age can be a foyer, an elevator, or the entire space. Intelligently monitoring and managing this space is one of the most important characteristics of the third media age. As an extension and upgrade of elevator advertising in the second media age, we first examine the differences between elevator space in the third media age and in the second media age, taking the Elevator Guard of China Mobile's IOT as the research object. China Mobile

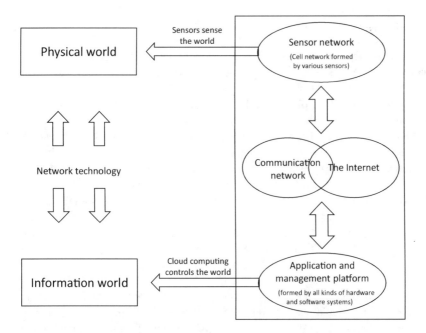

Figure 6.2 Composition principle and functions of IOT

112 *Application and verification of the models*

Elevator Guard is an elevator safety information management product launched by China Mobile. According to its white paper, China Mobile Elevator Guard collects information on elevator lifts, rafts, power outages, and other faults, as well as elevator maintenance information, through sensors installed outside the elevator. It then transmits the data through a wireless GPRS transmission module to the elevator operation management platform. As a result, the platform achieves the various functions of elevator safety management, helps engineers and maintenance workers address any threats to elevator safety, and greatly improves the overall elevator operation management (CART, 2011).

From the perspective of communication, we can see that the basic functions of Elevator Guard include (1) information acquisition and transmission and (2) information management. First, Elevator Guard has terminal data collection functions, that is, sensors installed on the periphery of elevators, that can collect information on elevator floors, door status, speed, top-down faults, bottom-end faults, maintenance status, and other information and then transmit the data to the elevator operation management system platform through a GPRS communication module to provide basic data for elevator safety management. Likewise, it enhances platform security and basic information management, including real-time monitoring.

Therefore, Elevator Guard not only provides intelligent data management services for elevator manufacturers, maintenance companies, government elevator supervisory departments, and residential properties that require remote real-time monitoring of the elevator's operating status but also serves as a 24-hour news medium. The benefits are already evident. For example, in 2010 a 9-year-old boy fell out of an elevator at the Hyatt Regency Hotel. A news report on the tragic story highlighted the monitor's role (Figure 6.3):

A 9-year-old boy was trapped and wormed himself in the cracks, then was stuck, and finally vanished and fell to the ground floor. This process takes at least 20 minutes! The child's family cannot help but ask: "It can be seen clearly in the monitor, but where is the security?" (Li & Wu, 2010)

To give another example, a March 2011 story from Guangxi News Net, titled "A Youth Dissuading Smoking in Elevator Was Beaten by a Man, Recorded by the Monitor," reported that a teenager was violently beaten for asking others not to smoke in the elevator. The incident, which happened on March 9 in Jinhuwan Community in Nanning, was recorded by the monitor in the elevator. On March 10, the suspect was located through clues provided in the monitor, arrested, and taken to the police station. When Guangxi News Net editors processed this news, they also added a special note: "This video has been uploaded to the Morning News Forum 'News Interactive' with this post" (Xu, 2011).

These are just functions that an ordinary elevator monitoring video can achieve. The ubiquitous technology-supported intelligent monitoring system will not be limited by distance. For example, China Mobile's GSM network and GPRS wireless data transmission technology can greatly reduce the difficulty and cost of terminal installation and break the bottleneck of information transmission distance in wired and short-range wireless transmission technologies, possessing greater adaptability. Immersive communication is accomplished in an open space,

Application and verification of the models 113

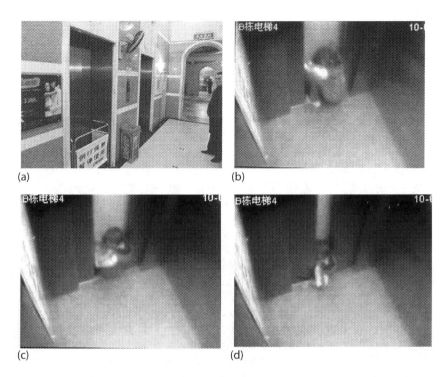

Figure 6.3 The elevator monitor recorded the fall of a 9-year-old boy

in which the object-to-item, person-to-person, object-to-person, and person-to-person connections and information transmission are realized. The Foshan Little Yueyue incident mentioned previously happened in an open space. The market monitor serves the same function as the one in the elevators.

Such places can truly be "any place"—factories, rural areas, transportation, urban management, and other areas—but can also include daily life. In China, the early development and application of the IOT has achieved remarkable results in various fields. The automatic drip irrigation control system of Shihezi in Xinjiang is an example. After the drip irrigation system is connected to the wireless network, the drip irrigation valve can be controlled at any time through a mobile phone, allowing fine irrigation. Intelligent management is adopted in terms of safety production, and the data collection and transmission also broke the previous physical boundaries.

3. High-intensity intersection of "connectivity" and "want"

The ubiquitous network is changing from the government's strategic vision to the reality of our lives. Some leading application services have appeared in many areas as revolutionary changes take place worldwide. From the trials of smart

114 *Application and verification of the models*

connections started in some pilot cities in Japan and South Korea to the launch of mature devices, products, and rich applications, people have begun to live in a post-information society based on the ubiquitous network. The ability to meet the want is strengthened by connectivity, so the application of the ubiquitous network has greatly improved the level of informatization and intelligent automation in many industries, bringing about changes in government management, financial services, logistics, and environmental protection.

As a telecom operator who is taking the lead in the research and application of IOT in China, China Mobile's "Wireless City" has covered more than 30 provinces; China Mobile has also established an IOT Research Institute and Base in Jiangsu, Chongqing, and other places, while 40 industry application templates and standard products such as Yijutong and Wuliantong have been developed. These applications are widely used by cities, individuals, families, businesses, and rural IOT sites.

The IOT has begun to be widely used in all walks of life to enable our cities and daily lives to operate in an orderly manner. Elevator monitoring is a part of our analysis. Ubiquitous communication technology can deploy machine-to-machine (M2M) terminals with photoelectric sensors for elevators and connect elevators to intelligent management systems. When an elevator fails, passengers do not need to panic, since the elevator management department will receive the information immediately and get to the scene faster to handle the problem. In the field of transportation, the intelligent management of vehicles is achieved by installing wireless terminal equipment on taxis and buses. Wireless terminals have been installed on taxis and buses in Beijing, Shanghai, and Liaoning to implement vehicle management and dispatch. Shanghai Mobile has likewise installed chips on taxis and buses, and many cities and provinces in China have launched digital city management and digital transportation. M2M has also been widely used in smart buildings, streetlamp monitoring, animal traceability, mobile wallets, and environmental monitoring. China Mobile has launched a series of IOT services including mobile payment, logistics management, terminal monitoring, electrical guards, and monitoring of agricultural vegetable greenhouses (China Academy of Telecommunication Research of Ministry of Industry and Information Technology, 2011).

The promotion of the ubiquitous network, including the IOT, has not only stimulated economic development and increased the degree of informationization in human society but also brought great convenience to people's social lives and production. This is reflected in our daily experiences: we will find that "any want" can be satisfied. It's not just that newspaper information has become a multimedia format and that you can send and receive emails on the road, but that any information service you want will be realized at your fingertips: even without lifting a finger, you can know what's going on around you and enjoy the surrounding services.

4. High-intensity intersection of "connectivity" and "who"

In China, the IOT has moved from the laboratory to practical application, emerging in the areas of logistics, national grids, and airport security. Experts predict

Application and verification of the models 115

that IOT technology will be popularized and developed into a trillion-scale high-tech industry within three to five years. On February 3, 2010, the China Communications Standards Association (CCSA) established a ubiquitous network technical committee in Beijing, which brought together experts from China's telecommunication, power, transportation, logistics, and meteorology industries. At present, China Telecom's information service has been successfully applied in network video surveillance (Global Eye), intelligent transportation, and green communities; China Mobile has already had 3 million M2M modules with an annual growth rate of more than 80%. It has also been successfully applied in elevator monitoring, remote meter reading, etc. Huawei, ZTE, Putian, and other companies have researched and developed corresponding chips and modules. Tsinghua University, Beijing University of Posts and Telecommunications, and Nanjing University of Posts and Telecommunications are also conducting related research (Pan, 2011).

Although China may not have seized many opportunities on the Internet, in the field of sensor networks, China is undoubtedly at the forefront of the world, joining with the United States, Germany, Britain, etc. to lead the formulation of international IOT standards. When the "connectivity" and the "who" achieve a high-intensity intersection, the resulting immersive communication affects everyone. So, what does this mean for "anyone" living in this new world?

The three-dimensional spiral diagram of the immersive communication process given in Chapter 5 describes the process of "positioning–communication–feedback" in immersive communication. Expanding the previous communication models, the "positioning" function is added. This is an embodiment of completely personalized and customized services, an important feature of immersive communication. For instance, when you are walking in a public space, you may suddenly receive a message on your mobile phone: there is a vending machine 50 meters ahead. This is because the Bluetooth on the vending machine and the Bluetooth of your mobile phone reach each other when they are within a certain distance, so the set software will give a reminder to the mobile phone. When you input the verification code, you can use the vending machine and pay for goods through your mobile phone.

This process starts by positioning you: it discovers your location with GPS and other navigation systems and adjusts your positioning as you move. For example, there are people who like to go for a run with a mobile phone. A fitness app can be installed on the phone to tell you how many calories you burned. If you get lost, the mobile phone positioning function will immediately tell you where your new location is and then show you the way home on the map. This is just a small manifestation of all-around personalized service.

Since Weiser first proposed the ubiquitous network concept in 1991, ubiquitous technology and cognition have continued to develop. Japan has proposed U-Japan; South Korea has proposed U-Korea; the European Union has proposed I-Europe; and the United States has proposed "Smarter Planet." For its part, China has proposed "Sensing China," in which a ubiquitous network is the infrastructure. Under the ubiquitous network's perception, it can realize panoramic monitoring

116   *Application and verification of the models*

and intelligent management of people's production and lives, potentially providing personalized services to everyone. Some people may feel that the panoramic surveillance is too similar to a modern panoramic prison, leaving people with no privacy and less freedom, so they may consider switching off the portable terminal. However, these people may find that if there is no intelligent service, life will become difficult again.

A "selective attention" factor has also been demonstrated by the "transmission model of news learning" in the literature (McQuail, 2008, p. 78). There is a "positioning" factor in the immersive communication process model of this study. One of the key points and prerequisites for the realization of modern "selective attention" can also be to control the switch on each person's or communicator's hand.

In hisbook *The Nerves of Government*, Karl W. Deutsch (1956) discussed how social science models have structural functions that reveal the order and interrelationships between systems, enabling us to gain an overall image of things. The immersive communication model has both explanatory functions and predictive functions for processes and results, which provide the basis for analyzing and estimating the probabilities of different outcomes. Researchers can thus establish their own hypotheses accordingly. Based on the immersive model described earlier, this study will analyze and predict the future of the third media age and the immersive communicator guided by immersive communication.

6.3 Summary

This chapter applies and validates the immersive communication models proposed in the previous chapter. These models can be used to investigate and solve the problems of the communication process and the function realization of immersive communication. Analyzing the intersections on the diagrams helps clarify why a given effect is not achieved or why it is only partly achieved, and they can also be used to identify and classify the characteristics of communication methods. This chapter includes three research steps: general applications of the models; using the model, the function model matrix of immersive communication (Figure 5.9), to divide the three media ages; and finally, analyzing representative examples.

1. Discussion of general applications

The use of the immersive communication model matrix diagram (Figure 5.9) is examined in terms of both technical dimensions (hardware and software) and communication dimensions (time and place, etc.). The degree of immersion is reflected in the intersection point on the immersive communication matrix diagram, from low to high, representing the improvement of communication technology and communication capabilities. When all points reach high-intensity intersections, that is, when the CII index reaches the highest value, it is the full realization of immersive communication.

Application and verification of the models   117

Table 5.1 listed 25 specific intersections and the forms of media communication forms and communication effects they represent. The number and strength of the intersections demonstrate the level of immersion, as follows.

1. *Differences in "connectivity" capabilities.* The core technology of immersive communication is its full connectivity, which is the high-intensity intersection of "connection" (C4) and "5W," respectively. Real-world data supports this model: at the beginning of 2012, about 2.3 billion people around the world were connected to the Internet, while the number of connections to the IOT had risen to 1 trillion. The number of mobile phone users globally exceeded 3.3 billion in 2007. Forrester, a market research institution, predicts that the world's interoperable business will be 30 times as large as the human-to-human communication business by 2020.

2. *Differences in "computing" capabilities.* In the immersive communication matrix model diagram, the emergence of computing and later, cloud computing forms a watershed between the three media ages. Another factor that promotes the development of communication is the development of Big Data, which is also supported by computing power. Looking at the five intersections between "computing" and "5A" in the model diagram, we can see that the low-intensity intersection belongs to the earlier media, while the high-intensity intersections allow communication to appear at "any time," at "any place," and on "any network," with the data now in the cloud. When the "computing" and "want" variables achieve a high-intensity intersection, a ubiquitous social communication architecture will be formed.

3. *Differences in "place" and space.* On the immersive communication function model diagram, following the line where "place" intersects with "5C," we can see that whether communication can reach "any place" depends on its intersections with communication, computing, connectivity, and other technical factors; they are positively related. The reality is exactly the same: the developmental level of these factors determines the area where the communication can reach, as well as the effect and intensity of its arrival. China's TV development is given as an example of how the changes in "place" affect the communication of content, and the intersections between "place" and "anytime" and "anybody" are used to study changes in viewer presence. When "connectivity" and "any place" form a high-intensity intersection, the mobile ubiquity is fully realized, as well as communication in any open space.

4. Differences in the ability to meet the "want." The immersive communication model diagram uses "Want" as the first entry in "5W." The level of intersections between "want" and "content," "communication," "computing," and "connectivity" directly corresponds to the level of the immersion index, CII. The display/attention model proposed by McQuail in 1987 focused on how "the attention potential of the available audience is limited, and one channel or display's gain must be another's loss" (McQuail, 2008, p. 52). Taking advertising communication as an example, this chapter examines the strengths and weaknesses of the intersections between "want" and "5C,"

118 *Application and verification of the models*

along with the relevance of differences in communication effectiveness, as well as the relevance to people's active choices or passive acceptance.

5. *Differences in "convergence."* Convergence is a core issue in modern communication, which determines the level of communication ability as well as the ability to solve the "synchrony" of communication. Convergence can be a fusion of "content" and technology, a fusion of "Web" and "connectivity," or a combination of "computing" and "want." To consider the convergence intersections in the immersive communication model, we take China's radio and TV as an example. The high-intensity intersection between the cloud computing technology in the "computing" and "Web" categories can speed up the process of integrating the three networks, optimizing media resources to achieve faster communication anytime, anywhere, and with anyone.

These differences prove that, by examining the conditions of these intersections, there is a great deal of common-sense and research evidence to support the phenomena and meanings described in the model diagram.

2. Dividing the first, second, and third media ages with the immersive communication model

The immersive communication model also helps clarify the differences and boundary lines of the three media ages. As shown in Figure 6.1, the first media age, supported by technology, witnessed the formation of content for communication and telecommunications, along with the ability to communicate to meet certain needs and reach certain places. The main forms of media that emerged were newspapers, telegrams, etc. The second media age is distinguished by the appearance of computing and the Web, as the pre-computing age was the first media age. The third media age is characterized by computing at any time and with any object; for example, cloud computing and ubiquitous computing.

The intersections of "connectivity," "convergence," and "object" are also the intersection and convergence of reality and virtuality. "Place" distinguishes the media age attributes of telegrams, magazines, telephones, etc. The infinite expansion of space is an important feature of the third media age that distinguishes it from the first two media ages. When everything in technology is "converged," and communication can meet the needs of any object at any place, at any time, or through any network, immersive communication will be realized. There is mass communication in all three media ages, but the need for complete personalization can only be realized in the third media age. Finally, this graph is backward compatible, and the third media age is the simultaneous satisfaction of all intersections.

3. Case study analysis

Lastly, this chapter selects typical cases of the three media ages to conduct case validation of the immersive communication model. The maximal realization of the "4Any" goal of the immersive communication model lies in the realization of

Application and verification of the models 119

all intersections of 5C and 5W. Taking the development of advertising in China and the related media as an example, the immersive communication model was examined and verified.

The first media age is exemplified by lobby leaflets and unidirectional transmission. Lobbying is basically human communication, but it is often accompanied by the distribution of leaflets. Leaflets can be said to be the prototype of early newspapers, and they are the original forms of media in the first media age. In the immersive communication model diagram, the communication behavior of the lobby leaflet at least occupies an intersection of "content + place," which of course is far from the "any" level in "any place." The leaflet distributor must choose a "place" and typically uses a point-to-point, one-on-one distribution. In a physical lobby space, there are a lot of people, but they don't spend a lot of time there, so they may not pay close attention to information provided there. Therefore, the effect of communication is similar to that of a "fairy maiden scattering flowers," as communicators often do not know who will receive their message. In general, the distribution of leaflets in the foyer is basically a one-way communication in fixed places. Likewise, lobbyists rely mainly on words, yet do not have computing, the web, and other modern functions.

The second media age is demonstrated by elevator television and focus awareness. The elevator, as a communication space, is still a fixed "place" like the hallway, but it is enclosed. Print advertisements and television advertisements began in the first media age, but the communication method of focus awareness was mainly characteristic of the second media age. Focus Media's elevator advertisements reflect the realization of some intersections and also reflect the lack of some intersections. The replacement of information is not "any time," nor is it immediate; it is mainly done through manual replacement. Likewise, it is not individualized, but it is focused, often on high-income customers. Overall, it is still the merger of similar resources; that is, the homogeneity of "connectivity" or "channel" is not a qualitative mutation.

Compared with the direct delivery of flyers, there are more audience choices. However, this is not the ubiquitous and pervasive phenomenon of immersive communication, as "place" and "content" are still at a low intensity here. Media communication carries and releases content in the communication environment. In the immersive communication model diagram, to maximize the effect of content communication, it is necessary to form a high-intensity intersection with "want," "time," "Web," and "who," and to choose a communication method to execute it strategically. For instance, elevator television was established based on the community marketing and focus communication theory, representing a form of development of outdoor advertising media in the second media age. Therefore, it is a good case to verify the description of the media development process in the immersive communication model. While elevator television gains the attentional advantages of a confined space, it also confines the space that the communication reaches. The trend of modern communication is constantly entering an increasingly large open space.

120 *Application and verification of the models*

The third media age features panoramic monitoring and personalized service. Compared with the first media age and the second media age, which focused on defined places, the third media age prefers open space. Because of the comprehensive connection, the communication of the third media age can reach any time, any place, and anybody. This panoramic monitoring may be similar in form to a modern panoramic prison, but functionally it can achieve full-scale personalized service. The immersive communication model proposed in this study attempts to characterize the intersections from low intensity to high intensity through relevant factors, reflecting the relative activeness and motivation in information communication. This is also a manifestation of the personalized services of immersive communication.

This chapter separately verifies the performance of the super-intersections between "connectivity" and "where," "want," and "who." It also demonstrates the three-dimensional spiral diagram of the immersive communication process presented in the previous chapter, describing the process of immersive communication as "positioning–communication–feedback." Compared with the previous communication models, it mainly adds the "positioning" function. This is an embodiment of completely personalized and customized services, an important feature of immersive communication.

7 How immersive communication guides the formation of "the third media age"

According to Mark Poster's *The Second Media Age*, the media on which human society depends for survival and development not only has an evolutionary significance in terms of materiality, but also has a symbolic function in the era of cultural representation. Utilizing historical depth and philosophical thinking, Poster combines philosophy, history, and media to form a major argument concerning human self-development (Poster, 1995). *The Second Media Age* systematically established the ideas of Western criticism from the perspective of postmodern theory and examined the implications of new communication technologies. Poster's book was born in the era of Web 1.0 but clearly stated that the "two-way decentralized communication" is the defining characteristic of the second media age. About five years later, a conference named Web 2.0 announced the birth of this eponymous new Internet era. The most prominent feature of the Web 2.0 era is that the recipients of information can also create information, changing from a passive to an active role.

However, the change is far more pervasive: Web 2.0 and ubiquitous network technologies have transformed the relationship between people, media, and society. The level of technological mediation in human society continues to deepen, and humanity has entered a completely new social pattern that is different from the second media age. Here, both the real society and the virtual society are integrated in a social form dominated by immersive communication. Behind this lies a state of human existence in which information is highly intelligent, networked, and pan-mediated. In this era guided by immersive communication, people cannot live without communication. Since 2000, technology has driven an unprecedented level of profound social change. In particular, due to the development of the IOT and the ubiquitous network, people live in both the physical and the virtual world, which permeate each other. From receiving information to obtaining entertainment, from the channels of shopping and consumption to the space of social interaction, great changes have taken place.

The world has begun to enter the early days of the ubiquitous era of high-speed connectivity. Human society has not only provided basic material needs such as food and shelter, but has also provided information through various print and electronic media. Society itself has become the content, channel, and space

122 *The formation of "the third media age"*

of information communication—a new form of immersive communication has begun to penetrate the muscle and marrow of human society.

In this era of immersion, the ubiquitous network covers everywhere, terminals occupy every corner, and people become their own media. The concept of media communication is thus undergoing a qualitative revolution, becoming omnipresent and omnipotent. Intelligent survival under immersive communication has become a typical feature of this new society. Immersive communication has gradually enabled society to transcend the initial function of information exchange and has taken shape as a powerful force that affects people's daily life and values, changes people's ways of understanding and experiencing the world, changes people's way of thinking, and even reconstructs people's lifestyles, emotional worlds, and group awareness. In this immersive society, the "immersive people" living in it enter into each other and change each other through immersion, anytime and anywhere. Understanding the status quo and trends of this social change and grasping the function and communication mode of this in-depth mediated society are of great significance for the cognition of human thinking and the influence on the landscape of the future.

7.1 The inevitable cause of the formation of "the third media age"

From interactive communication to immersive communication, the entire social scene has undergone large-scale and profound changes. The main issues include the formation and development of communication of information, the generation and interpretation of meaning, the structure of information, the motivations for the interaction between the disseminator and the recipient, how rights and resources are distributed in society, how culture is generated, and how the various sectors of society interact. In the research on public information, public service, the expansion of advertisements, and the drive of market interests, humanity has gradually established immersive communication as a central position in the process of human survival and life.

The goal of the EU is to achieve an "ever-ubiquitous" information society by 2020. The "Smart Planet" of the United States is a similarly huge concept. It will be matched with many practical ways to boost all industries and increase employment. Early in 2005, China proposed a vision for future communications to the International Telecommunications Union (ITU) and designed a smart environment full of terminal equipment. The form of these terminals can be changed at any time as needs and tasks change. This controlled, supported soft service environment has a beautiful name: MUSE (Mobile Ubiquitous Service Environment). The information superhighway, which brought a stormy impact 20 years ago, is still making its presence felt. The task we face is to make the earth more intelligent, to bring people closer to nature and even to space-.

Human life will soon be more informative, intelligent, and personalized. According to IBM, a real-time analytics technology in development can customize information for users based on their network preferences and performance on

The formation of "the third media age"   123

social networking sites. Spam email will be extinct, as ad emails utilize more targeted and personalized customization, and as email filters become more accurate, so users will not have to worry about getting a lot of irrelevant information. IBM also predicted that the rapid development of mobile communications technology would eliminate the "digital divide" and result in tremendous development in areas such as e-commerce and telemedicine (IBM, 2011b). These innovative technologies and innovative ideas are pushing human communication and society into a new era of development.

7.1.1 The revolution of media ontology and changes in social productivity

In immersive communication, the concept of media is undergoing profound changes. People are media, society is media, and the environment is media. Can the media be defined as human-centered existence? "More than two centuries ago," Mattelart noted, "the concept of communication entered the modernity through the 'road', and the advent of the postmodern era characterized by non-material networks and intangible flows was completed under the metaphor of the highway network" (Mattelart, 2007, p. 121). Freedom of commercial expression leads to the homogeneity of society- intrinsically unified in the market, but it will inevitably lead to the fragmentation of society. The tension between market rationality and cultural diversity, the tension between the popularization of science and technology, and the absence of attribution are all intensifying. These turbulent patterns of postmodern imbalances and the integration of humanity tend to create unpredictable patterns of change. The meaning of the media as the "intermediary" and soul of the society is increasingly becoming manifest.

As Poster said, "[e]ach method of preserving and transmitting information profoundly intervenes in the network of relationships that constitute a society." (Poster, 1990, p. 7). If the media is only defined as a communication system, then the media is only the center of communication to the general public, and it is only the transmitter that sends signals to distant communities. In the book *No Sense of Place*, Meyrowitz showed how the particular relationship between the media and its audience has remarkably reshaped the social order. Meyrowitz's ideas are based on those of Erving Goffman, who believed that the media mixes people who are otherwise separated from each other in everyday life, thus changing society. In his eyes, the technical achievement of television was to eliminate the influence of space and time, thus making it possible for heterogeneous people to have an asynchronous "party."

Each person in the hierarchy has a sense of position, allowing us to maintain a social order based on grade differences. The print media and human literacy can be said to be a corroboration of this conservative principle and to support his claim: "The media is a different type of social environment that accepts or excludes, unites, or distinguishes people in various ways" (Meyrowitz, 1986). However, in an age dominated by immersive communication, the meaning of the media will evolve further into a kind of service centered on people. This study

124 The formation of "the third media age"

proposes a new concept of "ubiquitous mass communication," in which the "ubiquitous mass" is both "with people" and "without people." Immersion seems to pull us back to the ancient era of communication without people, but this kind of communication is based on overall public comprehension.

Because of this, things that seem to be purely for personal consumption have a common symbolic meaning in the space for immersive communication, even things that were rarely recognized as a medium in the past, such as clothes, houses, and cars. Regardless of whether they have been in the virtual world or in real life, in the immersive communication society that embraces conspicuous consumption as a potential culture, these symbolic objects have also become mediators. They convey different ideological information and indicate the owner's social hierarchy and attitude toward life: in China, for instance, owning a recreational vehicle (RV) represents the middle-class standard of living and the liking for natural freedom. To a certain extent, this can be said to represent a conciliation of a contradiction between the individualization and socialization of immersive communication.

The ubiquitous network turns everything around people into media. The tangible media and the intangible media, including the environment itself, become media that can transmit and collect information. They can interact with people at any time and in any place. Information communication is deeply buried in life and profoundly changes the relationship between media and people. "What's the significance of using your own 'incarnation' in 'Second Life'? The answer is: Compared with the rest of the Internet, 'Second Life' has the charisma of 'full-heart'" (Levinson, 2011, p. 153). This is the charm of immersion. After entering Second Life, your "incarnation" moves about in a highly simulated and surreal environment, and a strong hallucination develops from it. You really feel full of heart and soul, not just watching, listening, or reading. However, the more profound change is that people have fully integrated into the two worlds of the virtual and the physical, and they are able to move in and out freely, because immersive communication completely fuses these two worlds.

Since the invention of the electronic media, the temporal and spatial parameters of people's social communication have undergone great changes, providing the possibility for anyone to communicate with anyone at any time. However, before immersive communication became a socially dominant model, McLuhan's vision of the global village was mainly an imaginative possibility, as there was still some distance from actual reality. Only by immersive communication can long-distance communication and ubiquitous communication become possible, creating a global village where the world is closer and making human information exchange become more productive in the process of globalization.

Wiener, the founder of cybernetics, pointed out in *Cybernetics*: "Information is information, neither material nor energy" (Wiener, 1948). However, information in any society has the nature of its public goods. In the era of immersive communication, it is a manifestation of higher productivity. It adds value to barrier-free communication anytime and anywhere, forms social productivity and strong creativity, and effectively promotes social changes.

7.1.2 Changes in the media space and the transformation of human living space

Immersive communication relies on the environment of the network and the networking of that environment, reconstructing the media "space" and extending the concept of media "space" to the overall human environment. Tim Berners-Lee, the founder of the Internet, once said: "The World Wide Web is more a kind of social creation than a creation of technology. I designed it for a social purpose—helping people work together—rather than designing a technology toy. The ultimate goal of the World Wide Web is to support and promote the survival of the world's networks" (Berners-Lee, 2000). The Internet has been in existence for more than 40 years since its inception in 1969. However, its development history has proved that this is a process in which technology both influences communication and changes life.

Beyond its industrial impact, the rapid development of the Internet as an information communication technology has led to the large-scale development and structural upgrading of information and related industries, resulting in a series of emerging industries. But the first 20 years of Internet development remained in the virtual world, until the emergence of the ubiquitous network of the world and the convergence of the Internet and the IOT enabled the network to truly move from virtuality to reality, completely changing the "spatial" meaning of the media.

In the ubiquitous network, people and people, people and things, and things and things are all connected, as humanity has entered into a truly full-scale networked existence. That is, full network environmentalization and environment networkization are ever-present. The ubiquitous network is not only a carrier of information communication but also creates a completely socialized media while also stimulating society as a whole to be fully intelligent and multi-medialized. Forrester, the world's leading market research institution, predicts that by 2020, the demand for the world's interconnected business will exceed the demand for human-to-human communication by 30 times.

As early as 2007, the number of mobile phone users globally exceeded 3.3 billion, and according to the ITU's 2011 final report, that figure reached 5.9 billion just four years later. Mobile Internet access has brought about great changes in life:

"Access to the Web on mobile devices outside the home thus not only frees us from the sticky spiderweb of seat and screen, but makes the home nest more convivial. The growing availability of media outside the home, not only in libraries and cyber-cafes but in cars and pockets, makes each of us a nest or hearth of communications – a hearth we can explore and enjoy without clipping or short-circuiting the hearth at home" (Levinson, 2004, p. 47).

The mobile phone is still a product of the second media age. The high-speed and constantly upgraded Internet and the IOT have brought about tremendous changes in human communication and life. In contrast, the number of "things" connected to the IOT has exceeded 1 trillion, and the number of object-to-object communications is far greater than the number of people-to-people communications.

126   The formation of "the third media age"

These connections are the technological foundation of immersive communication, and they also brought about the physical entities that support immersive communication—the development of smart buildings, smart cities, smart communities, and smart worlds.

From an international perspective, smart cities must not only make the public service system of the city fully informatized, but also completely and thoroughly universalize the urban space from the inside to the outside, like the smart city that Korea has promoted in 2004 under the concept of UCK. The realization of the "Broadband China Strategy" will likewise promote intelligent transportation, smart security, smart environment, and smart energy, and will transform the cities' and governments' management cores into a highly connected intelligent database, allowing intelligent management and information communication anytime and anywhere.

In a society with highly intelligent and networked immersive communication, people and things are all media, and each terminal can send information to all people instantly. In the physical sense, in an immersive society, the media is ubiquitous, from reality to virtuality and from virtuality to reality. Society's needs for commercial security and personal safety have connected devices such as surveillance videos to form a ubiquitous and omnipotent network in the real world. The Little Yueyue case mentioned in Chapter 1 is the most obvious example. A tragic incident befell Little Yueyue, a two-year-old girl from Foshan, Guangdong. The incident was able to arouse extensive and rapid attention from the whole of society because the surveillance video in a nearby market played a key role. The surveillance camera recorded that a car had run over the little girl twice, while none of the 18 people passing by stopped to help the poor girl. The resulting video was spread across the traditional media, Internet, and interpersonal communication systems, entering the cyclical communication stage. In the ubiquitous network world where monitors are everywhere, obviously, monitors are the tools and carriers of media, and can be said to be a social medium, though still in the basic media form of immersive communication.

As seen from the previous chapters, the mode of immersive communication encompasses all previous modes and forms of communication, especially as ubiquitous networks, which exist as a kind of technology concept that contains the Internet, completely subverts the traditional mode of information communication. Not only does it have the non-linear characteristics of the Internet that make information communication break through the mode of mass communication, but it also has great tolerance for immersive communication, enabling the ubiquitous network information model to fully incorporate and integrate various forms such as information push, actively searching for information, information booking, and information monitoring.

When the Internet was born, the intellectual community hoped it would become a true "public space," but Poster was cautious about this. When we talk about public spaces, we think of salons, the congress hall, and churches where people can meet. The place for communication is not the Internet, and most importantly, the exchanges on the Internet are based on the information processing machine as a

The formation of "the third media age" 127

mediating center. Although we are establishing contact, our object is not people but machines.

> With representational machines such as the computer the question of the interface becomes especially salient because each side of the human/machine divide now begins to claim its own reality; on one side of the screen is Newtonian space, on the other, cyberspace. Interfaces of high quality allow seamless crossings between the two worlds, thereby facilitating the disappearance of the difference between them and thereby, as well, altering the type of linkage between the two. Interfaces are the sensitive boundary zone of negotiation between the human and the machinic as well as the pivot of an emerging new set of human/machine relations.
>
> (Poster, 1995, p. 21)

In another paper, Poster also talks about how machines used as tools, such as the Internet, have much greater capabilities than in the past and thus have more than just tool-level meaning. He suggested that instead of applying the old theories of the public sphere and civil society, the Internet should be studied in a broader political and economic context, because the Internet is more like a collective space than a public space.

In fact, just like the continuous evolution of human society from low to high, the network continues to produce higher-level forms. First, the center of economic structure was changed from industrial production to information communication, and then the power structure changed from a pyramid to a network, which makes the space of human existence and creation infinitely three-dimensional. It is in this sense that immersive communication reconstructs the three major spaces of human beings, fully integrating psychological space and physical space, spiritual space and intelligent space, and virtual space and real space into a large living space, that is, the large space of immersive communication.

The French scholar Armand Mattelart stated in the introduction to *The Globalization of Communication*:

> The real-time communication network is the way to organize on Earth. The material flow customarily called the globalization and cross-boundary and non-material flow co-occur ... The communication machine accelerates the gradual integration of the whole to society by constantly expanding the flow of people, material and symbolic wealth, and constantly moves the boundary of matter, knowledge and spirit.
>
> (Mattelart, 2007, p. 1)

The fully networked ubiquitous society is completely different from the previous industrial society and information society. It has features such as economic globalization and organizational networking; due to ubiquitous network-based immersive communication anywhere, it realizes ubiquitous information communication beyond the time and space of globalization, breaking through the

128 *The formation of "the third media age"*

boundary between life and work, and its labor production methods have become completely individualized. The nature of the network, its inherent temporal and spatial separation and openness and equality, has reconstructed the living space of human society, bringing about a profound effect on human production and living methods and social structure.

7.1.3 *Changes in the social functions of media bring changes to social relations*

While immersive communication has brought about changes in the concept and spatial meaning of media, its own social function as a medium has also undergone corresponding changes. The main feature of immersive communication that distinguishes it from previous communication is that it has changed from an information system to a full-service system: from the information core of the society to its command core.

In immersive communication, media is not an accessory or an optional extra like the icing on a cake. Due to the comprehensive ubiquitous information survival of human beings, media has become the oxygen on which people rely for survival. Media information is the basis for a society to make key decisions—the commander of everyone's life. If the mobile phone has become the remote control of all media, then the media is the switch of our life. See the next chapter, on immersive communicators, for further details.

Walter Ong studied the "second dictation period" after electronic media were introduced into a written society, which is essentially different from the "basic dictation period" of the former written society. The "word" returned in electronic form is significantly different from the original word in its spiritual and psychological meaning. This difference can be compared to the concept of "without people" in the era of immersive communication and in the spoken language. The ancient "without people" was a complete one-to-one communication, while the non-public" contained in the immersive ubiquitous communication refers to the personalized service provided to a specific person in the context of the general public.

Daniel Boorstin, in his study on the influence of electronic media on thought patterns and social structures, described how electronic media mass-produce a certain scene to make experiences repeatable and make full use of various technologies to produce time and space at the same level. Immersive communication can "de-batch" and "de-duplicate" based on the "batchable" and "repeatable" functions of electronic media, rendering the "batch" and "repeat" functions of the media "obsolete" and bringing back the originals.

The strength of immersive communication is different from the exclusive authority of mass communication. The communication function of immersive media inherits the characteristics of "de-authority" and "de-centering" that began in the electronic age. The communication characteristics of the immersive communication era are most clearly manifested in the reconstruction of the communication hierarchy and the elimination of authority. The theory of the two-level flow

The formation of "the third media age" 129

hypothesis in mass communication, proposed by Paul F. Lazarsfeld, is a classic theory of mass communication. It describes how information usually reaches "opinion leaders" through mass media and is then transmitted by opinion leaders to ordinary people. This reflects the two levels and processes of communication—first the process of information transmission, and then the process of interpersonal influence. Immersive communication includes multi-polar forms of "point-to-point" and "point-to-surface," and it generalizes the communication hierarchy, using "de-authorization" and "de-centrality" to reconstruct social interpersonal relationships.

On "de-centering," Poster also made an interesting statement:

> The poststructuralist position illuminates the decentering effects of the electronically mediate communication on the subject and, reciprocally, the electronically mediated communication subverts the authority effects of the poststructuralist position by imposing the social context as a decentering ground for theory. Hence I couple TV ads and Baudrillard, database and Foucault, electronic writing and Derrida, science and Lyotard.
>
> (Poster, 1990, p. 18)

Immersive communication does not generally "de-authorize" the media but completely "de-centralizes" it. The media itself is no longer the center for collecting and disseminating information, while people become the center. The pursuit of making everyone the center makes immersive communication the most democratic communication function.

Of course, from another point of view, immersive communication transforms people into the center only by turning people into media. This resembles Gilles Deleuze's commentary on Foucault that humans' power is interconnected with the power of information technology and their third-generation machines to create something that is not human, but a 'human-computer-individual' system (Deleuze, 2001). We know that when the variable caused by the change is large enough, a qualitative paradigm shift occurs.

The media directly influences social relations by shaping social interactions, and after reaching a certain level, it achieves direct influence on the social structure. It can be said that every historic transition of media inevitably brings about changes in both social structure and the forms of social interaction. At the level of social relations, the more unified the logic of the media composition, the more unified the interaction forms, and the more unified the overall structure of social relations, the easier they are to control. In the Internet era, especially in the era of immersive communication, interaction continues to become more complicated, eventually achieving media integration and complementary advantages, thereby achieving the optimization of interpersonal relationships and social structures and increasing individuals' satisfaction and sense of accomplishment in the social structure.

Immersive communication and its ubiquitous network are not only technological, but also have a conceptual and social existence. When ubiquitous connectivity

130 *The formation of "the third media age"*

and the related information and communication technologies fully penetrate all aspects of society, they will cause the transformation of communication modes and relations in both the virtual world and the physical world. This will further lead to changes of production and lifestyle, political and economic systems, and the cultural values of human society. It will bring about a qualitative change in the entire social relationship. At the same time, this change in social relations will infiltrate into the historical field of immersive communication or renewed communication relations.

7.2 The concept and characteristics of "the third media age"

After the preceding discussion on the relationship between media forms, modes of transmission, and the development of social structures, it is possible to demonstrate the transformative relationship between social relations and modes of communication that promote each other. The first media age was characterized by reading, listening, and watching, mainly passive forms of one-way communication. The second media age featured interactive and interpersonal communication. Now, in the era of immersion, individuals have jumped in and become avatars, becoming a part of computer games and media. Once immersive communication became the main mode of communication, the advent of the third media age was announced.

7.2.1 The concept of "the third media age"

Based on the preceding analysis, this study defines "the third media age" as the age of ubiquitous communication, which is based on ubiquitous networks and is characterized by immersive communication. The following sections explain this definition.

1) The maturation of the ubiquitous network is the material basis and technical prerequisite for the emergence of the third media age.

As discussed in the first chapter and in later chapters of this book, based on the omnipresent concept of ubiquitous communication, the world will rise to build a grand vision for future development beyond the information society—a ubiquitous network society (UNS). The new information-based development strategy that focuses on U (Ubiquitous) characteristics replaces the electronic rejuvenation strategy with E (Electronic) characteristics that emerged at the turn of the century. In 2009, the ITU defined the key features of the ubiquitous network in its "Y. 2002 Standards Proposal" and proposed "5C" and "5Any," emphasizing the omnipotent function of the ubiquitous network and its ubiquitous coverage characteristics. The construction and functional realization of the ubiquitous network mainly rely on the existence and interaction of three ubiquitous physical layers: network transmission, terminal units, and intelligent applications.

The formation of "the third media age"   131

As discussed in the previous chapter, the core technology and implementation foundation of immersive communication is its overall "connectivity" capability, namely the high-intensity intersections of "connectivity" (C4) and 5W, which also reflects the core target appeal of U strategy. The ubiquitous nature and demands of U strategy will inevitably promote the comprehensive integration of various communications technologies into human production and life. It emphasizes that the development of information technology must not only meet the needs of economic growth, but also promote the transformation and improvement of people's daily lives. The goal is to enable anyone to enjoy the convenience of modern information technology, at any place and at any time. The United Nations is also actively promoting global recognition and following this new goal of human information communication. It also believes that this goal is higher than the information society and represents the new highest realm of modern information technology for human production and life.

2) Immersive communication is the dominant form of communication in the third media age.

Chapter 5 of this book proposes three immersive communication models based on the ubiquitous connection target; these models are verified in Chapter 6. Drawing on the assumptions and arguments of the previous chapters, the verification of the three model diagrams results in the table of immersive communication proposed in Chapter 5, especially the 25 intersections shown in the table and the media forms and communication effects they represent. We analyze and exemplify the differences in connectivity ability, the differences in computing ability, the differences in places and spaces, the differences in ability to meet wants, and the differences in convergence. The results show that the number and strength of the intersection points represent the level of immersion index, denote the ability to solve the core problems of communication, and ultimately determine the level of communication ability.

In Section 6.1.2, on the basis of the immersive communication model, we offered a division map of the three media ages—the immersive communication function model matrix diagram. After analyzing the various intersections, a model for dividing the three media ages was proposed. It points out that in the first media age, in terms of technical support, there was both content and communication, and communication was able to meet certain needs and reach certain places. The main media forms were newspapers, telegrams, and so on. The presence of computing can be regarded as the dividing point between the first media age and the second media age, while the full use of cloud computing can be regarded as the dividing point between the second media age and the third media age. The infinite expansion of space is an important feature of the third media age that distinguishes it from the previous two ages. This map is downwardly compatible, and the third media age is the simultaneous satisfaction of all intersections.

We can see that when all intersections achieve high intensity, when everything in technology is integrated and communication can meet any needs of any object

132 *The formation of "the third media age"*

at any place, any time, and through any network, it is the full realization of immersive communication, showing the characteristics of the third media age. That is, when immersive communication is fully realized, it is also when a new media age, different from the past, takes shape.

3) Ubiquitous communication distinguishes the third media age from the first media age of mass communication and from the second media age of focused communication.

Mass communication is a process of information dissemination. It is a process in which certain social groups use newspapers, magazines, books, radio, movies, television, and other mass media to send messages and knowledge to most members of society. This definition was first used in the UN Charter of Science, Education and Culture, published in London in November 1945. Obviously, this definition describes a one-way process of communication and does not reflect the existence of feedback and the two-way process later developed in mass communication.

Focused communication refers to the selection of specific media according to different characteristics of social groups. It is a one-to-minority group communication, also called demassified communication or sub-communication. All three media ages have mass communication and focused communication, but completely personalized needs can only be truly realized in the third media age.

The new concept of ubiquitous mass communication proposed in this book is so named because it is based on the ubiquitous network. Ubiquitous mass communication refers to ubiquitous network–based personalized communication provided to all people. It is simultaneously many-to-many and one-to-one communication. It is both "with public" and "without public." It is the communication of all people to all people, and it is also a one-on-one communication. Immersive communication seems to pull us back to the ancient communication without a public, but the immersive non-mass communication is different from the original. It is based on the "non-public" of the overall mass communication, but the personalized information service is realized under the background of being "with public" and is also the result of any service provided to any person at any time and in any place.

The main differences between the concepts of "mass," "focused," and "ubiquitous" are as follows. Mass: one-to-many, one-to-all; focused: one-to-minority, one-to-some; ubiquitous: many-to-many, one-to-one. Many-to-many means that ubiquitous communication is the communication of all people to all people; one-to-one refers to the personalized information services that it provides on the basis of positioning a single service object, and it is also the effect after the realization of any service provided anytime, anywhere, to anyone.

The definition of new media by *Wired* magazine is similar: "[t]he communication of all people to all people." Contrasting with the original "non-mass" and mass communication, the concept of ubiquitous mass means that one person becomes a public and the public is everywhere. In the context of ubiquitous communication, the meaning of media will evolve into a personalized service centered

The formation of "the third media age"   133

on everyone. It is both mass and non-mass communication, which is both focused and non-focused.

Television was the most powerful medium in the first media age dominated by traditional media; the second media age was characterized by interaction and two-way communication after the "media information" revolution in the 1990s, so the Internet was the most influential. After the first media age and the second media age, humans entered the third media age, dominated by immersive communication. People live in both the physical world and the virtual world at the same time. The society is fully mediated. Society, the environment, and people themselves become media, forming a unique method and mode of communication. This has profoundly changed the production and lifestyle of the immersive communicators living in it and reconstructed their social forms.

If we say that the physical meaning of the earth is the first space on which human beings rely for survival, and the spiritual meaning of space is the second living space for human beings, then the environment with physical and spiritual dimensions, connected by the IOT, the ubiquitous network, and the virtual world, is the third space. The integration of these three spaces forms immersive space, the overall space for human existence that is produced by the third media age and what human beings rely upon in the third media age.

7.2.2 The characteristics of "the third media age"

The third media age is characterized by immersive communication. Because immersive communication is people-oriented, ubiquitous, omnipresent, and omnipotent, it forms its own unique media age characteristics.

1) The era of ubiquitous integration: the era of borderless sharing

The third media age is the media of social form based on ubiquitous connection as the main technology, so it must have the characteristics of the U era. It is an era of integration and an era of borderlessness; it embraces all forms of media and embraces all forms of culture.

In 1984, Toffler wrote that an information bomb is exploding among us. It's an image of shrapnel. It's like a heavy downpour coming to us. It drastically changes the way in which each of us feels and acts in the inner world ... It also changes our psychology. "Value systems splinter and crash, while the lifeboats of family, church, and state are hurled madly about" (Toffler, 1980, p. 18). Today, it is no longer an information bomb but a new revolution in information technology that changes human existence and lifestyles and determines human self-cognition. How do different regions and different groups understand the integration of the ubiquitous network with globalization? How do they welcome or resist, succumb or adapt, or simply accept it? In *The Amish Get Wired*, published in 1993, Levinson describes an interesting example. Amish people, who are not supposed to be easily influenced by new technologies, do not simply reject all the new technology around them, but select it carefully on the basis of being helpful without

134   *The formation of "the third media age"*

disrupting their existing lives. For example, they do not want to set up telephones at home, but many years ago, they built personal "telephone booths" on the edge of their property and used them occasionally. Later, they also finally got online, and this major change in the way they accept information has affected their overall lifestyle (Levinson, 1993).

Ubiquitous strategy uses connectivity in technology but sharing in culture. It is in just such a process of cultural technology hybridization or questioning modernity that human society is constantly moving toward modernity and postmodernity. In the process of promoting all cultural and institutional models of hegemonic countries to the world, people of different cultures and nationalities have different reactions. Some oppose annexation, while some are infected and start to imitate. For example, Aztecs changed the etiquette imposed by Spanish conquistadors and utilized "syncretisme" with their own conventions; there are also reterritorializations of foreign things. This is the view of Michel de Certeau in his book *Art de faire. L'invention du quotidian.* He argued that there is a constant interactive relationship between the imposed system and its users, which can be extended to the marginal practice of disciplinary settings currently engaged in by "ordinary people" (Certeau, 1980).

From the so-called "network determinism," we can see the process from the emergence of the Internet to the third media age based on "Internet determinism." Of course, the so-called "mobile civilization" begins with entity. It can be said that it began with the laying of the first railway in the United Kingdom. Chevalier believes that the material network of transport and the spiritual network of financial credits have the function of connecting large social organisms. Transportation not only shortens the distance between people but also reduces the gap between classes. It is also the only way to create equality and implement democracy.

Let us trace history back to the internationalization of social networks. When the First International was founded in London in 1864, its charter read: "Liberation labor is not a local or national issue but a social one. It includes all countries that exist in modern society." The large-scale international expo, another form of political cooperation, came into being and made Paris, which has hosted five of the international expos, the "cultural capital of the 19th century." The first exposition was held in the Crystal Palace in London in 1851. It witnessed the start of the first international underwater cable connecting Dover and Calais, while the 1900 exhibition gave the world a glimpse of the cinema. Movies brought the wide communication of myths into the age of images and are often considered another symbol of the end of inequality between different classes and countries.

As early as 1852, *The Silent Revolution* predicted the harmony of human society based on a computer network. The submarine cable is closely related to the prosperity of Great Britain. The first submarine cable was started in 1851 and connected to the financial districts of Calais and Dover as well as Paris and London. The telephone was invented by Edison in 1876 and managed by a bilateral agreement. It was not until 1956, when the first transatlantic submarine cable came into service, that the telephone became truly international. In 1962, the launch of the first artificial satellite, "Telstar One," ushered in the age of television.

The formation of "the third media age" 135

In the ten years after the first wave of mergers and acquisitions in the 1980s, the information superhighway promoted another wave of networks: the desire to restructure the content of the television networks spurred the union of studios and networks such as Disney-ABC and the amalgamation of communication groups, most notably the formation of the Time-Warner-Turner Communication Group. The electronic society had begun to prepare itself for the whole-network era.

2) The age of humanity: the age of freedom for the physical and the spiritual cutting across each other

The third media age emerged on the basis of the overall promotion of information communication technology, and it occurred under circumstances in which the communication technology and communication elements had a strong intersection. It was also an inevitable result of the trend of humanization. It was driven by humans' yearning for more advanced life forms and higher quality of life.

Judging from the common trend of technology and human nature, higher-level media forms will be driven by the latest technology, which can meet the needs of human production and life to the maximum extent. Biological media will be the most likely new media form in the future, from which the highest form of immersive media development can be inferred, because it can better meet the needs of humanization and individuation.

As a biological person, symbolic person, and social person, the identity of a "human" changes with the change of media composition, which then directly affects the multiple relationships of social compositions or social systems. Benjamin is optimistic about how to evaluate the media and its role in society, while Adorno and Habermas are pessimistic. Poster agrees more with Benjamin that the disappearance of traditional communities brings people psychological discomfort, but new media can be used to try to solve this problem.

Any interactive process of communication integrating into society will reconstruct social relations. The word "cell" in "cellphone" is polysemic, which means that the mobile phone can not only move like the "cell" of an organism but also, like those cells, generate a new society, new possibilities, and new relationships wherever it goes. From another point of view, the word "cell" (as in prison) describes the function of a cell phone, which not only opens up new possibilities for reproduction but also forces users to keep in touch, thus locking us into a cage with nowhere to hide and where we are always on call (Levinson, 2004).

Today, the telephone is no longer a luxury but a necessity. The old cells continue to generate new cells. With the continuous humanization of technology, people can dial, surf the Internet, and go shopping anytime and anywhere. Everything can be realized in mobile life. A statistical report released by The Mobile World, a British telecom analysis company, says that the global telephone penetration rate has reached 100%; that is, the number of global telephone users is equal to the total population (Gao, 2012). Specifically, the total number of telephone users in the world has reached 6.92 billion. Mobile phone users account for the vast majority of them, reaching 5.6 billion, while fixed phone users only number 1.32

136 *The formation of "the third media age"*

billion.[1] John Tysoe, principal analyst at The Mobile World, said: "The telecommunications industry has once again subverted the forecast that growth will slow down" (Gao,2012).

The ubiquitous network is a large space that contains the mobile Internet and the IOT. 2005 was the year of Myspace, the rise of the online community. 2006 was the year of YouTube when online video sparked. 2007 was the Second Life year, when the virtual society officially entered the life of human beings and opened up another aspect of life. Second Life, which is a combination of Web 1.0 and Web 2.0 and 3D, has become a new sought-after favorite. The dynamic venture capital circle has smelled numerous business opportunities, and it doesn't care how many unresolved problems exist between the virtual and the real. Only when the virtual world is integrated with the physical world can it achieve great development. China's Second Life has problems such as currency not being able to circulate within the real world, which affects the penetration and expansion of the virtual world in the real world. Following the Second Life pattern, China's "Kaixin" ("Happy Network") was formed. Although it can't realize the direct exchange of virtual currency and real money, it also introduced the full "eat, live, and travel" needs of human life. It was sought after by white-collar workers, who are worried about the soaring price of real estate and the difficulty of parking. They squeezed into the Internet to cook, grow vegetables, snap up parking spaces, and realize the dream of buying a house. Office workers who "steal vegetables" and "buy houses" on the Internet are spending a lot of time and energy every day to participate in the construction of a virtual world because of the need for entertainment, wealth ownership, spiritual sustenance, and a sense of accomplishment.

With the continuous satisfaction of human needs realized by technology and creativity, human social relations are also reconstructed in the fusion of the physical world and the virtual world. Unlike the second media age, the third media age is the penetration of the virtual world and the real world. The boundary between the virtual and the physical is gradually blurred. At the same time, the reality is virtualized and the virtuality realized. People not only need to roam in the virtual world; they also need to interact in the physical world, including interactions on the earth and in space. People live in two worlds at the same time, and their identities in both worlds can be the same or different. Whether it is the physical existence or the spiritual existence of human beings, they can travel freely in both worlds, thus satisfying their information needs, psychological needs, aesthetic needs, and so on. The dividing lines between the physical world and the virtual world are rapidly fading out and disappearing in ways and at speeds that we can't imagine.

---

1 The Mobile World stated that the telephone penetration rate it makes is based on the U.S. Census Bureau's estimate of the world's population. The U.S. Census Bureau has estimated the total population of the world at 6.92 billion people.

The formation of "the third media age" 137

3) The era of intelligence: the era of highly automated information

The third media age is an age of intelligence. People's work, life, and entertainment are all accomplished under a highly automated information system. All this will be described in more detail in the next chapter, "Immersive communicators and their production and lifestyle characteristics."

We discussed the smart earth and the U era earlier in some detail, but a little historical review is in order. In February 1993, the Clinton administration announced Gore's plan for the construction of the information superhighway. At the end of the same year, a white paper submitted by Jacques Droll, then president-in-office of Europe, launched the European Information Highway Project, advocating the mobilization of the overall industrial machinery in Europe. Growth, competitiveness, and employment were his three themes. In May 1994, under the chairmanship of Martin Bangemann, a team of 20 major industrialists presented a report entitled "Europe and the Global Information Society," which details the financial and strategic orientation of the Information Superhighway Project (Mattelart, 2007, p. 118).

All technologies are the embodiment of people's thinking, and changes in the media form have distinct characteristics of the times. In the United States, the era of print communications produced the "newspaper president" Grover Cleveland; the age of radio broadcasting gave birth to President Roosevelt and his warm-hearted "Fireside Chat." President Kennedy began and ended with live television, while the online interaction era of national microblogs produced the first online president, Obama. These are the direct results of the interaction between social environment and media forms in different historical times. The role and function of media in social development have changed from being a part of society to becoming the characteristics of society itself. Freya Mathews believes that the holism theory connects every specific self (each self is a self-developing system) with its entirety. The whole purpose of the universe itself will be integrated with the existence and purpose of the individual self (including humans) (Mathews, 1991). Various factors influence the existence of media and human beings. The overall concept of media ecology in immersive communication demonstrates, to some extent, the common countermeasures and the survival wisdom of mankind in the face of the future development of the earth.

In the age of the third media, guided by immersive communication, human productions and lifestyles are highly intelligent. These intelligences are embodied in the fact that the media is an extension of the human brain, an extension of the human hand, an extension of human will, and an extension of human imagination. The human environment in the third media age is full of intelligent terminals, which at any time and in any place constantly send and collect information (in a way without our awareness), affecting our judgments and even determining our behavior. The function of the human brain as a command center can sometimes give way to a cloud-driven brain that exercises the power to perform the tasks of life and work on our behalf through a preset agenda. We can buy food and switch on the air conditioner by remote control. We don't really need to do anything:

138 The formation of "the third media age"

as soon as the thought flashes through our mind, our body and the surrounding intelligent terminals will automatically enter the work immediately, through the ever-connected "ubiquitous" network, completing a series of procedures such as making a phone call, setting up an appointment, or arranging a trip.

In the third media age of wisdom, various smart services are invisible around us. Because they are invisible, intangible, or even insensible, some fear a modern panoramic prison, but in general, as the center of all this intelligent service, humans can fully enjoy extreme convenience of work and life, leading to physical and psychological satisfaction.

The revolutions of communication technology and humanization trends bring about change of communication modes, and the change of communication mode brings about deep change of social forms and social structures. Historically, human communication has been experienced through ancient oral communication, medieval handwritten communication, modern printing communication, modern electronic communication, and the immersive communication discussed in this book. These five major historical stages alternate and feature different media upgrades, which are, to a certain extent, a manifestation of human communication's desire to expand the scope of communication, to increase the efficiency of communication, and to satisfy diverse information needs.

Modern print communication produced the first media age. Modern electronic communication produced the second media age. Today's immersive communication forms the full integration of human and media, the physical world and the virtual world, and realizes the provision of any information service to anyone at any time and anywhere, producing a new media age guided by immersive communication—the third media age.

7.3 Summary

After the preceding discussion on the relationship between media forms, modes of transmission, and the development of social structures, it is possible to demonstrate the transformative and mutually reinforcing relationship between social relations and modes of communication. The first media age was characterized by reading, listening, and watching, mainly passive one-way communication. The second media age featured interactive and interpersonal communication. Now, in the era of immersion, individuals have jumped in and become avatars, becoming a part of computer games and media. Once immersive communication became the main mode of communication, the advent of the third media age was announced.

There are three inevitable reasons for the advent of this third media age. First, the transformation of media ontology brings about the transformation of social productivity. Second, the reform of the media space brings about the transformation of the social space. Third, the change of the function of the media in society brings about changes in social relations. The ubiquitous network turns everything around people into a medium, tangible or intangible, including the environment itself. They all become media that can transmit and collect information, interacting with people at any time and in any place. Humans deeply integrate information

The formation of "the third media age" 139

communication into their lives without being aware of it, profoundly changing the relationship between the media and people.

In this era of ubiquitous communication, which is physically based on the ubiquitous networks and characterized by immersive communication, several elements are important.

(1) The maturation of the ubiquitous network is the material basis and technical prerequisite for the emergence of the third media age. Based on the concept of ubiquitous communication, the UNS, a new global informationization development strategy that focuses on U (ubiquitous) characteristics, replaces the e (electronic) rejuvenation strategy that emerged at the turn of the century. In 2009, the ITU defined the key features of the ubiquitous network in its "Y. 2002 Standard Proposal" and proposed "5C" and "5Any," emphasizing the omnipotent function of the ubiquitous network and its ubiquitous coverage. The foundational technology for immersive communication is its comprehensive "connectivity" capabilities, namely the high-intensity intersection of "connectivity" (C4) and 5W, which also reflects the core target appeal of the U strategy. The U strategy's ubiquitous nature and needs must inevitably promote the full integration of various communications technologies into human production and life. This new goal of human information communication is higher than the information society and represents the new highest realm of modern information technology for human production and life.

(2) Immersive communication is the dominant form of communication in the third media age. The assumptions and arguments in the previous chapters, especially the three model diagrams and the table of immersive communication proposed in Chapter 5, provide the basis for the demonstration of the arrival of the third media age. In Chapter 6, on the basis of the immersive communication model, we presented a division map of the three media ages—the immersive communication function model matrix diagram. After analysis of the various intersections, the division of the three media ages was proposed. When all intersections are high intensity, and when everything in the technology has converged, communication can meet any need of any object anywhere, at any time, and on any network. In other words, when immersive communication is fully realized, the new media era will come into existence.

(3) Ubiquitous mass communication distinguishes the third media age from the first media age of mass communication and the second media age of focused communication. The ubiquitous mass communication model proposed in this book refers to the ubiquitous network–based, personalized communication provided to all people. It is both many-to-many and one-to-one communication. The main differences between the concepts of "mass," "focused," and "ubiquitous" are as follows. Mass: one-to-many, one-to-all; focus: one-to-minority, one-to-some; ubiquitous: many-to-many, one-to-one. Many-to-many means that ubiquitous communication is the communication of all people to all people; one-to-one refers to the personalized information

140 *The formation of "the third media age"*

services that provide on the basis of positioning a single service object, and it is also the effect after the realization of any service provided at any time, anywhere, and to anyone.

Television was the most powerful medium in the first media age dominated by traditional media; the second media age was characterized by interaction and two-way communication after the "media information" revolution in the 1990s, so the Internet was the most influential. After the first media age and the second media age, humans entered the third media age, dominated by immersive communication. People live in both the physical world and the virtual world at the same time. Society is fully mediated. Society, the environment, and people themselves become media, forming a unique method and mode of communication. This has profoundly changed the production and lifestyle of the immersive communicators living in it and has reconstructed social forms.

The third media age features a media society technically based on the ubiquitous connection, so it must have the characteristics of the U era.

(1) The third media age is an age of ubiquitous integration, a boundless sharing age. It embraces all forms of media and also incorporates all forms of culture. The third media age emerged on the basis of the comprehensive promotion of information communication technology and occurred under the conditions of communication technology and communication elements generating a strong intersection.
(2) The third media age is the most humanized media age, a completely human-centered media age, and an age in which both physical and spiritual freedoms are traversed. Unlike the second media age, the third media age deepens the integration of the virtual world and the physical world. Whether it is the physical existence of human beings or their spiritual existence, it is possible to realize the freedom to cross between the two worlds. Humans' information needs, psychological needs, aesthetic needs, and so on are thus satisfied.
(3) The third media age is an age of intelligence. People's work, life, and entertainment are all realized under a highly automated information system. Various kinds of smart services are invisible around us. Although they are invisible, intangible, or even insensible, people can fully enjoy extreme convenience in work and life and gain physical and psychological satisfaction. All this will be described in more detail in the next chapter.

8 "Immersive communicators" and their production and lifestyle characteristics

As discussed earlier, immersive communication brings about a revolution in the relation between humans and media: humans are media and media are human. This study defines such people as "immersive communicators": they are in the ultimate media state, representing the true super-medium. Immersive communicators also include the subjects of biological media or virtual people. Compared with the past, immersive communicators fundamentally change access to information, lifestyles, production methods, and entertainment methods. Let us first look at the "ubiquitous surprises" described by China Mobile's white paper.

- *Animals have identities:* a QR code is stuck to every sheep in the field and then to every piece of lamb in the supermarket. Consumers can scan the QR code with their mobile phones to learn about the history of the sheep's growth and eating habits, ensuring they eat high-quality meat.
- *Automobiles recognize ownership:* in your car, a radio-frequency tag is embedded with information such as your name and license plate number, with which the car can automatically "recognize" its owner. If car thieves do not decode this tag, the vehicle alarm will automatically sound.
- *Mobile phones are wallets:* an electronic tag with a "wallet" function is combined with the SIM card of a mobile phone, so users can scan their mobile phones to buy groceries, movie tickets, and subway passes.
- *Cameras send photos:* professional cameras can not only take photos intelligently but also send those photos immediately. Their data chips allow photojournalists to transmit their photos to presses in real time.
- *Twenty-four-hour doctors:* the Wireless Sensing "Medical Health Care System" allows doctors to obtain the patient's pulse, blood glucose, and other information remotely, in real time, through sensors placed on the patient's body. The family members of the patient can be authorized to access this information at any time via the Internet.
- *Fully automatic bathroom:* an automatic service system can be installed in the bathroom to help set up flushing modes. If the toilet leaks, the Internet monitoring system will close the valve. You can also remotely monitor the toilet to see if it has been flushed or not. People who did not pass the RFID prescan will be sent home by a spurt of water. Once the toilet paper runs out,

142 *"Immersive communicators" characteristics*

you can press a preset button to ask the supermarket-linked service platform to send toilet paper to your house, checking out automatically through the convenience button in the bathroom.

These are dreams that are constantly being turned into reality. Today, at least 1 billion livestock have QR codes, while hundreds of thousands of citizens take city railways with a casual wave of their mobile phones. At the Beijing Olympic Games, the Xinhua News Agency used several cameras that could support shooting and sending photos simultaneously, which turned out to be a great advantage in communication. The networking and communication technology underlying these dreams is also rapidly gaining popularity in China. China's three major telecom operators, along with many provinces and cities, have issued their respective goals one after another, raising the overall level of competition.

8.1 Information acquisition by immersive communicators

In immersive communication, there are no obstacles to receiving and sending information, and people no longer even feel the presence of media. At the same time, people themselves become media, able to communicate freely with other people or things. Since the advent of electronic media, especially after humans entered the state of interactive communication, the concept of "audience" has been shifting to the concept of "media user." Immersive media not only fully develops the concept of media users, but also completely breaks the boundary between humans and media ontology.

8.1.1 Enhanced identity as audiences/recipients

In immersive communication, the concept of the audience has been further strengthened. People unknowingly receive abundant information from their environment, the latest proof of the "retrieval" and "reversal" of old media forms in McLuhan's famous "four laws of media"(Levinson, 1999, p. 188).

In the traditional media age, people gained most of their knowledge from media; media views, by default, represent views of the majority. Media coverage can influence policies and even international relations. Nowadays, people cannot do without the media, mainly because their communication and life increasingly depend on those media—Xiaonei, MSN, QQ, etc. At the same time, the relationship between humans and media has become alienated and seriously interdependent. People even ask, jokingly, "what will happen to my QQ if I die?" That is because a QQ profile does not just represent a string of numbers but an online identity and a symbol of interpersonal communication, just like the virtual farm, virtual city, and virtual family established, developed, and maintained with this identity symbol. People are unknowingly building a harmonious relationship with media.

The relationship between children, the Internet, and television consistently arouses a mixture of worry and delight among parents and social workers, making it an important concern for scholars. According to a survey by Nielsen in 2010, 36% of children between the ages of 2 and 11 use both media simultaneously. Altogether, children between the ages of eight and ten spend about 5.5 hours each day using media—eight hours if you count the additional media consumed while multitasking (Nielsen, 2010a).

When it comes to the age of immersive communication, immersive communicators, whether they have grown up or not, exhibit more "unconsciousness" in the way they obtain information. Pervasive information in the environment can affect people's judgment at any time, but people seem not to have taken the initiative to obtain that information. All of it has been smartly embedded into their surroundings. For example, a vending machine will recommend the most popular products to you, passing on the product marketing information and advertising to you insensibly. The identity of immersive communicators as the audiences of media is extremely strong. They receive a large amount of information without recognizing the process, which exactly corresponds to the trait of immersive communication as the "hottest" medium: it needs no cooperation from humans.

8.1.2 Enhanced identity as "we media"

If the media is an extension of humans, then immersive communicators have become media for themselves and others, and people are media. In immersive communication, people's identities go from an extension of media to being media themselves. At the same time, the identity of a disseminator returns, seeking not authority but publication. This is the difference between an immersive communicator as a disseminator and a mass media disseminator.

Immersive communicators are habituated to center on "I" to publish information, absolutely practicing the idea that what you publish determines your image. "You are just like what you have published," said Steve Goldstein, the CEO of Alacra, a leading provider of financial business information. "It's better to be famous than not." The development of ubiquitous networks and virtual reality technology for immersive communication enables immersive communicators to have more convenient opportunities for empowerment and release. They express their opinions through real identities and virtual realities, owning more tangible or intangible chances and rights to express their ideas and deliver free speech.

Immediacy and ubiquity have fundamentally changed the limitations of previous media society, where a large-scale communication effect could only be realized by depending on the so-called "big media." In the world of immersive communication, the identities of communicators do not matter. What matters is whether the information disseminated is worthy of attention and of social value. In the eyes of immersive communicators, big media is more often just a readily available database.

The immersive communicator, as a medium, can be said to fully satisfy Levinson's anthropotropic theory: "Man is the active master owner of media. They are not sent out in the media, but to give orders to create media content. For the content that others have created, people have an unprecedented capacity

144 *"Immersive communicators" characteristics*

for self-selection" (Levinson, 1999, pp. 40–41). People are naturally interested in being disseminators. Internet news has been called the "pajamas media," and independent bloggers are called "pajama pundits" because they can pull all-nighters on virtual networks, making it a priority in their lives to deliver messages. If they are willing, every immersive communicator can write a book and play the role of publisher. They dominate the content and channel of dissemination.

The "power" status of news communication needs to be redefined. For a long time, news served as the "fourth force" in the United States after the president, the Congress, and the Supreme Court. In *Agents of Power*, scholar J. Herbert Altschull claimed that the media is the institution of social control. News is power, or to be clear, in order to obtain and maintain power, it is necessary to control the means of news dissemination (Altschull, 1988). The authority and power of traditional media are reflected in the fact that the audience will not question the authenticity of the information they transmit. Under sophisticated arrangements such as agenda setting, the media will influence their audience's thoughts, feelings, and judgments. Traditional media try hard to obtain and maintain the status that can determine their audience's values and cultural orientation. Their power is reflected in their influence on recipients. In an immersive communication system, everyone becomes a communicator (disseminator), with our society being a major news agency. It is true that the power of the overall news dissemination in society has been not whittled down but greatly enhanced, which can be said to represent a transfer of power.

In the schematic diagram of the immersive communication relationship model given in Chapter 5, each person has a personal information space centered on himself or herself, and each person's space is intertwined with and contained in the larger information space of the society. So, what happens to the bodies of the "immersive communicators" when they act as media? They become discarnate (Levinson, 1999, p. 57): though separated from the physical body, they can be heard on the phone, seen in the video, and transmitted anywhere in a flash via electronic media. An immersive communicator as a medium, so to speak, reflects a spiritual existence divorced from the body.

8.2 The lifestyle of immersive communicators

What kinds of changes will people's lives undergo in immersive communication?

In Japan, the Ministry of Internal Affairs portrays the lifestyle of immersive communicators in its fantastic vision of the U era. It shares great similarity with ideas about the U era in China and other countries. Figures 8.1 through 8.8 depict the morning of an old Japanese man. His residence is far from the hospital and none of his grandchildren are around. The old man relies on ubiquitous terminals to keep in touch with his family and the outside world (Guo, 2007).

In this case of "intelligent" or "ubiquitous" living, sensors in the environment can sense the old man at any moment. In immersive communication, your information is constantly collected by sensors, while sometimes you also serve as a

Figure 8.1 The old man is doing morning exercises in the park

sensor for others. Hence, the exchange of information is constantly carried out between the two parties and in the entire space.

In a society of ubiquitous intelligence, information collection and management are processed intelligently through a logistics network and ubiquitous network. Terminal readers hidden in the environment are collecting information constantly. When customers pick goods up, they know simultaneously which ones are popular and which are in short supply. Customers can also enjoy the most thoughtful and customized service. There seems to be an "invisible man" reading your thoughts and helping you get things done at the same time. Immersive communication does give rise to new problems, such as personal privacy issues. People do not realize that they may be monitored at any moment. The whole environment may function just like a modern panopticon. In the meantime, your information collected by immersive media can also be used as a tool to discriminate against you.

In general, though, immersive communication is in many cases distinguished from traditional monitoring. Immersive communicators can choose self-surveillance, participating in a "voluntary panopticon" by actively choosing to monitor themselves or be monitored. Generally speaking, self-surveillance occurs in the moments involving consumption, fame, or security. When people think it is in their interests, they will choose to do so. For example, an immersive communicator may have others (or himself) record his performance or natural behaviors for later playback, or re-examine a secular behavior from a new perspective and endow it with new meanings, so as to make himself feel fulfilled and delighted.

e-Commerce linked with the ubiquitous network also infiltrates itself into the life of immersive communicators. People purchase a large number of goods from the Internet, such as electronic products and clothing. Online sales have begun to greatly affect the sales of offline consumer goods. Immersive communicators

146 *"Immersive communicators" characteristics*

Figure 8.2 A live sensor in the park reminds the old man: "Your heart rate is higher than normal"

do not only shop or consume this way; they relate to the world differently than before. Immersive communication enables people to have an all-around understanding of the world via various channels. As a result, the sense and sensibility of life are improved. Immersive communicators seek the joy of life and emotional attachment in both the physical world and the virtual world at the same time, thus earning a sense of belonging in both these worlds and integrating them together naturally.

Figure 8.3 The old man receives a remote diagnosis by a doctor

"Immersive communicators" characteristics 147

Figure 8.4 The doctor pulls up the man's electronic medical records and determines that excessive exercise leads to high blood pressure

8.3 The production mode of immersive communicators

The production mode of immersive communicators is also intelligent: "remote presence" and "ubiquity" exist simultaneously in both the virtual and the physical world. People can work and most likely entertain themselves anytime and anywhere. As aforementioned, the boundaries between the production, life, and entertainment of immersive communicators have disappeared. Instead, these

Figure 8.5 Ubiquitous terminals tip (alert): the man's granddaughter Shizuka wants to talk with him

148 *"Immersive communicators" characteristics*

Figure 8.6 Shizuka wants to learn how to make a paper airplane

spaces are overlapping, and mutually inclusive. Work is like entertainment, and people keep working in daily life.

When people lived a farming lifestyle, there was no boundary between work and leisure. For example, in traditional American Amish and Mennonite communities, people work from sunrise to sunset and do weaving or carpentry labor at their leisure, along with some singing or reading. These activities are both practical and productive from material and spiritual perspectives. Of course, such a primitive life based on farming seems to have stagnated in our time node of

Figure 8.7 The old man teaches Shizuka how to make a paper airplane through video

Figure 8.8 Shizuka waves goodbye to the old man

technology and spiritual development. Is this the only way humans can produce and entertain themselves at the same time? Of course not.

Immersive people constantly seek out activities that are not only productive but also bring the most immersive experiences to life. In the past, people often divided their lives into boring work and unchanging entertainment, in which neither working all day nor devoting all their time to entertainment was an ideal state. What immersive communicators are looking for is a perfect combination of the two. Of course, such a state of intersection seems to have emerged from the telephone's entry into people's bedrooms as a more modern form of life than farming. It intensified after the invention of the mobile phone; it became pervasive after the online virtual world became popular; and in the era of intelligent ubiquitous networks, we have finally achieved great integration of production, life, and entertainment.

The way in which immersive communicators create work value is bound to change fundamentally to be very efficient and convenient. Especially with the support of cloud computing in ubiquitous communication, we can travel anywhere in the whole world, completing work anytime and anywhere, all without being trapped in the office. We need not even carry laptops with us, because the terminals that allow us to search for information or enter work are all around. A large electronic head hangs in the sky to carry all your data, accompanying you at all times. You can log in at any time and in any place and start to work, no matter whether it is local, remote, or mobile. Products needed to facilitate the work of immersive communicators are also constantly being created. For example, in December 2011, the American company Autodesk released a simple and practical China-specific online software for AutoCAD in its R&D center in Shanghai, announcing that it might satisfy the cloud requirements.

150 *"Immersive communicators" characteristics*

Just as we often find that making the best use of leisure requires work-like intellect and concentration, immersive communicators will also find that to make work really interesting, one must put aside cultural prejudice and make the work personally meaningful. As Csikszentmihalyi mentioned in *Flow: The Psychology of Optimal Experience*, highly personalized occupations are more likely to bring people inherent gains, because the people concerned can freely choose goals and set the task difficulty. The work experience of artists, entrepreneurs, politicians, and scientists with high productivity and creativity is mostly similar to that of our ancestors in the hunting period, who fully integrated work into life. Such work is also the most likely to lead to an immersive sense of happiness.

Novel gadgets that contribute to the integration of work and entertainment keep entering the market. On April 5, 2012, Google's smart glasses debuted. According to a YouTube video showcasing the new product, by wearing these stylish glasses with a modern high-tech feel, you can use map navigation by voice commands, interact with friends, start a video chat, and even shoot pictures and video. You can also add calendars to manage your daily routine. If you want to know what the weather is like today, you only need to look up at the sky to see an automatic display of weather information, which is achieved through virtual reality technology. Once wearing these eyeglasses, you can get a lot of work done by simply giving commands.

It should be a pleasant state for immersive communicators to integrate work with entertainment and merge life with work. However, when something shifts from scarcity to excess, it often changes from a popular innovation to an annoyance. For example, when people can enter entertainment from work at any time, it becomes an overload. Mobile phones have become a necessity for work and life. On the one hand, the phone is your mobile office and remote control for everything in your house. On the other hand, it will eventually give you almost nowhere to escape. Can you really refuse to communicate? Recall Levinson's words in *Cellphone: The Story of the World's Most Mobile Medium and How It Has Transformed Everything*:

> The first way to deal with the avalanche that haunts people all day is to admit that refusing to communicate is a reasonable choice … Freedom of communication—mobile homes provided by mobile phones—of course includes the freedom not to communicate. In fact, if we live in a world where we constantly communicate with everyone no matter we are willing or not, that kind of communication is almost meaningless … In that sense, it is no longer humanized and it is no longer a free expression of personal will but an unconditioned reflex like eating and drinking.
>
> (Levinson, 2004, p. 58)

Although Levinson optimistically believes that "the world of irresistible, ubiquitous communication will never come," the changes in production and life caused by ubiquitous communication are already a reality, even without the awareness of immersive communicators. It took 75 years for the phone to enter 50% of U.S. households.

"Immersive communicators" characteristics 151

Not until the 1950s did the earliest mobile phones enter the cars of the rich. By contrast, it only took 10 years for the commercial television developed in the late 1950s to completely penetrate American households. Starting in the early 1980s, Macs and personal computers reached over 50% of U.S. homes in less than 20 years. Now, driven by national determination, the rate of optical fiber-to-home is rapidly growing on a global scale. The U era, which is connected by a fiber ribbon and serves as the basis for social operations, is already here, while the space where the immersive communicators work and live resembles a smart and fun Disney-like fairytale world with rapidly rotating technology wheels.

It can be said that immersive communicators are more likely to secure achievements in their work, because successful people tend to be those who can perfectly combine work and leisure. Csikszentmihalyi (1997) noted that in nearly 100 interviews with Nobel laureates and leaders from all walks of life, he heard two ideas over and over:

> "You could say that I worked every minute of my life, or you could say with equal justice that I never worked a day." The historian John Hope Franklin expressed this blending of work and leisure most concisely when he said, "I have always subscribed to the expression 'Thank God it's Friday' because to me Friday means I can work for the next two days without interruptions."
>
> (p. 61)

The flow of mind elicited by immersion is also most often seen in those professional activities where work and leisure are integrated. Although the use of cutting-edge knowledge and technology is inseparable from inner struggles and arduous explorations, the gains after laborious work and the joy when you expand your mind to a new field are the greatest features of a fulfilled life. From the perspective of work, the American poet Mark Strand makes the concept of psychological immersion very clear: "'you're right in the work, you lose your sense of time, you're completely enraptured, you're completely caught up in what you are doing ... when you are working on something and you are working well, you have the feeling that there's no other way of saying what you're saying'" (Csikszentmihalyi,1997, p. 62).

Immersive communicators improve their personal life quality through work, which happens to prove that the sense of pleasure brought about by immersion does not depend on external conditions, but on our working attitude and the experiences and feelings we gain in the face of challenges. Of course, work is definitely not the entire life of immersive communicators: even the workaholics among them lead colorful lives.

8.4 The entertainment of immersive communicators

Since the end of the 20th century, the idea of an entertainment economy has fascinated many people. It seems that everything in the world is just for fun. If many entertained out of commercial interest at that time, then in the current era of

152 *"Immersive communicators" characteristics*

immersive communication, entertainment seems to be an integral and constitutive part of an immersive communicator's life.

The quality of a person's life depends largely on his or her use of leisure; likewise, the quality of a society is also influenced by the leisure methods its members adopt. Therefore, whether it is on a personal level or on a social level, leisure habits are both causes and effects for the quality of human life. The importance of leisure is evident. However, excessive reliance on leisure may also cause people to exhaust too much energy and time that should have been saved for the challenges of a high-difficulty technology and economy. Immersive communicators find a balanced solution. As mentioned in the previous section, immersive communicators combine work and leisure, making work as entertaining and enjoyable as leisure. In addition, when you stop working, leisure will be completely entertaining and will not slow you down mentally.

The age of immersive communication is also an era of innovation and creativity. This era, whether in the physical world or the virtual world, is filled with attractive things to do, as long as you have imagination and energy. Immersive communicators develop their full potential during leisure time, thus making themselves scientists, artists, inventors, or any social role they dream about. These roles can be realized in either the physical world or the virtual world, or in both.

Immersive communicators live partially in the "virtual society." The virtual world represents some of humanity's dreams. Virtual societies such as online forums in the early days, such as China's "Xici Hutong," have their own set of social rules—in this case, forum rules representing the simple and honest folk customs of the South Nanjing Hutong. The people in Xici Hutong have their own names. "Xiangma" was the first renowned name in Xici, and the oldest household recognized is Aunt Zhang of the 15th Hutong, who is the director of the neighborhood committee of Xici Hutong. In the physical world, Nanjing is seen as the place where the sense of Chinese civil life is the most obvious. People did not expect the emergence of a virtual society such as "Nanjing's Zero Distance," a civic TV news program, which is as sincere as the host Meng Fei. There was also "Love Apartment" in the early days of the virtual world, along with the "Cohabiting Dreamland" game launched by a Taiwanese female website that was earlier known for its Internet cohabitation. Initially, seeking cohabitation online was viewed as "challenging secularism." However, by 2005, instances of "online cohabitation" had reached 100,000 (Netease Technology, 2005).

As most immersive communicators inhabit the virtual world, "immigrants" there have put forward higher and higher requirements for the management and life quality of virtual societies. Immersive communicators create content on their own, and at the same time, managers for the virtual world are also constantly improving their professional standards as "world makers." Simulation technology must make the virtual world more attractive than the physical world, giving free rein to an important function of intelligence or post-informatization, which is to give people "entertainment to death," that is, great satisfaction and joy in entertainment.

As to the satisfaction obtained in the virtual world, people naturally hope that they can get a copy in real life. The Ghent city research team found that people's positions in modern big cities in the world depend to a large extent on variants of consumerism advocating the principle of happiness. These variants are constantly creating and implementing the prevalence of "satisfaction and joy," and they thus become a very important economic driver of urban material and social development (Ghent Urban Studies Team, 2005). It is worth pondering that social reality can be considered man-made as well. The world around us can be seen as the virtual world of various buildings and products brought about by industrialization. The modern cities where people live are only the continuous recreation of artificial and virtual reality, and the artificial world contains all the natural landscape.

Immersive communicators seek happiness in the real world, on the one hand, but on the other hand, they immerse themselves in the virtual world. Leisure is often seen as a necessary condition for happiness, but in fact it is not. Some things can enrich people's lives in moderation but will have counterproductive effects in excess. As a result, psychiatrists and sociologists in the mid-20th century warned that too much leisure time could be a social disaster.

Of course, when the virtual world is truly integrated with the physical world, there will be problems such as false information and legal issues. For example, cyberbullying uses false identification to hurt people. One well-known case is Lolita Drew of Myspace, who achieved the purpose of harming people in the name of love. Similarly, because students get preferential treatment when buying tickets for the Chinese Spring Festival, some criminals sell fake student ID cards on the Internet, which are even equipped with magnetic strips and anti-counterfeiting measures. Because of these fraudulent purchases, genuine students could have trouble buying tickets (Bao, 2012).

Negative examples like this have historically aroused sighs of concern in theoretical circles worldwide, especially after the invention of such media as telephones, movies, and television. At the beginning of the 20th century, critics worried that movies would have a negative impact on children's development. For example, in a 1910 article in *Good Housekeeping Magazine* entitled "Motion Pictures: A Primary School for Criminals," Kansas professor William A. Mckeever argued that because children spent their afternoons in dark and humid cinemas, movies were destroying the backbone of our future. Mckeever's complaints about films included that they were "instilling directly in the senses" (Mckeever, 1910). In the middle of the 20th century, the danger zone became comic books and television. Marie Winn's *The Plug-In Drug* is probably the most famous attack on TV. She believed watching TV was addictive, like taking drugs (Winn, 1977). Jerry Mander was even more aggressive. He said seriously in his 1978 publication *Four Arguments for the Elimination of Television* that watching TV might result in cancer (Mander, 1978). Postman's *Technopoly: The Surrender of Culture to Technology*, called computer and television pollution a good way to contaminate the spiritual life (Postman, 1993).

Sven Berkitz is also famous for his critique of electronic media. In 1994, he mourned the fate of reading books in the electronic age in *Gutenberg's Elegy*.

154 *"Immersive communicators" characteristics*

However, many parents think that computers are actually helping children instead of preventing them from doing their homework. At the end of the 20th century, the Internet became the culprit. In 1996, the federal government of the United States wanted to implement the Communication Decency Act, but it was eventually ruled unconstitutional by the Supreme Court. The provisions of the bill included the following: if you publish "indecent" materials which can be easily seen by children on the Internet, you may be fined $100,000 and sentenced to two years' imprisonment (United States Congress, 1996).

Correspondingly, the data from the Survey Report on the Use of Internet/ Social Networks by Chinese Minors in 2011, issued by China's Young Pioneers Career Development Center, shows that most Chinese parents also believe that surfing the Internet does more harm than good. The report also pointed out that the prevalence of Internet use by minors in China then exceeded 90%, reaching 91.4% and increasing 14.2% over the previous year. Among those minors, children under seven years old accounted for 26.2%. Social networking is likewise popular among Chinese minors: 66.5% of the respondents use QQ, and the penetration rates of Tencent Weibo and Sina Weibo are 18.8% and 11.4%, respectively (China Young Pioneers Career Development Center, 2011).

Compared with the television era, the influence of media on U.S. children is even more intense in the Internet era, as attested by data released by the U.S. non-profit educational institutions Joan Ganz Cooney Center and Sesame Studio in May 2011. Their study aggregated seven statistical studies and pointed out that American children's consumption on digital media keeps increasing. Eighty percent of 0–5-year-old children use the Internet every week, often using more than one digital medium. In addition, of the time that children spend on all types of media, television accounts for a whopping 47%. In one of the surveys, parents indicated that more than 60% of children under age three watch videos online (Gutnick, Robb, Takeuchi, & Kotler, 2011). Accordingly, *USA Today* reported that 80% of children under five use the Internet weekly, drawing the attention of the world (Kessler, 2011). But even given this data, should we try and stop the ubiquitous network? The world will not stop but move forward: as the "Four Laws of Media Effects" point out, it will be enhanced, made obsolete, retrieved, and finally revered, shifting back and forth.

8.5 The future of immersive communicators: The commencement of biological media

What is the result of these highly immersed immersive communicators? Could it be the beginning of the purported "biological media"? Stephan Littlejohn, Karen Foss, and John Oetzel put forward the possibility of the emergence of communibiology in *Theories of Human Communication*:

> As the study of genetics assumed increasing importance, psychologists and other behavioral researchers became interested in the effects of brain function and structure, neurochemistry, and genetic factors in explaining human

behavior. These researchers believe that many of our traits, ways of thinking, and behaviors are wired in biologically and derive not from learning or situational factors, but from inborn neurobiological influences. These theories, which began to gain prominence in the 1990s, are probably best labeled psychobiology, which may be an emerging tradition in its own right ... The term communibiology refers to the study of communication from a biological perspective.

(Littlejohn & Foss, 2008, p. 39)

IBM's 2011 annual report identified five major innovations expected to bring about major changes in human life within five years, including biocommunication, especially related innovative technologies such as "thought reading": "Now the commonly used alphanumeric passwords will be replaced by biometric indicators such as facial recognition, retinal scanning, and voice information." Another innovation is the identification of a person's state of mind. The moment you want to talk to a friend, your phone may automatically dial that number. Bioinformatics research scientists have devised a headset with a sensor that can identify facial expressions, levels of excitement, and even specific thoughts by analyzing human brain waves (IBM, 2011b). IBM has issued technology forecasts for five consecutive years, some of which have already been fulfilled. For example, in 2008, they predicted that people would be able to ask questions and obtain answers directly from the Internet within five years. Apple's iPhone 4S phone came with the artificial intelligence voice assistant Siri, which can be considered to partly achieve this goal.

Professor Xiong Chengyu wrote in 2011:

The future media form will inevitably consolidate the latest scientific and technological achievements to satisfy people's needs to the maximum. After digital media, biological media will be the most likely new media form in the future, because it can better satisfy the more humane and personalized needs.

(Xiong Chengyu, 2011)

Can immersive communicators become the most anticipated "biological medium"? According to relevant research, the relationship between human DNA and organisms is somewhat like the relationship between computer programs and instructions. DNA can combine proteins into living organisms, while ideas can reshape things. The result of thoughts acting on matter is likely to be the emergence of new technologies. It is believed that human thinking will make the biological media technology a material result.

8.6 Summary

This chapter discusses people in immersive communication—immersive communicators—and describes their production and living characteristics. The information acquisition methods, lifestyles, production methods, and entertainment

156 *"Immersive communicators" characteristics*

methods of immersive communicators represent a fundamental change from the past. Many of the good things previously seen as scientific dreams are now being realized.

The information acquisition method of immersive communicators has the characteristics of "receiver" and "self-media" at the same time. In immersive communication, information is accessible in reception and sending, so people no longer feel the presence of media. People themselves become media and can communicate freely with each other and with things. Sensors in the surrounding environment can sense immersive communicators at any time, while information collection and management operate intelligently through the logistics network and the ubiquitous network. Immersive communicators can thus enjoy the most considerate and customized information services.

The lifestyle, production methods, and entertainment methods of immersive communicators are extremely integrated, as they live or work in the media at all times. Immersive communicators find a balanced solution that combines work and leisure, making work as entertaining and enjoyable as leisure. The way immersive communicators create work value has also undergone great changes and become very efficient and convenient. In particular, with the support of cloud computing in ubiquitous communications, a large electronic brain is suspended in the sky, and immersive communicators can access their private data anytime and anywhere to enter a working state, whether they are local or remote, or even on the move.

Immersive communicators are also different in how they connect to the world. Immersive communication enables people to understand the world with an all-around view at any time and place, and thus the rationality and sensitivity of life are improved. Immersive communicators seek the joy of life and emotional reliance in the physical world and the virtual world at the same time, to integrate and obtain a sense of belonging in both worlds. Given these characteristics, the future of immersive communicators may include the commencement of biological media.

9 Conclusion: Immersive communication opens a new chapter in human communication

This study explores immersive communication: its definition, morphological characteristics, modes of communication, and goals and effects. It analyzes the laws of communication and social development, using them to deduce that immersive communication is a new mode of communication based on ubiquity and that it pioneers the arrival of a new communication era—the third media age. If the first media age was a one-way mass communication era, and the second media age emphasizes interactive focused communication, then the third media era is an era of immersive and ubiquitous mass communication.

Immersive communication ushers in a new page in the development of human media. In terms of communicative targets, human communication has roughly gone through a development process of 1) interpersonal communication, 2) mass communication, 3) focused communication, and finally 4) ubiquitous mass communication. Likewise, in terms of communicative characteristics, it has gone through 1) primitive communication, 2) one-way communication, and 3) interactive two-way communication, before finally reaching 4) immersive communication.

The electronic technology invented 100 years ago enabled human communication to begin to emphasize interaction and focus. But "interaction" and "focus" are insufficient terms to describe the current status of human social communication: immersion has succeeded interaction. Immersion is a new concept that communication scholars have attended to throughout the 21st century. It was originally used to describe people's state of "remote presence" and obliviousness of themselves in virtual reality and the Internet world. In the past decade, however, immersive communication methods have become more popular. They have had a profound impact on our lives with the development of the mobile Internet, the IOT, the ubiquitous network, and even budding biological communication technologies, along with the spread of "smart cities" and "smart worlds."

As a novel concept, immersive communication represents a brand-new approach to information communication. It describes an ever-present, omnipresent, and omnipotent media that is people centered and based on a broad environment connecting all forms of media. It is also a dynamically customized communication process that enables a person to fully focus and be fully focused

158 *Conclusion*

on. The ideal communication effect it achieves is an imperceptibly ubiquitous experience (invisible, intangible, and insensible) that transcends time and space. Immersive communication has brought about breakthroughs in people's information communication methods, production, and lifestyles.

The immersive communication defined in this study is built on the global ubiquitous connection. It expands human communication from "remoteness" to "ubiquity" and then expands the communication space to the entire human environment that integrates the virtual world and the physical world. As a result, it reconstructs the three "spaces" of human society and the relationship between the media and humans. Immersive communication extends, in an all-around way, humans' vision, hearing, touch, and smell. It is not only an indispensable tool for people's wisdom but is also bound to boost the transformation of human beings into biological media.

Immersive communication represents the communication paradigm of the third media age. Compared with any form of communication in the past, immersive communication is nothing less than a profound media revolution:

- Immersive communication is human centered: everything is a medium, and people are media forms.
- Immersive communication is ever-present: the present, the past, and the future are merged; the virtual and the physical exist together; and the instant and the eternal coexist.
- Immersive communication is omnipresent: remoteness and ubiquity are fused together. The fixed, the mobile, and the virtual coexist.
- Immersive communication is omnipotent: boundaries between entertainment, work, and life disappear, as cloud computing and Big Data integrate everything.

9.1 Revolutions in human–media relations

Immersive communication completely reconstructs the relationship between humans and media. It is a people-centered, open media form that contains all new and old media: all tangible and intangible forms of media that can produce, disseminate, display, and receive information. It also includes the environment and even humans themselves as forms of media. People are media forms, and everything is media.

Immersive communication enables the humanization of media to be fully realized. Its communication is completely human centered, but the forms and combinations of communications vary from person to person. According to Levinson's anthropotropic theory, the choice of media in the evolutionary process both formally and functionally supports the "pre-technology" human communication mode. In immersive communication, the role of human beings further evolves: people appear on the core stage as active operators of media and media entities. The human is the ultimate media state, the real super-medium, and the subject of future biological media.

Conclusion   159

This study's schematic diagram of the immersive communication mode (Figure 5.12) illustrates the transformation of the relationship between humans and media. The big circle in the picture represents the entire environment; the many small circles inside it represent remote, ubiquitous, physical, and virtual spaces. This diagram highlights the characteristics of people-centered immersive communication and personally customized information, the essential characteristic of immersive communication. The diagram emphasizes the integration of the virtual world and the physical world in which people live during immersive communication. Likewise, it stresses the existence of cloud computing in immersive communication and its role in allowing people to enter a ubiquitous presence from a remote presence. Finally, it emphasizes the mutual and comprehensive integration of people and the environment, people, and media, as well as the environment and media.

The self is the command center and service center for immersive communication. Arguably, in speech communication, the self is embedded in the face-to-face relationship of direct communication; in print communication, the self is constructed as an actor located in the center of self-discipline; and in electronic communication, the self is in a continuous state of uncertainty and decentralization. However, in immersive communication, the self is in an unambiguously central position, and information can be presented in the form of giving orders or in the form of services that satisfy this requirement.

The revolution brought about by immersive communication does not only alter the traditional information dissemination chain and subvert the concept of "audience" in the traditional sense: it completely reconstructs the definitions of human and media. In immersive communication, people are not only passive information receivers but also active and passive information spreaders. They can be the media itself and part of the environment. Furthermore, the environment itself is a medium. In immersive communication, media have no interface, but are fully integrated with the environment and humans. What lifts immersive communication to the highest level of "humanization" will be the commencement of biological communication.

9.2 Revolution of communication content

The ubiquitous presence of immersive communication leads to a revolution in the content of communication. Timeliness is the dividing line between the old media and the new media: the immersive medium distinguishes itself from all old media in its "ever-present" form. Likewise, its content changes from traditional information to personally customized services anytime and anywhere, from the traditional "sometimes" to the ubiquitous "all the time."

The content of immersive dissemination follows a human-centered open pattern. All new and old media are its contents—immersive communication is the synthesizer and container of all media forms and contents. There are four main forms of immersive language: (1) all previous media languages, (2) pan-media languages in large environments such as city surveillance cameras and

160   *Conclusion*

environmental advertisements, (3) humans as media languages and information content, and (4) the language of the virtual world.

The content of immersive media enters aggressively with its unique language hegemony. However, when it comes to the way immersive communication expresses its ideas, it is a kind of subtle and silent personalized customization, mainly manifested in the packaging of information thoughts into personalized services and demands. After it conducts one-to-one precise positioning, collecting and analyzing the clear requirements of an exclusive object, immersive communication determines the specific means and content of communication with constant adaptation. This process, though, is only an instant flash in the electronic brain of cloud computing and Big Data, which occurs without the conscious awareness of immersive communicators.

The content of immersive communication is also packaged as an entertainment game, which can appear in people's life and work at any time. Therefore, the media advertising and social discourse of immersive communication present a corresponding uniqueness. Immersive media are embedded in our surroundings in the form of various terminals, connected with the ubiquitous network into a common space. Consequently, large environments, including "Smart Earth," are themselves media and media content at the same time. Immersive communication can therefore absorb all the information from the surroundings at all times and then send the information to various terminals (including people). This completely breaks the "central power" of traditional mass communication, making immersive communication a dynamic, multi-polar, and all-encompassing new form of information communication.

Such communication breaks the boundaries of entertainment, work, and life. Communication contents are ever-present and omnipresent. With the help of ubiquitous networks and the virtual world, work and entertainment are often integrated by immersive communication. Games are jobs and jobs are games. This has become an inevitable form of work and life for many people, often promoting the efficiency of work and giving people spiritual pleasure. When people play games, there is a sense of liberation that creates a sense of pleasure, which can also be considered psychological immersion. More and more people are now combining work and games, immersing themselves in this kind of work–life blending scenario. This provides new ways and opportunities for human emotional expression and psychological satisfaction, fundamentally subverting the stereotypical mode of traditional communication.

The profound revolution of immersive communication content is also embodied in the transcendence of time and space, such as agenda setting. For example, after death, because the computer program has already set the agenda, people will continue to receive and send information, and in spirit and in substance, they will exercise their rights and obligations such as voting on issues. Will this not only make people's thoughts infinite, but also make their thinking ability eternal? These possibilities bring new issues to communication and human sociology.

9.3 Revolution of communication methods

Immersive communication supported by the ubiquitous intelligent network truly realizes the omnipresence of communication: the integration of remote presence and ubiquitous presence; the coexistence of the fixed, the mobile, and the virtual; and the co-presence of the instant and the eternal.

Immersive communication methods and processes are based on the all-around connection of modern information technology. The more invisible and the more profound the technology, the more fully integrated it is into everyday life, until no trace is left. All the media functions of immersive communication are hidden in our surroundings, naturally breathed in and serving us invisibly like air.

Immersive communication is likewise interface-free communication, breaking all the limitations of the traditional media. The ubiquitous network turns everything around people into a medium, which can transmit and collect information at any time and place, as well as conduct in-depth interactions and imperceptibly disseminate information into people's lives. There are fewer laptops in Starbucks, and many people no longer even surf the Internet in coffee shops, because there are more mobile terminals connected to the Internet anywhere and anytime: ubiquitous smartphones, iPads, and all the ubiquitous virtual and real worlds under the unified layout of cloud computing. Cloud computing frees us from physical dependence on devices such as computers and provides a unified and ever-thinking brain for all media that are connected to the ubiquitous network, so that we can carry our work and our life with us. The clouds are in the air, making it easy to move around.

The immersive communication method also distinguishes itself from traditional communication methods through its "positioning + customization" service. The three-dimensional spiral diagram of the immersive communication process (see Figure 5.11) emphasizes that the immersive communication process is a dynamic process of constant positioning and three-dimensional ascent. The human-centered trait of immersive communication similarly creates dynamic messages, completely customized to each individual and centered on each individual person. Therefore, each communication process is in fact a cyclical process: positioning, dissemination, feedback, re-positioning, re-dissemination, and re-feedback.

Immersive communication constructed on the ubiquitous connection also perfectly implements location-based services (LBS), which allows you to be discovered by the media at any location and to freely use any information in any location near you. LBS is increasingly becoming a necessity, allowing people to immerse themselves in media services anytime and anywhere. According to ABI Research (2009), "LBS comprises the fastest growing sector in Internet technology businesses with forecasted profit growth from $515 million in 2007 to 13.3 billion in 2013" (Silva & Daniel, 2011).

The concept of "space" in communication has also been redefined by immersive transmission. The difference between immersive communication and traditional media's information movement methods is not confined to the range of "point to surface" or "surface to point." In fact, immersive communication is the

162　*Conclusion*

transmission of information not simply between one or more environments, but across the entire human environment.

Immersive communication methods therefore have the characteristics of environmental media, including physical and virtual spaces. They take all available space and materials as the carriers to advertise information, including infiltrating into virtual space to build new human societies and a new order.

9.4　Revolution of media function

Immersive communication brings about the overall sublimation and core revolution of media function. In immersive communication, communication is omnipresent. Communication can traverse time and space, pulling past, present, and future together. Communication can allow people to freely roam in two worlds all the time, combining the virtual and the physical without boundaries.

While technological determinism "determines" the emergence of immersion as a new mode of communication, media evolution theory renders people able to choose what is best suited to their needs in order to survive. Media technology and social development have created the conditions and environment for the evolution of immersive communication. Human beings are changing from information survival to post-information survival, from localized survival to ubiquitous survival, as we live not only physically but also virtually.

Immersive communication links all types of media to solve the growing demand for information communication in human society, so that both intentionally invented media and media that solve problems coincidentally, such as surveillance videos, are indispensable in serving the new highest information goal of omnipresence and omnipotence in human society.

The virtual reality created by immersive communication, supported by the ubiquitous network, means the full penetration of the virtual world into the physical world. It is the full integration of the cognitive styles and lifestyles of the two worlds. One of the attractions of the virtual world versus the physical world is that the virtual world is infinite. For example, a physical clothing store has space limitations, while the rack space in a virtual clothing store is unlimited. In the physical world, one has limited time and energy to make money, while people seem to have more possibilities to make money in the virtual world. People in the virtual world seek dreams that they cannot realize in the real world, while the joy and satisfaction they achieve in the virtual world is real. The breakthrough of the physical and the virtual boundaries brought about by immersive communication has not only fully expanded the living space of human beings, but is also a breakthrough of present and historical space and time, not to mention a full-scale upgrade of media functions beyond time and space.

This book uses the matrix chart of the immersive communication function model (see Figure 5.9) to study the development and revolution of immersive media functions. It can analyze the functions of immersive communication from the intersection point of the "5W" communication elements and the "5C" communication capabilities in immersive communication. Unlike the earliest "5W"

Conclusion 163

model of news communication, this element updates the original Lasswell model by changing "What" to "Want," emphasizing that the focus of immersive communication is what recipients want. Likewise, the original "In Which Channel" becomes "Web," highlighting the significance of the emergence of the Web as a specific channel in the history of communication. It is the watershed of the first media age and the second media age.

If we use Table 5.1 to compare the Internet model with the immersive communication model, for instance, the first thing we notice is the difference in connection capabilities. One of the core technological advancements of immersive communication is the realization of the overall ability to connect people and people, people and things, and things and things. With the advent of the IOT, the Internet began to move from virtual reality to reality. At the beginning of 2012, about 2.3 billion people worldwide had access to the Internet, while more than 1 trillion things were connected in the IOT. Forrester, an authoritative consulting agency in the United States, predicts that the world's "thing connection" business volume will be 30 times that of human-to-human communications business by 2020, and the IOT is therefore called the next trillion-class communications business. Everything we imagined in movies and in science fiction is becoming a reality based on ubiquitous connection. The IOT and the ubiquitous network have become revolutionary products that connect everything, while immersive communication is the inevitable product, built on the ubiquitous network and the smart planet, necessary to guarantee humanity's information survival. Above the ability to meet the information demand of humans, immersive communication has super-functions that go beyond all previous media.

This study deduces the division of the three media ages from the immersive communication function model matrix diagram. It can be seen that the third media age led by immersive communication has brought about qualitative changes in human production, life, and entertainment. The third media age is an era of smart living—an era in which communication is ever-present, omnipresent, and omnipotent.

The American scholar Mark Poster(1995) argued in his famous *The Second Media Age* that the first media age was dominated by the one-way broadcasting mode of communication, featuring a small number of information producers and a large number of information consumers. By contrast, the second media age is dominated by the two-way, decentralized communication mode, including the media's producers, sellers, and consumers as a whole. But this division is inadequate to describe the momentous changes that the new mode of immersive communication has brought to human society: a third media age is emerging.

Immersive communication makes media interfaces disappear, formed by the fusion of the communication technology supporting a U strategy. It makes possible things we once thought impossible. The fast pace of technology application and industrial integration has boosted the emergence of various new technologies, new products, new industries, and new lifestyles. From smart cities to smart planets, from digital entertainment to smart travel, and from mall shopping guides to telemedicine—they are all the product of the rapid integration of the mobile

164   *Conclusion*

Internet, the IOT, and ubiquitous networks on multifaceted levels such as the Internet, terminals, businesses, and industries. U strategy is spreading around the world. The United States is implementing the "smart planet" strategy, Singapore is building "Smart Island," South Korea is building the "ubiquitous dream hall," Europe is building a ubiquitous European information society, while China has the "Experience China" Mobile Ubiquitous Service Environment (MUSE) plan and the striding "Broadband China" strategy. In the ubiquitous era, China already has a certain leading edge.

Of course, the third media era will constantly give rise to new problems in human society. How can we define "virtual existence" and "infinite existence"? How should we perceive the relationship between technological application and social civilization? What does it take to control the technology so that it can be an angel instead of a devil? First and foremost, there are data security issues. As more and more critical applications and data are ported to the cloud, the security risks justify some concern. Recently, the Cloud Security Alliance conducted a series of surveys on cloud computing security, documenting the "seven sins" of cloud computing, including data loss, leakage, and insecure application program interfaces. It is imperative to establish cloud industry operation management and legal protection, and to improve new rules for wise digital living.

When the ubiquitous network is everywhere and the smart environment invades the private sector, issues of personal privacy will become even more striking. Will anyone be resistant to becoming biological media? Levinson noted, "Some people commented: I don't think people will accept implanting chips in their brains … My answer is that there is no problem. The essence of new media is choice" (Levinson, 2011, p. 192). If this is true, then is the essence of immersive media having no choice—or simply no other choice? Just think: what if you are the medium itself and it leaves no choice for you? These are serious problems, but we believe that the development of technology and the wisdom of humanity will also constantly propose new solutions.

In short, the revolutionary nature of immersive communication is bound to herald the advent of a new media age, as well as a new model of production and lifestyle for human society. We have reason to expect the comprehensive and imminent arrival of the third media age, guided by immersive communication.

Afterword to Chinese edition

Sporadic feelings about the book began five years ago, or even earlier, but the real focus on its ideas began in 2009 during my Ph.D. research. After three years of research and two years of manuscript development, in Beijing's continuous foggy days, the construction of "immersive communication" and the future of "the third media era" are becoming clearer and clearer. In such a prosperous world, it is extremely luxurious to steal half a day's leisure. I have shut myself up for three and a half months to finish the final sprint of this book. I sincerely thank all the people who gave me support and encouragement.

Thanks to my father and mother for their nurturing and cultivation. They made me self-confident and self-reliant, which is the greatest wealth of my life. If this book reflects some feelings of bold imagination and careful evidence-seeking, it is inseparable from my parents' unconditional support, active maintenance, encouragement, and relaxed atmosphere. They supported me in pursuit of journalism and communication as a career, and also supported me to abandon my work at the central media agency to study abroad, and most of all they supported my unconstrained personality and courage to let my imagination fly.

I would like to thank Professor Xiong Chengyu for his meticulous guidance of this research. His words and deeds will benefit me all my life. I would like to express my gratitude to Professor Jin Jianbin for his continuous attention from the beginning of the research concept and his important help in modeling and quantitative research. I thank Professor Yin Hong for his inspiration and guidance in thinking about modes and methodology. Thanks to Professor Lei Jianjun, Professor Shi Anbin, Professor Cui Baoguo, Professor Li Bin, Professor Guo Qingguang, and Professor Zhao Shuguang for their guidance and help. Thanks to the teachers and students of Tsinghua University's School of Journalism and Communication for your enthusiastic help and support!

The research process of this book was also a process of self-satisfaction. The research originated from a speculative perception and a trust in life that I insisted on. I believe that the most important learning comes from life, whether we actively or passively draw knowledge and inspiration from life, so thank you, life.

I write this postscript on a plane flying to New York. In a world changing with each passing day, any documentary argument will not catch up with the rapid progress of time, so we can only hope that the glimpses of forward-looking light

166 *Afterword to Chinese edition*

and laws of thought and inherent foresight will hold on. So I let this monograph go to press now.

A day of doing research is a day of meditation. I miss these very pure days, just as we human beings often miss the very simple times gone by—no mobile phones, no computers—but we can't go back. We all become immersive communicators. Imagination promotes science and technology, and the combination of science and technology and creativity will paint a beautiful picture of future life.

The human imagination is inexhaustible, and I believe that in this book I have not exhausted my own brain. Exploring the relationship between information communication and human survival and development will be my eternal concern in the future.

References

Altschull, H. J. (1988). *Agents of power: The role of the news media in human affairs* (Y. Huang & B. K. Qiu, Trans.). Beijing: Huaxia Publishing House.

Anderson, J. Q., & Lee, R. (2008). The future of the Internet III. Pew Internet & American Life Project. Retrieved from http://www.pewinternet.org/~/media//Files/Reports/2008

Aukstakalnis, S., Blatner, D., & Roth, S. F. (1992). *Silicon mirage: The art and science of virtual reality*. Peachpit Press.

Bao, X. J. (2012). *Alert: Fake student ID card disturb spring festival travel ticket buying.* Retrieved from http://news.xinhuanet.com/edu/2012-01/21/c_122613332.htm

Bell, D. (1976). *The coming of post-industrial society: A venture in social forecasting.* Basic Books.

Berners-Lee, T. (2000). *Weaving the Web: The original design and ultimate destiny of the World Wide Web* (1st ed.). HarperBusiness.

Best, S., & Kellner, D. (2002). *The postmodern adventure* (G. Chen, Trans.). Nanjing: Nanjing University Press.

Bourdieu, P. (1997). *Cultural capital and social alchemy: Interview with Pierre Bourdieu* (Y. M. Bao, Trans. & Ed.). Shanghai: Shanghai People's Publishing House.

Cai, K. R., & Huang, Y. X. (2003). *Transcend time and space: On broadcast television communication*. Beijing: Xinhua Publishing House.

Canalys. (2019). Canalys estimates and forecast, mobility services. Retrieved from https://www.canalys.com/, http://www.199it.com/archives/822460.html

Carpenter, E. (1974). *Oh, what a blow that phantom gave me!* (1st ed.). Austin: Holt, Rinehart and Winston.

CART. (2011, May 20). *China Mobile Internet White Paper (2011)*. Beijing: Ministry of Industry and Information Technology of the People's Republic of China.

Certeau, M. D. (1980). *L'invention du quotidien 1. Arts de faire (nouvelle edition)*. Paris: Gallimard.

Chen, F. Q. (2004, February 15). Overall communication dialogue: A brief talk on the development status of domestic elevator media. *Voice & Screen World* (Z1), 187–189.

Chen, Y. (2006, August 1). Focus M & A Framework: 1+1=?. *Brokerage*, (8), 68–70.

Chinese Young Pioneers Career Development Center. (2011). 2011 China minors Internet/ social network usage survey report. Retrieved from https://style.mla.org/citing-a-comp any-report/

Chyxx. (2015). *2015–2011 China elevator market supply and demand and future investment evaluation report*. Beijing: China Industrial Information Network.

168   *References*

Chyxx. (2018). In 2017, China's TV comprehensive population coverage rate reached 99.07%, and it is expected to continue to grow steadily by 2020. Retrieved from http://www.chyxx.com/industry/201812/698560.html

CNNIC. (2012). The 29th statistical report on the development of China's Internet. Retrieved from http://www.cnnic.net.cn/hlwfzyj/hlwxzbg/hlwtjbg/201206/t20120612_26720.htm

CNNIC. (2013). The 31st statistical report on the development of China's Internet. Retrieved from http://www.cnnic.net.cn/hlwfzyj/hlwxzbg/hlwtjbg/201403/t20140305_46239.htm

CNNIC. (2019). *The 43rd statistical report on the development of China's Internet*. China Internet Network Information Center.

Csikszentmihalyi, M. (1975). *Beyond boredom and anxiety: Experiencing flow in work and play*. San Francisco, CA: Jossey-Bass.

Csikszentmihalyi, M. (1990). *Flow: The psychology of optimal experience*. New York, NY: Harper and Row.

Csikszentmihalyi, M. (1996). *Creativity: Flow and the psychology of discovery and invention*. New York, NY: Harper Perennial.

Csikszentmihalyi, M. (1997). *Finding flow: The psychology of engagement with everyday life*. New York: Basic Books.

Cui, B. G. (2003, October 5). The medium is a fish—some thoughts on media ecology. *Media Watch*, (10).

Cui, B. G. (2004). *Media environment: 25 lectures on media*. B. Li & J. C. Wang (Eds.), Beijing: Tsinghua University Press.

Cui, B. G. (2011). *Report on development of China's media industry*. Beijing: Social Sciences Academic Press.

Dance, F. E. X. (1967). "A helical model of communication", in Dance, F. E. X. (ed.), *Human Communication Theory*. New York: Holt, Rinehart and Winston.

De Mauro, A., Greco, M., & Grimaldi, M. (2016). A formal definition of Big Data based on its essential features. *Library Review, 65*(3), 122–135.

Debord, G. (2007). *La société du spectacle* (2nd ed.) (Z. F. Wang, Trans.). Nanjing: Nanjing University Press.

DeFleur, M. L. (1970). *Theories of mass communication.* New York: David McKay.

Deleuze, G. (2001). *Foucault* (Q. Z. Yu & J. Yang, Trans.). Changsha: Hunan Literature and Art Publishing House.

Deleuze, G., & Guattari, F. (1987). (B. Massuri, Trans.). *A Thousand Plateaus: Capitalism and Schizophrenia (2nd ed.)*. Minneapolis, MN: University of Minnesota Press.

Deutsch, K. W. (1956). *The nerves of government: Models of political communication and control*. The Free Press.

Fang, M., & Liu, Y. (2005). Online cohabitation challenges the secular world – the number of "online cohabitation" has reached 100,000. Jiefang Daily, July 20.

Fidler, R. (1997). *Mediamorphosis: Understanding new media*. Thousand Oaks: Pine Forge Press.

Foucault, M. (1977). *Discipline and punish: The birth of the prison* (A. Sheridan, Trans.). New York, NY: Pantheon.

Freud, S. (1930). *Civilization and its discontents* (J. Riviere & J. Strachey, Trans.). New York, NY: Cape & Smith.

Fuchs, P., & Moreau, G. (2006). *Le traité de la réalité virtuelle*. Vol. 2. Paris: Presses des Mines.

References 169

Gao, X. (2012). Latest history version: Global mobile phone users. *Science and Technology of China*. Retrieved from http://www.techcn.com.cn/index.php?edition-view-181642-8.html

Gauntlett, D. (2000). *Web.studies: Rewiring media studies for the digital age* (pp. 348–350). London: Arnold.

Gauntlett, D. (2000). *Web.studies: Rewiring media studies for the digital age*. Hodder Education Publishers.

Geirland, J. (1996). Go with the flow. *Wired, 4*(9). Retrieved from http://www.wired.com/wired/archive/4.09/czikpr.html

Ghent Urban Studies Group. (2005). *The urban condition: Space, community and self in the contemporary metropolis* (D. Jing & Q. Xie, Trans.). Beijing: China Water Power Press.

Goffman, E. (1959). *The presentation of self in everyday life*. New York, NY: Doubleday.

Guan, L., & Zhang, M. L. (2010, February). Analysis on the propagation advantage of confined space—comparison with the propagation effect in open space. *Xin Wen Jie*, (2), 39–41.

Gutnick, A. L., Robb, M., Takeuchi, L., & Kotler, J. (2011). Always connected: The new digital media habit of young children. Retrieved from http://joanganzcooneycenter.org/Reports-28.html

Guttentag, D. A. (2010). Virtual reality: Application and implication for tourism. *Tourism Management, 31*(5), 637–651.

Hang, Y., & Su, B. H. (2007). The formation of virtual reality and immersive communication. *Modern Media, 149*(6), 21–24.

Hudson, S., Matson-Barkat, S., Pallamin, N., & Jegou, G. (2019). With or without you? Interaction and immersion in a virtual reality experience. *Journal of Business Research, 100*, 459–468.

Huntington, S. P. (2011). *The clash of civilizations and the remaking of world order*. Simon & Schuster.

IBM. (2011a). 2011 annual report. Retrieved from www.ibm.com/annualreport/2011/

IBM. (2011b, , December). IBM: 5 great innovations will change people's life. *Science & Technology for China's Mass Media*, (12), 16.

IEEE. (2019). *About IEEE*. Retrieved from https://www.ieee.org/

Innis, H. A. (1999). *The bias of communication* (2nd ed.). Toronto: University of Toronto Press.

ITU. (2005). ITU Internet reports 2005: The Internet of Things. Retrieved from http://www.itu.int/osg/spu/publications/internetofthings/

ITU. (2015). *ITU's 2015 IOT report*.

Kessler, S. (2011, March 15). Study: 80 percent of children under 5 use internet weekly. *USA Today*. Retrieved from http://content.usatoday.com/communities/technologylive/post/2011/03/study-80-percent-of-children-under-5-use-internet-weekly/1#.T8Ypoph5W6V

Lasswell, H. D. (1948). *The structure and function of communication in society*. New York: Harper & Bros.

Lefebvre, H. (1991). *The production of space* (D. Nicholson-Smith, Trans.). Oxford: Blackwell.

Levinson, P. (1993). The Amish get wired—the Amish? *Wired, 1*(6), 124.

Levinson, P. (1997). *The soft edge: A natural history and future of the information revolution*. New York, NY: Routledge.

170   *References*

Levinson, P. (1999). *Digital McLuhan: A guide to the information millennium.* New York, NY: Routledge.

Levinson, P. (2004). *Cellphone: The story of the world's most mobile medium and how it has transformed everything!* New York: Palgrave Macmillan.

Levinson, P. (2011). *New new media* (D. K. He, Trans.). Shanghai: Fudan University Press.

Levinson, P. (2014). *New new media* (2nd ed.) (D. K. He, Trans.). Shanghai: Fudan University Press.

Levinson, P. (2019). Human Replay: A Theory of the Evolution of Media. Connected Editions.

Li, L. Y., & Wu, X. P. (2010). A 9-year-old boy was monitored falling from an elevator into serious injury. Retrieved from http://news.sohu.com/20100406/n271326363.shtml

Li, Z. G., Cai, L., & Huang, D. (2007, April). "Yuyingtang" soars up to national brand with two-pronged service and delivery. *Modern Marketing: Business Edition,* (4), 36–37.

Lippmann, W. (2006). *Public opinion* (K. W. Yan & H. Jiang, Trans.). Shanghai: Shanghai Century Publishing Group.

Lippmann, W. (2010). *Public opinion.* CreateSpace Independent Publishing Platform.

Littlejohn, S. W., & Foss, K. A. (2008). *Theories of human communication* (9th ed.). Cengage Learning.

Lum, C. M. K. (2006). *Perspectives on culture, technology, and communication: The media ecology tradition.* Cresskill, NJ: Hampton Press.

Lyon, D. (2001). Surveillance after September 11. Retrieved from http://www.socresonl ine.org.uk/6/3/lyon.html

Mander, J. (1978). *Four arguments for the elimination of television.* New York, NY: Morrow.

Marx, K. H., & Engels, F. (1848). *Manifest der Kommunistischen Partei; The Communist Manifesto (Manifesto of the Communist Party).* S. Fischer Verlag.

Mathews, F. (1991). *The ecological self.* London: Routledge.

Mattelart, A. (2000). *Networking the world 1794–2000* (L. Carey-Libbrecht & J. A. Cohen, Trans.). Minneapolis, MN: University of Minnesota Press.

Mattelart, A. (2007). *Mondialisation de la communication* (Z. M. Zhu, Trans.). Beijing: Communication University of China Press.

McKeever, W. A. (1910). Motion pictures: A primary school for criminals. *Good Housekeeping.*

McLuhan, M. (1951). *The mechanical bride: Folklore of industrial man.* New York, NY: The Vanguard Press.

McLuhan, M. (1962). *The Gutenberg Galaxy: The making of typographic man.* Toronto: University of Toronto Press.

McLuhan, M. (1994). *Understanding media: The extensions of man* (L. H. Lapham, Intro.). Cambridge: The MIT Press.

McLuhan, M. (1976). Inside on the outside, or the spaced-out American. *Journal of Communication, 76*(4), 46–53.

McLuhan, M. (1994). *Understanding media: The extensions of man* (L. H. Lapham, Intro.). Cambridge: The MIT Press.

McLuhan, M., Fiore, Q. & Agel J. (1967). *The Medium is the massage.* Corte Madera: Gingko Press.

McLuhan, M. & Parker, H. (1969). *Counterblast.* Corte Madera: Gingko Press.

McLuhan, M., & Powers, B. R. (1989). *The global village.* New York: Oxford University Press.

References 171

McQuail, D., & Windahl, S. (2008). *Communication models for the study of mass Communications* (J. H. Zhu, Trans.). Shanghai: Shanghai Translation Publishing House.

McLuhan, M. & Nevitt, B. (1972). *Take today: The executive as dropout*. New York: Harcourt Brace Jovanovich.

Mell, P., & Grance, T. (2011). *The NIST definition of cloud computing*. Special Publication 800-145,National Institute of Standards and Technology, U.S. Department of Commerce.

Meyrowitz, J. (1985). *No sense of place: The impact of electronic media on social behavior*. New York, NY: Oxford University Press.

Meyrowitz, J. (1997). Shifting worlds of strangers: Medium theory and changes in "them" versus "us". *Sociological Inquiry, 67*(1), 59–71.

Min, J. (2012). Cloud computing awarded marks for the integration of three networks. China Electronics Newspapers. March, 21st. Retrieved from http://yjs.cena.com.cn/a/2012-03-20/133222196066071.shtml

Naisbitt, J. (1982). *Megatrends: Ten new directions transforming our lives*. New York, NY: Warner Books.

Negroponte, N. (1996). *Being digital*. New York, NY: Vintage.

Nielsen. (2010a). The increasingly connected consumer: Connected devices—a look behind the growing popularity of iPads, Kindles and other devices. Retrieved from https://www.nielsen.com/us/en/insights/article/2010/the-connected-devices-age-ipads-kindles-smartphones-and-the-connected-consumer/

Nielsen. (2010b). What Americans do online: Social media and games dominate activity. Retrieved from http://blog.nielsen.com/nielsenwire/online_mobile/what-americans-do-online-social-media-and-games-dominate-activity/

Nixon, R. (1989). *1999: Victory without war*. Pocket Books.

Novak, T. P., & Hoffman, D. L. (1997). Measuring the flow experience among Web users. Paper presented at Interval Research Corporation, July 31, Draft 1.0. Retrieved from http://www2000.ogsm.vanderbilt.edu/

Novak, T. P., & Hoffman, D. L. (2000). Measuring the flow experience among Web users. Retrieved from http://www.ucr.edu/about/promise/hoffman_novak.html

Nye Jr, J. S. (2004). *Soft power: The means to success in world politics*. PublicAffairs.

Pan, F. (2011). The ubiquitous network is the infrastructure to "Sensing China". Retrieved from http://www.ptsn.net.cn/article_new/show:article.php?article_id=cyzx_67df12a8-7f3f-cddb-9c7c-4b6a8258d0c9

Pool, I. D. S. (1984). *Technologies of freedom*. Belknap Press of Harvard University Press.

Poster, M. (1990). *The mode of information: Poststructuralism and social context*. Cambridge: Polity Press.

Poster, M. (1995). *The second media age*. Cambridge: Polity Press.

Postman, N. (1994). *The disappearance of childhood*. Vintage/Random House.

Postman, N. (2000). The humanism of media ecology. In C. M. K. Lum (Ed.), *Perspectives on culture, technology and communication: The media ecology tradition* (pp. 61–69). Cresskill, NJ: Hampton Press.

Postman, N. (2005). *Amusing ourselves to death: Public discourse in the age of show business* (revised edition). London: Penguin.

Richards, I. A. (1929). *Practical criticism: A study of literary judgment*. New York: Harvest Books.

Schramm, W. (1954). "How communication works", in Schramm, W. (ed.), *The process and effects of mass communication*. Urbana: University of Illinois Press.

172 *References*

Shannon, C. & Weaver, W. (1949). *The mathematical theory of communication.* Urbana: University of Illinois Press.

Silva, A. D. S., & Daniel, M. S. (2011). Theorizing locative technologies through philosophies of the virtual. *Communication Theory, 21*(1), 23–42.

Sohu. (2018). The first downturn in China's smartphone market in 2017, winter arrives. *Sohu Finance.* Retrieved from http://www.sohu.com/a/219677364_99950678

Soja, E. W. (1996). *Thirdspace: Journeys to Los Angeles and other real-and-imagined places.* Oxford: Basil Blackwell.

Strategy Analytics. (2018). Q3 global smartphone shipments are 360 million units in 2018, down 8% year on year, November 2, 2018. Retrieved from http://www.199it.com/arch ives/790833.html

Temporal, P. (2010). *Advanced brand management: Managing brands in a changing world* (2nd ed.). Hoboken: Wiley.

The Economist. (2019, January 12). The maturing of the smartphone industry is cause for celebration. Retrieved from https://www.economist.com/leaders/2019/01/12/the-m aturing-of-the-smartphone-industry-is-cause-for-celebration

The Video Bus. (2012). *Apple iPhone 4S's sales speed broke the Guinness world records.* Retrieved from http://iphone.tgbus.com/news/class/201201/20120130133755.shtml

Toffler, A. (1980). *The third wave.* New York, NY: William Morrow and Company, Inc.

Trevino, L. K., & Webster, J. (1992). Flow in computer-mediated communication: Electronic mail and voice mail evaluation and impacts. *Communication Research, 19*(5), 539–573.

United States Congress. (1996). Communication Decency Act.

Wang, S. T. (2008, March). Poet CEO: Elevator ads make great fortune. *Business Culture,* (3), 50–53.

Weiser, M. (1991). The computer for the 21st century. *Scientific American* Special Issues on Communications, Computers and Networks.

Weiser, M. (2012). Retrieved at May 2012, from http://sandbox.xerox.com/weiser/

Wiener, N. (1948). *Cybernetics: Or control and communication in the animal and the machine.* New York: MIT Press.

Winn, M. (1977). *The plug-in drug.* Viking Penguin Publications.

Xici Hutong. (n.d.). *Online registration.* Retrieved from http://www.xici.net

Xinhua News Agency. (2017). Official: Revenue of Big Data products and services business will exceed one trillion yuan in 2020. Retrieved from http://www.xinhuanet .com/yuqing/2017-01/18/c_129451572.htm

Xiong, C. Y. (2009, January 15). The pattern and trend of media development in the digital age. *Science & Technology for China's Mass Media,* (1), 76–77.

Xiong, C. Y. (2011, December 15). Thoughts about the future of new media. *Modern Communication,* (12), 126–127.

Xiong, L. (2012). Guo Xiaoqi, 15-year-old "Loveliest Girl" given free medical treatment. Retrieved from http://www.hlj.xinhuanet.com/news/2012-02/09/c_131400973.htm

Xiong, W. Y. (1988). *A dictionary for modern army men.* Beijing: Xinhua Publishing House.

Xu, B. (2011, March 11). A teenage monitored being beaten up by a man for discouraging smoking in the elevator. *Guangxi News Network—Nanguo Morning Post.* Retrieved from http://www.gxnews.com.cn/staticpages/20110311/newgx4d7952f4-3658793-1. shtml

Zhang, P. (2009). Future broadband wireless network: From heterogeneous fusion to ubiquity. *China Electronic Newspaper*. Retrieved from http://ydhl.cena.com.cn/a/2009-10-23/125626475935157.shtml

Zhou, X. (2012). An analysis of the phenomenon of false information spreading in microblog. *Modern Communication, 34*(1), 151–152.

Zhu, P. S., & Duan, S. H. (2009, July 15). Ubiquitous network development status analysis. *Telecommunications Network Technology,* (7), 18–22.

Index

Page numbers in **bold** reference tables. Page numbers in *italics* reference figures.

3D artistic advertisements 68
3In 87
4A communications 86
4Any 87–8
5Any 32
5C 32, 88
5W 88
5W Model 79
2006 ITU Radio Frequency Identification Symposium 34

"acoustics" space 62
Adams, Harold 78
Adidas, Second Life 35
advertising 105–6; environmental advertisement 68; media advertisement 72–3; "want" 102
age of humanity 135–6
AGPS (assisted GPS) 28
AI (artificial intelligence) 27
Akira, Fujitake 59
Altschull, J. Herbert 144
The Amish Get Wired (Levinson, 1993) 133–4
animals, QR codes 141–2
anthropotropic theory 8, 143, 158
anthropotropic trends survival 46–8
anthropotropicness 6–8
"anti-wolf underwear" xviii
"any" 88
"anytime" form 58
Apple 25; iPhone 4S 155; iPhones 27; iTV 29
AR (augmented reality) 45
Art de faire. L'invention du quotidian (de Certeau, 1980) 134
artificial intelligence (AI) 27
assisted GPS (AGPS) 28

audiences: human-centered communication 86; immersive communicators 142–4
auditory immersion 20
augmented reality (AR) 45
authority 4
Autodesk 149

Bangemann, Martin 137
Baoguo, Cui 9, 10
bathrooms, fully automatic 141–2
Beijing Conghui Advertising Co., Ltd. 107–9
Bell, Alexander Graham 44
Bell, Daniel 26, 60–1
Berkitz, Sven 153
Berners-Lee, Tim 125
Best, S. 73
Betamax 7
Bi-circulating Model of Mass Communication 80
Big Data 99
big media 143
biological communication technology 46
biological media 135, 154–5
Boorstin, Daniel 128
boundaries xvii–xviii, 62–3, 72
Bourdieu, Pierre 71
Broadband China 'Optical Network City' Project 39
"Broadband China Strategy" 39, 126
Broadband Forum 39
broadcasting 26, 44
Burdea, Grigore 45
Burgess, Ernest 11

C2C (customer-to-customer) 36
cable TV subscribers 103–4

Canalys Mobility 27
Carpenter, Edmund Snow 54
CCSA (China Communications Standards Association) 115
cellphones 50, 125, 135
changes in media forms 137
characteristics of: first media age 2–3; second media age 4–5; third media age 133–8
Chen Tianqiao 102
children, media and 142–3, 153–4
China: "Broadband China Strategy" 39; Internet platforms 4; Internet use 24; Little Yueyue case 38; MUSE (Mobile Ubiquitous Service Environment) 34; virtual worlds 36–7
China Communications Standards Association (CCSA) 115
China Internet Network Information Center (CNNIC) 24
China Mobile 115, 141; Elevator Guard 111–12; "Wireless City" 114
China Telecom 115; Broadband China 'Optical Network City' Project 39
Chinese netizens 24–5
CII (Communication Immersion Index) 84, 86–8
city 61; intelligent city 68
Clear Channel 106
cloud computing 39–40, 49, 52, 62–3, 104, 149
CNNIC (China Internet Network Information Center) 24
Coca-Cola, Second Life 35
coevolution 6–8
coexistence 6–8
"Cohabitating Dreamland" 152
Coiffet, Philippe 45
commercialization of the world 73
communication content 159–60
Communication Immersion Index (CII) 84, 86–8
communication methods 161–2
communication models 78–83
communication modes 75
Communications Decency Act (U.S.) 38, 154
communication space 51
communicative action 5
communities 3
compensating media 13
composition principle and functions of IOT *111*

computing differences, immersive communication models 99–100, 117
connectivity: immersive communication models 98, 117; super-connectivity 110
consumption space 51
content 66–7, 159–60; humans 69; language forms 67–71
convergence, immersive communication models 118
convergence media 62; immersive communication models 103–4
Cook, Tim 25
copyrights, virtual worlds 36
CSI 59
Csikszentmihalyi, M. 17–18, 150–1
customer-to-customer (C2C) 36
cybernetics 124
cyberspace 50

"Damocles' Sword" 19
Dance, F. E. X. 81
Dangdang electronic book platform 29
Dear Enemy (Xu) 37
de-authority 128–9
Debord, Guy 73
de-centering 128–9
de Certeau, Michel 134
DeFleur, M. L. 80
Deleuze, Gilles 129
Depew, Chauncy 63
de Souza, e Silva 52
Deutsch, Karl W. 116
Dianping 28–9
display/attention model (McQuail, 1987) *83*, 102
DoCoMo 33
"Dream Transmission" 72–3
Drew, Lolita (Myspace) 153
Droll, Jacques 137
Duan, Shihui 100

ecological theory 9
e-commerce, immersive communicators 145–6
E-Japan 32
E-Korea 32
electronic erosion 61
electronic media 14–15; virtual worlds 70–1
electronic terminals 29
Elevator Guard, China Mobile 111–12
elevator leaflets 100–1
elevator monitoring 111–14

176 *Index*

elevator television, second media age 107–9

"Eleventh National Radio and Television Working Conference" 101

Engels, F. 24

entertainment, immersive communicators 151–4

environment: for evolution of immersive communication 24–6; pseudo environment 59; relationships with humans and media 9–13

environmental advertisement 68

environmental limitations 15

environmental media 67–8

environment networkization 125

ESM (Experience Sampling Method) 17

European Information Highway Project 137

European Information Society Congress 33

evolution of immersive communication, media technology and social development 24–6

evolution of media: coevolution, coexistence and anthropotropicness 6–8; first media age 2–3; second media age 4–5

evolution of networks 61–2

evolutioreplay 46

"Experience China" 164

Experience Sampling Method (ESM) 17

Facebook 28, 59

facebrushing 30

Fidler, Roger 6

film 3

Finding Flow (Csikszentmihalyi) 17–18

First International 134

first media age 2; characteristics of 2–3; immersive communication models 119; lobby leaflets and unidirectional transmission 106–7

Fitbit xix

"Flow Experience" 17

flow of space 51

flow state 17–19

"Flow Theory" 17

focus awareness, second media age 107–9

focused communication xiv, 132

Focus Media 106, 108

Forrester 163

Foss, Karen 154

Foucault, Michel 5, 110

Four Arguments for the Elimination of Television (Mander, 1978) 153

Four Laws of Media model (McLuhan) 7

Foursquare 28

four-tiered policies 101

Framedia 106, 108

Franklin, John Hope 151

Freud, Sigmund 11

functional models 79

function model matrix of immersive communication *93*

Fusion Network 103

Gauntlett, David 87–8

general application of immersive communication models 97–104

General Morphology (Haeckel, 1866) 9

geographic information system (GIS) 28

globalization of commodities 73

The Globalization of Communication (Mattelart, 2007) 127

global village 34–7; ubiquitous networking 45

Goffman, Erving 14–15, 123

Goldstein, Steve 143

Google, smart glasses 150

Gore, Al 137

GPRS 112

Grance, T. 99

Guan, Lu 100

Guangxi News Net 112

Guo, Xiaoqi 68–9

Gutenberg's Elegy (Berkitz, 1994) 153

Haeckel, E. 9

helical model 81

Hoffman, Donna L. 18–19

home AI assistants 27

human-centered communication 86

human-centered, open media form 56–8

human communication history 56–8

human living space, third media age 125–8

human-media relations 158–9

humans: life in the virtual and physical worlds 34–7; media and 53–4; relationships with media and the environment 9–13; source of media language and information content 69

Huntington, Samuel P. 11

i2010 33

IBM 123, 155; Second Life 35; "Smart Planet" 85

ICASSP (International Conference on Acoustics, Speech, and Signal Processing) 21–2

IC matrix 88–91
IC schematic 92
IC stereo helix 91
identities: immersive communicators 142–4; "we media" 143–4
IEEE (Institute of Electrical and Electronics Engineers) 21
I-Europe 115
imaginary space 12
immersion xiii, 38, 157; concept of 16–18; virtual reality 18–20
immersive communication xiii, xiv, 157–8; definition of 48–9
immersive communication function model matrix diagram *105*
immersive communication models 83–8, 131; first media age 106–7; general application of 97–104; IC matrix 88–91; IC schematic 91–2; media ages 104–5; second media age 107–9; third media age 110–16
immersive communicators 141–4; biological media 154–5; entertainment 151–4; lifestyle of 144–7; production mode of 147–51
immersive dissemination, content 159–60
immersive media 160
Industrial Revolution, rational cognition 10
information 124
information movement 74–6
information presentation 73–4
information society 26–7
information superhighway 137
Institute of Electrical and Electronics Engineers (IEEE) 21
intelligence, third media age 137–8
intelligent city 68
intelligentization 30
intelligent space 52
interaction, humans and media 53–4
International Conference on Acoustics, Speech, and Signal Processing (ICASSP) 21–2
internationalization of social networks 134
International Telecommunications Union (ITU) 32, 85–6, 122; ubiquitous networks 130
Internet 69
Internet determinism 134
Internet environment, flow state 19
Internet interaction 4
Internet model, versus immersive communication model 98

Internet of sensors 84
Internet of Things (IOT) 34, 73, 83–6, 98, 114–15, 163–4; connectivity 110–11; SIM cards 30
Internet use 24–6
intersection points, IC matrix 89
invisible man 58
invisible tool era 46
IOT (Internet of Things) 34, 73, 83–6, 98, 114–15, 163–4; connectivity 110–11; SIM cards 30
iPhone 4S 155
iPhones (Apple) 27
Iraq War 51
ITU (International Telecommunications Union) 32, 85–6, 122; ubiquitous networks 130
iTV 29

Japan 32; NTT (Nippon Telegraph and Telephone) 33; U-Japan 115; U-Japan Best Business Award 75
JCO of France 106
Jiang Nanchun 102, 108
Joan Ganz Cooney Center 154
JVC, VHS 7

Kaixin.com 59, 136
Kalker, Tom 21
Kant, Immanuel 11
Kellner, D. 73
Kinect (Microsoft) 27
Korea Telecom (KT) 33

LangMedia 108
language forms 67–71
language of virtual worlds 70–1
Lanier, Jaron 20
Lasswell, Harold Dwight 79
Lasswell formula (Lasswell, 1948) *79*
latent morphosis 6
Lazarsfeld, Paul F. 129
LBSs (location-based services) 28–9, 75, 161
leaflets 100–1, 119; first media age 106–7
Lefebvre, Henri 12
Levinson, Paul 7, 8, 13, 34, 40, 46–7, 50, 53–4, 62–3, 67, 69, 133, 143, 150, 158
LG Telecom 33
lifestyle of immersive communicators 144–7
linguistic hegemony of immersive media 71–3

178 *Index*

Lippmann, Walter 23, 59
literacy 3
Littlejohn, Stephan 154
Little Yueyue case 38, 126
lobby leaflets, first media age 106–7
location-based services (LBSs) 28, 75, 161
Lost 59
"Love Apartment" 152
Lyon, David 38

M (Mobile) 34
M2M (machine-to-machine) 114
magazines 7
Magic Media 106
mail filters 30
Maletzke, Gerhard 81–2
mandatory reading 108
Mander, Jerry 153
many-to-many 132
Marx, K. 24
mass communication xiv–xv, 132
massively multiplayer online role-playing game (MMORPG) 36
Mathematical Model 79
Mathews, Freya 137
The Matrix 35
matrix of immersive communication functions *93*
Mattelart, Armand 51, 71, 123, 127
McKeever, William A. 153
McLuhan, Marshall 6–7, 10, 14–15, 23, 35, 47–8, 50–1, 56, 58, 66–7, 69, 124
McQuail, Denis 81, 91, 102
media 48, 52; children and 153–4; environment 9–13; human beings and 53–4; third media age 128–30
media advertisement 72–3
media ages, immersive communication models 104–5
"media by appointment" 58
media convergence 57, 62
media ecology 9–10
media environment 10, 13
media evolution 46
media forms 44; changes in 137
media function 162–4
media geography 11
media humanization 57
media language, humans 69
media morphosis 1–2, 38–40; coevolution, coexistence and anthropotropicness 6–8; first media age 2–3; second media age 4–5

Media Nation 106
media ontology, third media age 123–4
Media Partner International 106
media sociology 11
media space 48; relationships between media, humans and the environment 9–13; third media age 125–8
media technology: from "informational survival" to "post-information" survival 26–30; from "localized" survival to "ubiquitous" survival 30–4; social development and 24–6
Mell, P. 99
message 67
Meyrowitz, Joshua 3, 14–16, 51, 61, 78, 123
Mickey Mouse 12
microblogging 5
Microsoft: Kinect 27; Xbox360 29
MMORPG (massively multiplayer online role-playing game) 36
mobile civilization 134
mobile media 67
mobile phones: productivity 150; as wallets 141; *see also* cellphones
mobile terminals 24
mobile ubiquitous 33
Mobile Ubiquitous Service Environment (MUSE) 34, 122, 164
mobile video 29
The Mobile World 135
The Mode of Information: Poststructuralism and Social Context (Poster, 1990) 4, 66
model of immersive communication 83–8, 131; first media age 106–7; general application of 97–104; IC matrix 88–91; IC schematic 91–2; IC stereo helix 91; media ages 104–5; second media age 107–9; third media age 110–16
Model of Mass Communication 81–2
models of communication 78–83
modernity 5
modern society 5
modes of communication 14–16
monitoring 38
monitoring cameras 68–9; panoramic monitoring 111–12
"more" 2
"More-Is-Better" communication theory 74
movement of information 74–6
movies 3, 6

MUSE (Mobile Ubiquitous Service Environment) 34, 122, 164
Myspace 136; Drew, Lolita 153

Naisbitt, John 26
narrowcasting 26
Negroponte, Nicholas 26, 59
network communication model 79
network determinism 134
network environmentalization 125
networks, evolution of 61–2
new media 132, 135
news 144
"Next-Generation I-Hub" 33
Nippon Telegraph and Telephone Corporation (NTT) 33
Nixon, President Richard 72
noise 80
Nokia 102
no-place spaces 51
Novak, Thomas P., 18–19
NTT (Nippon Telegraph and Telephone) 33
Nye, Joseph 71

Obama, Barack 85
object-to-object communications 125
Oetzel, John 154
olfactory system, VR (virtual reality) 20
one-way communication era, first media age 2–3
Ong, Walter 128
online communication 53–4
opinion leaders 129
"Opportunity and Need," media morphosis 7
"oral communication, self" 71–2
Orpheus in the Underworld, environmental advertisement 68
Orton, William 63
Osgood, C.E. 80
Osgood and Schramm circular model 80–1

pajamas media 144
pan-media language 68
pan-media theory 14
panoramic monitoring, third media age 110–16
Peng, Nicole 27
people-to-people communications 125
personalized service, third media age 110–16
phones 44

physical space 12, 50
physical world 34–7
places, immersive communication models 100–2, 117
The Plug-In Drug (Winn, 1977) 153
"point-to-point" 75, 129
"point-to-surface" 74, 129
political model of communication 79
Pool, Ithiel De Sola 57
pop culture 72
"positioning" 75
Poster, Mark 2, 4, 5, 66, 70, 121, 123, 127, 129, 135, 163
post-industrial society 26
post-information era 26
Postman, Neil 10
presence 40–1
print communication 2–3
production mode of immersive communicators 147–51
"propagation," media morphosis 7
pseudo environment 59
public space 126–7

QQ profiles 142
QR codes, lifestock 141–2

radio 7
rational cognition 10
real life 62
Reis, Philipp 44
relationships xv; between media, humans, and the environment 9–13
relative degree of immersion 97
remote presence 40–1, 147; immersive communication 21–3
renren.com 59
representative intersections in the matrix of immersive communication functions **90**
revolutions: communication content 159–60; communication methods 161–2; human-media relations 158–9; media function 162–4
RFID (radio-frequency identification) 85–6
Richards, I. A. 69
Rogers, Everett 2

Samsung Electronics 33
Santayana, George xvi
Schramm, Wilbur 80
second dictation period 128
Second Life 35–6, 59, 124, 136

180   *Index*

second media age xv, 2; characteristics of 4–5; elevator television and focus awareness 107–9; immersive communication models 119

The Second Media Age (Poster, 1995) 2, 121, 163

selective attention 116

self 71–2, 159

self-surveillance 145

Sensing China 115

Serres, Michel 52

Sesame Studio 154

Shanghai Mobile 114

Shannon, Claude 79

Shannon-Weaver Model *80*

"Shengda Network" 102

The Silent Revolution 134

SIM cards, Internet of Things 30

Sina 4

Singapore: "Next-Generation I-Hub" 33; "Smart Island" 164

SK Telecom 33

smart assistants 27

smart cities 126

smart glasses, Google 150

"Smart Island" 164

smartphones 25

"Smart Planet" 85, 122

smart space 13

smart speakers 27

smart TVs 29

social communication 5

social development and, media technology 24–6

social discourse power 72–3

social networks, internationalization 134

social productivity, third media age 123–4

social relations, third media age 128–30

"social scenario" 15

social system model 79

society, space and 11

sociological model 78

soft power 71–2

Sohu 4

Soja, Edward W. 13

Sony: Betamax 7; Second Life 35

South Korea 32, 164; U-Korea 115

space 10–12; "acoustics" space 62; imaginary space 12; immersive communication models 100–2, 117; media space 48; no-place spaces 51; physical space 12; public space 126–7; smart space 13; virtual space 12; visual space 62

spam email 30

"spectacles" 73

stereo-helical model of immersive communication process 84, 91

stereo helix model *94*

stereo-phantom 68

story of 'more' 2, 14

Strand, Mark 151

structural models 79

submarine cables 134

super-connectivity 110

super-modernity 51

Su Qin 107

"surface to point" 74–5

The Surrender of Culture to Technology (Postman, 1993) 153

surveillance 38; self-surveillance 145

survival, anthropotropic trends 46–8

"survival," media morphosis 7

Sutherland, Ivan 19

symbolic consumption 72–3

symbolic violence 71

symbol worship 73

tactile immersion 20

Target Media 106

"technical determinism" 10

technological determinism 43–4, 162; ubiquitous technology 45–6; virtual reality 44–5

technology 60–1

telephone communication 51

telephones 63, 135

television 3, 6, 54, 133, 140; children 153; invisible man 58; TV stations 101

television networks 135

"Telstar One" 3, 134

Tencent 4

Theories of Human Communication (Littlejohn & Foss, 2008) 154–5

third media age xiv, xv, 122–3, 140; characteristics of 133–8; concept of 130–3; immersive communication models 120; media ontology and social productivity 123–4; media space and transformation of human living space 125–8; panoramic monitoring and personalized service 110–16; social functions of media and social relations 128–30

thirdspace 13

thought reading 155

Toffler, Alvin 26, 99, 133

Toyota, Second Life 35

Index 181

traditional media 67
transition from "informational" survival to "post-information" survival 30
transportation 134
Trevino, Linda Klebe 17
TV stations 101
Twitter 28
two-level flow hypothesis 128–9
two-way cycle and interaction model 79
Tysoe, John 136

ubiquitous communication 30–4, 49, 139; third media age 132–3
ubiquitous computing 31
"Ubiquitous Dream Hall" 33
ubiquitous integration 133
ubiquitous mass communication xiv, 124, 132, 139
ubiquitous networking 43–6
ubiquitous networks 83–6, 114–15, 124; third media age 130
ubiquitous network society (UNS) 31, 100, 139
"ubiquitous surprises" 141
ubiquitous technology 45–6
ubiquity 147
U-Japan 32, 115
U-Japan Best Business Award 75
U-Korea 32, 115
unidirectional transmission, first media age 106–7
United States: Communication Decency Act 38, 154; global society model 11; "Smart Planet" 122; soft power 72
UNS (ubiquitous network society) 31, 100, 139
USA Today 154
U strategy xviii, 131, 164

vanishing boundaries xvii–xviii; modes of communication 14–16
VHS 7
Viacom 106
virtual currencies 36
virtual race 23
virtual reality 2, 59, 162; immersion 18–20; remote presence 21–3; technological determinism 44–5
virtual societies, immersive communicators 152
virtual space 12
virtual worlds 34–7, 59–60; immersive communicators 152; language of 70–1
visual immersion 20

visual morphosis 6
visual space 62
voluntary panopticon 145
VR (virtual reality) 20, 59, 162; immersion 18–20; remote presence 21–3; technological determinism 44–5

"want:" immersive communication models 102–3, 117
Warring States Period 107
Weaver, Warren 79
Web 2.0 121
Webster, Jane 17
WeChat 28
Weibo 28
Weiser, Dr. Mark xiv, 31, 87
"we media" 143–4
WhatsApp 28
White Horse Outdoor 106
Wiener, Norbert 14, 124
Winn, Marie 153
"Wireless City," China Mobile 114
Wireless Sensing "Medical Health Care System" 141
"without people" 128
"wolf-proof underwear" xviii
World Electronics Annual Conference 44–5
World Summit on the Information Society (WSIS) 33–4
written communication 2, 14
WSIS (World Summit on the Information Society) 33–4

Xbox360 (Microsoft) 29
"Xiangma" 152
Xici Hutong 152
Xinhua News Agency 142
Xiong, Chengyu 22, 39, 155
Xiong, Wuyi 106
Xu, Jinglei 37

Young Pioneers Career Development Center 154
YouTube 136
"Yurtangtang" 107

Zhang, Zhengyou 21
Zhang, M. 100
Zhang, P. 31, 39
Zhang, Y 107
Zhou, X. 5
Zhu, P. 100
Zuo, Si 107

Printed in the United States
By Bookmasters